◎本书系教育部人文社会科学研究青年基金项目"汉语二语学习者语用社会化进程中的身份构建研究"（19YJC740108）成果。

来华留学生
汉语语用能力
发展研究

The Pragmatic Development of
International Students in China

应洁琼 著

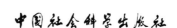

中国社会科学出版社

图书在版编目（CIP）数据

来华留学生汉语语用能力发展研究：英文／应洁琼著.—北京：
中国社会科学出版社，2019.5
ISBN 978 - 7 - 5203 - 4394 - 7

Ⅰ.①来… Ⅱ.①应… Ⅲ.①汉语—语用学—对外汉语教学—
教学研究—英文 Ⅳ.①H195.3

中国版本图书馆 CIP 数据核字 (2019) 第 085446 号

出 版 人	赵剑英
责任编辑	马 明
特约编辑	孙瑶鑫
责任校对	黄茜茜
责任印制	王 超

出 版	中国社会科学出版社
社 址	北京鼓楼西大街甲 158 号
邮 编	100720
网 址	http://www.csspw.cn
发 行 部	010 - 84083685
门 市 部	010 - 84029450
经 销	新华书店及其他书店

印 刷	北京明恒达印务有限公司
装 订	廊坊市广阳区广增装订厂
版 次	2019 年 5 月第 1 版
印 次	2019 年 5 月第 1 次印刷

开 本	710×1000 1/16
印 张	19.25
插 页	2
字 数	332 千字
定 价	89.00 元

凡购买中国社会科学出版社图书，如有质量问题请与本社营销中心联系调换
电话：010 - 84083683

Preface

It is my great pleasure to write this preface for Dr. Ying Jieqiong, who worked with me from 2014 to 2017 as a PhD researcher at Shanghai International Studies University (SISU). Before she approached me, Dr. Ying had finished her master degree at Leeds University, UK, majoring communication studies. Naturally, when she started to consider her PhD research topic, I suggested that she might take "intercultural communication" and "international students" into her consideration. As she attempted to integrate linguistics into her research, she found that "L2 pragmatic development among international students" was a meaningful and significant research topic to work at. As everybody knows, SISU has a rich pool of international students, which provides convenience for Dr. YING to select her participants and conduct her longitudinal observation. However, it was a long and hard journey for Dr. YING to complete her research. In order to meet the benchmark of originality of a PhD dissertation, Dr. YING worked strenuously and closely with me to establish a solid and profound theoretical model for her research topic, which obviously has made her research firmly stand in the frontier in the discipline of pragmatics.

In recent years, China has attracted more and more international students to study Chinese. Due to the diverse cultures throughout the world, misunderstandings and multicultural communication failures would occur if those students were incompetent pragmatically. This study explores international students' pragmatic competence by examining request speech acts made by Korean, Russian and French students, figuring out their pragmatic development trajectories and penetrating into the main factors that might aid or hinder their pragmatic development.

A mixed research method was employed. Three cultural groups were selected to investigate the cross-cultural variations of the pragmatic strategies in requests, based on which three international students were chosen to explore the changes of pragmatic strategies and factors that affected their pragmatic development.

The findings of the study demonstrate that the formulae Korean students employed are similar to that of Chinese, while French students differ from Chinese native speakers most and Russian students stand in the middle. According to the qualitative data, L2 learners' pragmalinguistic and sociopragmatic competence develop at different speed. And cultural background, motivation and acculturation attitudes, social activities and contextual factors serve as the main factors that affect their pragmatic development.

I fully believe this study provides language teachers, postgraduate students and cross-cultural researchers with insights as well as pedagogical implications in terms of rich empirical data, logical analysis and convincing discussion for multi-cultural studies, curriculum design, and administrative management of international students. Therefore, I strongly recommend this book to you.

Zheng Xinmin (PhD, The University of Hong Kong)

Professor of English in Education

Shanghai International Studies University

January 28th, 2019

Contents

List of Tables

List of Figures

Chapter 1

Introduction

1. 1 Research background

With the rapid development of Chinese economy and deepening of China's opening-up policy, the number of international students has been increasing significantly in recent years (Qu & Jiang, 2011; Yang, 2006), which results in a booming demand for changes and development of international students' education (Fang & wu, 2016; Li, 2012). According to the statistics from the Ministry of Education of the People's Republic of China (PRC) in 2017, there are 442,773 international students enrolled in 829 universities, research institutes or other educational institutions in 2016, which distributed in 31 different provinces, autonomous regions or direct-controlled municipalities. China became the fifth of most popular study abroad (SA) destinations during 2007 and 2008, and it had been ranked as the third most popular SA place all around the world, only followed the United States and the United Kingdom in 2013 (Kim et al. , 2015).

The number of the international students has increased considerably compared to that of previous years. Moreover, according to the statistics (2017), the source countries of international students in China had peaked at over 200 in 2016 since "the Belt and Road Initiative", which demonstrates the ever-increasing diversity of source countries. And the total number of the students from Asia, such as Korean, Japanese, ranked number one, followed by European and African students. With the growth of the number of international students in China, we are confronted with opportunities as well as challenges. Meanwhile, the international students not only face pressure from study, but also have to overcome the obstacles from cross-cultural communication (Yang, 2005). Kasper (1989) puts forward that the main barriers in intercultural communication are caused by pragmatic failure. Therefore, pragmatic competence is crucial for the international students to finish their study smoothly and live in China easily.

Kasper claims that interlanguage pragmatics (ILP) concentrates on learners' study and use of the target language. Accordingly, this research on the international students learning Chinese falls into this area. The emergence of interlanguage pragmatics was in 1980s, and became a heated area in the following years. Studies on interlanguage pragmatics have been published in more than 19 journals in English, such as Journal of Pragmatics, System, Procedia, Journal of Language Teaching and Research, Language Learning, EUROSLA Year Book, SPRING, Applied Linguistics, Teaching in Higher Education, Language Science, the Modern Language Journal, TESOL Quarterly, Foreign Language Annals, International Journal of English Studies, Studies in Second Acquisition, English Language Teaching, Journal of Language and Linguistic Studies, Language and Linguistics, Intercultural Pragmatics. Accordingly, a great number of research on interlanguage pragmatics can be found, which mainly classified into five types in terms of research perspectives, such as pragmatic awareness and cognition, pragmatic teaching and learning, theory elaboration, cross-cultural pragmatics, pragmatic development and assessment of pragmatic competence (see Table 1).

Table 1   **Types of studies on interlanguage pragmatics abroad**

Types of studies	Studies on ILP
Theory elaboration, research method on ILP	(Hong, 2005; Huang, 2010; Kasper, 1991, 2001; Saasaki, 1998; Yuan, 2001)
Pragmatic awareness, cognition	(Abolfathiasl & Abdullah, 2015; Bardovi-Harlig, 2009; Bardovi-Harlig & Griffin, 2005; Baron & Celaya, 2010; Halenko & Jones, 2011; Kinginger & Farrell, 2003; Taguchi, 2008)
Pragmatic instruction	(Abrams, 2014; Alcón-Soler, 2005; Alcón-Soler, 2015; Bardovi-Harlig & Vellenga, 2012; Bodycott & Walker, 2000; Eve & Josep, 2010; Farashaiyan, Tan, & Subakir, 2014; Glaser, 2013; Ifantidou, 2013; Koike & Pearson, 2005; Mehmet, 1991; Nguyen, Pham, & Pham, 2012; Soler & Martinez-Flor, 2008)
Cross-cultural comparison	(Blum-Kulka & House, 1989; Blum-Kulka, et al., 1989; Nishida, 1985; Thomas, 1982)
Pragmatic development, evaluation of ILP competence	(Alemi, Eslami, & Rezanejad, 2014; Kathleen Bardovi-Harlig, 1999, 2013; Baron & Celaya, 2010; Chang, 2011; Cohen, 2008; Kasper, 2001; Kasper & Schmidt, 1996; Kinginger, 2011; Rose, 2000)

There are also some important works on this topic (Kasper, 1992a; Schauer, 2009). In 1997, Rintell refers pragmatics to the study of speech acts, suggesting that learners' pragmatic competence manifest in how they use language to convey specific intentions. Therefore, there are tremendous studies on speech acts for pragmatic sake, among which request and apology are the most popular speech act (see Table 2).

Table 2   **Classification of studies on speech acts**

Types of speech acts	Studies on speech acts
Request	(Cohen & Shively, 2007; Rasouli Khorshidi, 2013; Economidou-Kogetsidis, 2010; Hassall, 2003; House & Kasper, 1987; Kahraman & Akkus, 2007; Koc, 2011; Kotorova, 2015; Li, 2012; Lin, 2009; Lundell & Erman, 2012; Rue & Zhang, 2008; Shively, 2011)
Apology	(Ghanbari, Gowhary, & Azizifar, 2015; Jebahi, 2011; Kim, 2008; Nureddeen, 2008; Rasouli Khorshidi, 2013; Warga & Schölmberger, 2007)
Refusal	(Felix-Brasdefer, 2004; Lin, 2014; Sa'd & Mohammad, 2014; Turnbull & Saxton, 1997)
Gratitude, compliment, complain, suggestion	(Lin, Woodfield, & Ren, 2012; Özdemir & Rezvani, 2010; Schauer & Adolphs, 2006; Yusefi, et al. , 2015; Li, 2010)

These studies on request speech acts are numerous with detailed elaboration of the coding scheme of pragmatic strategies, which paved the way for exploring cross-cultural difference. And we can also probe into the trajectories of learners' pragmatic development based on the changes of their pragmatic strategies.

However, studies on interlanguage pragmatics are not sufficient in China, and most of which are theoretical elaborations. And few empirical studies were conducted on speech acts (see Table 3) . As a result, it is urgent to conduct empirical studies for pedagogical implications and theory generation.

Table 3   **Research on ILP in China**

Research area	Type of researches	Some studies
ILP	Theory elaboration	(He, 1996; Hong, 2005; Huang, 2013; Liu & Liao, 2006; Shang, 1997; Xu & Ma, 2002;)
	Empirical studies	(Huang, 2013; Xu, 2015)

Research area	Type of researches	Some studies
Speech act	Request, apology, refusal, gratitude	(Wang & Li, 2007; Yang, 2009; Li, 2012; Lin, 2014; Su, 2014)

Note: including published on international journals.

More and more international students come to study in China, but few studies could be found on the interlanguage pragmatic development of the international students. As a result, this study attempts to fill this gap. Korean, Russian and French learners were selected for the cultural difference and the number of students at SISU in this study. Through discourse completion test (DCT), the features of their pragmatic features in request behaviors were found and their pragmatic developmental trajectories were defined, which is vital for pragmatic instruction and pedagogical implications. Furthermore, some main factors that affect their pragmatic development were also pined down so as to adjust administration to the international students and for other implications as well.

1.2   Purposes of the research

This study aims to capture the features of pragmatic strategies in request speech acts among the international students from different cultural backgrounds, and further our understanding of the process of their pragmatic development through a survey based on DCT and a case study of 3 international students, chosen for their cultural difference and their Chinese pragmatic competence. The purposes of this study are as follows:

1) This study intends to find out the features of the pragmatic strategies in request behaviors from the cross-cultural perspective. There are already some studies about the different choices of pragmatic strategies and linguistic usage for

the cultural difference. However, the studies on requests made in Chinese by the learners from different countries are hardly to be found. The target of this current study was to figure out the features of the pragmatic strategies so as to apply different types of instructions for the international students from different backgrounds.

2) It attempts to figure out the individual trajectories of pragmatic development in study abroad context. Many scholars have argued that study abroad context can help enhance L2 learners' pragmatic competence (Kinginger, 2008; Rasouli Khorshidi, 2013; Warga & Schölmberger, 2007) . China is study abroad context for the chosen participants in this study. Therefore, I chose 3 participants (1 Korean, 1 French, 1 Russian students) to test whether they have developed their pragmatic competence and how they developed their pragmatic competence.

3) It aims to find out the factors that affect their pragmatic growth. Some studies show that L2 learners' personality, attitudes towards the targeted culture, gender, explicit and implicit instructions and length of stay in study abroad context are all possible factors (Alcón-Soler, 2015; Bella, 2011) . However, there are few longitudinal case studies conducted to provide further evidence. Taguchi (2015) points out that future research should focus on the nature, domain and patterns of social contacts, activity types and learners' motivation orientation, thereby the types of personal experience and personality traits have impact on L2 pragmatic development could be figured out. The study employed case studies to describe, understand and explain the factors or activities that might facilitate or constrain the pragmatic development of the international students.

1. 3　Research design overview

This section displays a brief overview of the research design, with a more detailed description in chapter 3.

　　Shanghai International Studies University (SISU) was selected as the main research site (it is futher described in Chapter 3), which enjoys high reputation internationally with a large number of international students enrolled. In light of these search questions, 20 French, 20 Russian and 20 Korean students were chosen from short-term language course for the survey, and most of them enrolled in september 2015, and return to their own countries in July 2016. The criteria for selecting these 60 participants consisted of 1) Chinese Language proficiency (passing hanyu shuipin kaoshi (HSK) level 3 or at intermediate level); 2) Randomly chosen from language course. 20 Chinese undergraduates were chosen as baseline data at SISU. Moreover, I conducted a follow-up case study for further understanding of the pragmatic development. 3 participants from Korea, Russia and France respectively were among these 60 participants chosen for their willingness and cultural differences.

　　This research was carried out through collecting four types of data: 1) DCT eliciting questionnaire; 2) semi-structured interviews; 3) field notes; 4) natural recording. In light of Chapter 2, literature review and small-scale pilot study, the data collection instruments were shaped and refined. These different data sources intertwined and triangulated with each other. As for the data analysis, the coding scheme of pragmatic strategies through DCT was adapted from other scholars (Blum-Kulka & House, 1989). Concerning reliability and validity, I wrote journals and memos during the whole research process, and also consulted with colleagues, experts and supervisors to check coding schemes, and discussed findings with them as well.

　　As for a results of this study, the features of the pragmatic strategies in request behaviors among different cultures were found. Accordingly, teachers could be acknowledged for adapting appropriate teaching method to enhance international students' pragmatic competence. Furthermore, with the help of case studies, learners' pragmatic development process was found. The divergence and convergence of the developmental process in terms of the cultural difference could help teacher employ proper teaching method catering to the different needs of these international students. Main factors that facilitated or constrained their Chinese pragmatic development were also identified, which could possibly provide some reference for teaching and learning in study abroad, and also for the administration of the international students.

1. 4　Significance of the research

This study provides with some potential contributions to our knowledge of Chinese learners' interlanguage pragmatic development, which is related to cultural backgrounds, personal traits and other factors. Based on the data of this current study, this thesis could be a trigger for developing Chinese pragmatic competence of the international students. The significance of this research is elaborated from practical perspective as well as from theoretical perspective.

Kasper (1989) states that the main problem lies in multi-cultural communication still caused by the problem of pragmatics. Emphasis is laid on intonation, vocabulary and grammar in Chinese language teaching, while assessing learners' language proficiency, we mainly check whether the learners can use Chinese to communicate smoothly, in another word, the pragmatic competence stands out (LI & Xue, 2007). This study indicated that most international students didn't pay attention to Chinese pragmatics while using Chinese to interact. They tended to transfer their way of expression into Chinese directly, or they realize the difference but chose to remain their own way for maintaining their own cultural identities. The analysis of this study could arouse teachers' attention to the students' pragmatic features for different cultures, which could help enhance students' multi-cultural communicative competence and make their life easier in China.

This study employed longitudinal case study so as to explore the convergence and divergence of the pragmatic development of the international students from various cultural backgrounds. Accordingly, the pragmatic developmental rules were extracted for instruction implications. In addition to what has been mentioned, main factors that might facilitate and constrain their pragmatic development were also illustrated, which could provide implications for curriculum design, teaching Chinese as a foreign language and also for administration of the international students. Moreover, the international students could understand their own pragmatic features better in light of this study. As a result, they could avoid the negative pragmatic transfer and promote the positive pragmatic transfer. The international students' overall language proficiency also could be improved swiftly.

1. 5   Organization of the dissertation

This thesis is organized in seven chapters. As is shown above, Chapter 1 introduces the research background, purpose and significance of the present study. In Chapter 2, the important concepts related to interlanguage pragmatics and requests in politeness are identified and explained; theories relevant to L2 pragmatic learning, such as sociocultural theory, language socialization theory and dynamic system theory, are reviewed; key factors in empirical studies in the L2 requests are reviewed and research gaps are identified based on the review. Chapter 3 illustrates and justifies the research methodology. Moreover, issues of validity and reliability and ethical problem are also addressed.

Chapter 4 and Chapter 5 present the findings of the research. Chapter 4 provides and demonstrates a holistic picture of all the collected data, identifying pragmatic features of Chinese speakers provided as baseline data. The characteristics of pragmatic strategies produced by Korean, Russian and French students are also identified in comparison to those of Chinese speakers in terms of openers, head act (HA), external modifications (EM) and internal modifications (IM). The investigation of Chapter 5 evolves and emerges based on the previous chapter. By employing an ethnographic case study approach, this chapter analyzes and discusses findings from data of three case participants and explores the dynamic process of learners' pragmatic development. The pragmatic development trajectories of those participants vary for certain reasons. The main factors that might affect their pragmatic development are analyzed based on interview and observation data. An overview of cross-case analysis is described to understand the individual variation of pragmatic development. Chapter 6 gerneralizes the major findings in responses to the three questions and discusses the relations between pragmatic features and cultural backgrounds. Factors that result in the different pragmatic development trajectories are then examined and explained. This chapter concludes with the proposal of a model on the factors of L2 pragmatic development. Chapter 7 suggests possible contributions of the findings to the field of interlanguage pragmatic development, as well as the discussion of methodological considerations and implications for teaching, learning and administration of foreign students. Limitation of this research is elaborated, and possible directions for future research are proposed.

Chapter 2

Literature Review

2. 1　Introduction

The previous chapter illustrated the background, significance and purposes of the research and the overall structure of the thesis. This chapter aims to construct a conceptual framework for understanding interlanguage development in Chinese learners. This review of the following three parts of the literature sheds light on understanding of the research topic: （1）key concepts of pragmatics, politeness and request, （2）theoretical concepts on interlanguage development, （3）studies on interlanguage development.

This chapter attempts to address the following issues. First, it examines the key constructs on which this study is ground. Second, the review of different theories aims to develop a conceptual framework for understanding the phenomenon. Third, the literature review provides an understanding of the factors that affect L2 learners' interlanguage development, and which relates to the context, learners' cultural backgrounds etc.

This chapter is structured into the following four sections. Section 2. 2 identifies the concepts of interlanguage pragmatics, different perceptions of politeness and face between western and eastern cultures, and also reviews the situational factors in requests. Section 2. 3 reviews theories related to interlanguage development, and also examines the relationship between L2 learners living context, personal, sociocultural and linguistic factors and interlanguage development. Section 2. 4 reviews the existing research on interlanguage pragmatics and the speech act of requests from the cross-cultural perspective. Section 2. 5 presents a conceptual framework of pragmatic development of Chinese learners. Section 2. 6 concludes this chapter by pointing out the research gap and justifying the research questions.

2. 2   Key concepts

This review section illustrates four fundamental constructs, which are interlanguage pragmatics, politeness, face and request, which are also key terms to investigate this current study. Furthermore, this study focuses on the speech act of requests from cross-cultural perspectives. These constructs are redefined, elaborated and contrasted between western and eastern cultures, which highlight the differences of linguistic forms, functions and meaning in speech act performance for achieving politeness.

"Pragmatics" was first put forward by American logician, Morris (1938), who shows that language is composed of syntax, semantics and pragmatics. He states that syntax focus on interrelations between symbols and semantics, intend to study the relationship between symbols and the subjects that refers to, and pragmatics relates symbols to interlocutors. Yule (1996) states that pragmatics could be defined as a subject studying contextualized meaning. Pragmatics was established as a new discipline in 1860s, the emergence of which conforms to the regulation of language studies, because it relates language to those complicated factors, such as sociocultural, contextual and user factors, which shape the lens to reflect the overall scene of language studies.

There are more than 10 types of definitions of pragmatics. Crystal (1985) points out that pragmatics lays stress on users of the language, emphasized the process of discousal conversations in natural communication and the effects of discourse on interlocutors. He analyzed the evolution of the definitions of pragmatics in 2010, and he argues that the definition given by Yule seems the most appropriate one, although there is still some weakness. Pragmatics studies how speakers' express and hearers interpreter the implication, assumption and illocutionary force embedded in communicative discourse (Yule, 1996). Both of the definitions provide a good ground for this current study for its emphasis on actual language interaction, coding and decoding of sentences applied by interlocutors.

In the past thirty years, pragmaticshas developed tremendously, which involves context, speech act, deixis, conversational structure and pragmatic strategies. Moreover, the theories concerning pragmatics are booming, such as Gricean cooperative principle, Leech's politeness principle (leech, 1983), Brown and Levinson's principles of pragmatics (Brown & Levinson, 1978) etc.. Pragmatics brought into China not until the 1980s, which grew and spread fast afterwards in China for the significant contributions made by some scholars[①].

Levinson categorized the different understanding of pragmatics into two groups in 1983: the Anglo-American tradition and the European Continental tradition. The former restricts the scope of pragmatics, close to traditional linguistics, referring to the systematic elaboration of meaning derived from linguistic usage. The latter is much broader, which is comprised of such as discourse analysis, sociolinguistics, psycholinguistics, cross-cultural pragmatics and interlanguage pragmatics etc.. I will review cross-cultural pragmatics and interlanguage pragmatics in the following passage, which is tightly related to my research topic.

In 1970s, misunderstandings in intercultural communication results from

---

① Guozhang Xu, Ziran He, Zhaoxiong He

pragmatic issues had received numerous scholars' attention in this area. And then "cross-cultural pragmatics" emerged as an independent interdisci-plinary inquiry with its own conferences and journal in the 1990s. Cross-cultural pragmatics is also named intercultural pragmatics by Kecskes (2014), Hong (2005). House and Kasper (1987) points out that as a subdiscipline of contrastive pragmatics, cross-cultural inquiry focuses on pragmatic similarities, differences and pragmatic failures which raised from communication among various languages. The reason why it became an important newly established discipline is that people from different cultural backgrounds are prone to employ their own conventional expressions to communicate, and the misunderstanding emerges, which attracts scholars' attention extensively.

Although cross-cultural communication and cross-cultural pragmatics have a common ground, the scope of the former is broader than that of the latter. The former has to pay attention to body language, spatial distance and costume, besides linguistic issues (Wang, 2002), while the latter only focuses on the linguistic aspects of cross-cultural communication.

Kecskes (2014) indicates that cross-cultural pragmatics is based not only on pragmatic theory, but also on anthropology, communication, lingu-istics, discourse and second language acquisition, and its major source of development has always been Gricean pragmatics. Gricean theories regard intention as central to communication (Levisons, 2006), while recent studies against the continued placement of Gricean intention at the center of pragmatic theories. However, the linguistic-philosophical lines, such as Relevance Theory, Speech Act Theory and Politeness Theory, which are regarded as the basis of cross-cultural pragmatics, still consider intentions as center in communication. These theories all originated from western countries, which were challenged for overgeneralization without taking the different views from oriental countries into account.

In 1989, Blum-Kulka and House conducted a series of research to examine the pragmatic variations of request and apology speech acts from cross-cultural perspectives. He argues that this research was relevant to speech acts in 2010, contrastive pragmatics, cross-cultural pragmatics and interlanguage pragmatics. Request and apology made in different languages embody the pragmatic features of their first language, which is worth conducting research in this respect. The findings of the pragmatic difference among diverse languages could enhance understanding and bridge the cultural gap among people from different nations. Moreover, it is safe to make a conclusion from Blum-Kulka and House's study that contrastive pragmatics, cross-cultural pragmatics and interlanguage pragmatics are intertwined and correlated with each other in this kind of research.

　　As for this current study, I intend to find out the specific pragmatic features of L2 learners by studying their request speech acts in Chinese, and also try to seek their developmental trajectories of Chinese pragmatic competence from the cross-cultural perspective. To examine the international students' Chinese pragmatic competence and pragmatic development belongs to interlanguage pragmatics; to investigate the pragmatic features of these international students belongs to cross-cultural pragmatics; and to compare these international students' pragmatic features also involves contrastive pragmatics. In the following section, the interlanguage pragmatics will be reviewed for this study's sake.

2. 2. 1　Interlanguage pragmatics

　　With the emergence of *"interlanguage pragmatics"* coedited by Kasper and Blum-kulka, inerlanguage pragmatics (ILP) was established as an independent discipline. In 1989, Kasper defines interlanguage pragmatics as the discipline focusing on behavioristic patterns of second language learners' learning and using the second language. In 2010, He indicates that interlanguage pragmatics is not an independent language, but a kind of intelanguage existing between two languages, and embodies the features of these two languages and cultures. Interlanguage pragmatics belongs to pragmatics and second language acquisition involving sociolinguistics, psycholinguistics and language usage, which is now a heated research topic. As for this 'hybrid' nature of interlanguage pragmatics, In 2002, Kasper and Rose defined it that interlanguage pragmatics tend to examine how nonnative speakers understand and use the target language, and how L2 learners develop their capability to comprehend and produce action in the target language.

According to this definition, we could extract two main elements. First, it implicates that learner's pragmatic competence involves both comprehension and production of target language. Second, the learners have to get the ability of understanding the social variables in target language so as to produce appropriate linguistic behavior. These two elements are similar to pragmalinguistics and sociopragamtics respectively. And both of them constitute learners' pragmatic competence. The following subsection is going to review pragmatic competence.

2. 2. 1. 1　Pragmatic competence

In 1980, Chomsky defines pragmatic competence as the knowledge of realization of various purposes through appropriate use of the language in a particular situation. Fraser expanded the definition in 1983, and states that pragmatic competence includes the knowledge how a hearer interprets a speaker's intended meanings in saying and recognizes the illocutionary forces embedded in speakers' utterance. The most influential definition offered by Crystal (1997), which states that language is studied on the part of the users, especially the choices they make, focusing on the obstacles they confronted with durmg the interaction by applying the language and the effect of the use of language on others who participate in the conversation. Recently, Rose proposed the definition in 1989, which is extensively accepted in interlanguage pragmatics. He states that pragmatic competence is defined as the ability to employ linguistic knowledge (pragmalinguistics) in a particular context appropriately (sociop-ragmatics) .

Pragmalinguistics emphasizeslinguistic structures for utterances in a language, and describes how we must use them in a language in a correct way. Sociopragamtics emphasizes the sociocultural respects of social interaction, and lays stress on the situational factors, such as power, social distance, gender and etc. , (leech, 1983; Thomas, 1983). This study applied Leech and Thomas' definition of pragmalinguistic and sociopragmatic competence. Uso-Juan and Martinez-Flor (2006) argues that L2 learners often encountered some difficulties in their interactions with native speakers, so they need to be acknowledged of grammar and linguistic forms in target language (pragm-alinguistics), cultural norms and conventions in that language (sociop-ragmatics) . Consequently, L2 learners' smooth interaction with native speakers could be achieved through their familiarity of the linguistic knowledge and acknowledgment of social norms and conventions of the target language.

Abundant empirical studies on different types of speech acts have been conducted to investigate L2 learners' interlanguage pragmatic competence and its development (Allami & Naeimi, 2011; Bataller, 2010; Hassall, 2013). In 1997, Rintell states that the study of speech acts is central to pragmatics, claiming that how L2 learners produce utterances to convey particular intentions and how they interpret the intended meanings uttered by speakers are regarded as two important aspects of their pragmatic ability. The studies on various types of speech acts still remain as a hot area in interlanguage pragmatics.

In this current study, the request speech act was investigated to explore the features of pragmatic strategies of international students with different cultural and linguistic backgrounds, and also to understand the relationship among their pragmatic development, sojourn, cultural background and so on. In the pilot study, I found that transfer occurred from time to time, when they use Chinese to communicate. Based on interview data, they admitted that they translated some of the sentences or strategies directly from their native language. It seems that transfer is unavoidable, so this study attempts to find out how these international students get rid of negative transfer to develop their Chinese pragmatic competence during their stay in China. The following section reviews pragmatic transfer accordingly.

2.2.1.2 Pragmatic transfer

Apart from the popularity of studies on speech acts, transfer is also a hot term in interlanguage (Schauer, 2009). In 1981, Coulmas states that transfer occurred when L2 learners tend to translate certain norms, strategies of their first language into the targeted language to achieve a particular purpose. Transfer emerged in contrastive analysis (CA) period, which not only related to behaviorist views of language learning, but also structural view of language acquisition (Bu, 2010). Transfer consists of positive transfer and negative transfer. When two languages differ from each other considerably, negative transfer tends to occur since learners are likely to encounter difficulty in social language by employing L2, which would cause errors in communication; and when two languages don't differ much, positive transfer is prone to take place since L2 learners experience less difficulties in social language, which would lead to the facilitation of learning (Franch, 1998).

Pragamtic transfer is an important source of cross-cultural communication breakdown (Beebe, Takahashi, & Uliss-weltz, 1990). In 1992, Kasper defined that pragmatic transfer shall lay stress on the effects of L2 learners' pragmatic knowledge of languages and cultures on L2 learning rather than the target linguistic knowledge on their understanding, production and learning of pragmatic information.

According to Leech, pragmatic transfer encompasses sociopragmatic transfer and pragmalinguistic transfer. The pragmalinguistic-sociopragmatic dichotomy put forward by Thomas (1983) offered framework which helped to conduct studies on pragmatic transfer in ILP. Regarding the definition of pragmalinguistic and sociopragmatic transfer, Kapser (1992, P 226) defined as follows:

Sciopragmatic transfer operates when the social perceptions underlying language users' "interpretation and performance of linguistic action in second language are influenced by their assessment of their subjectively equivalent in first language context. Moreover, pragmalinguistic transfer designates the process whereby illocutionary force or politeness value assignedto particular linguistic material in first language influences learners' perception and performance of form-function mappings in second language."

As for empirical studies of pragmalinguistic transfer provided by Bu (2010) examined the suggestion strategies by Chinese learner of English. The results indicate that Chinese learners used more direct suggestion strategies for negative pragmatic transfer. Byon explored and described sociopragmatic features of Americans learning Korean as a foreign language through investigating request behaviors. The results show that learners demonstrated L1 transfer in terms of the analysis of semantic formula. More and more empirical studies involving quantitative and qualitative method have been conducted to assess pragmatic transfer in recent years (Bu, 2011; Dogancay-Aktuna & Kamisli, 1992; Hashemian, 2012)

Pragmatic transfer would be affected by numerous factors, eg, language proficiency, learning environment, instructional effects, learners' perception of language distance between their L1 and L2, length of stay in study abroad context (Beebe et al. , 1990; Felix-Brasdefer, 2004). However, It has been confirmed that prolonged length of stay in the target community could not guarantee the fade away of 'negative' pragmatic transfer (Kasper, 1992b) . In this current study, three case participants had been staying in China for almost one year, which could not predict their discard of negative pragmatic transfer. Although the central issue of this study is international students' pragmatic development, pragmatic transfer can't be neglected, which affects learners' pragmatic development. The development of pragmatic competence and pragmatic transfer interrelate with each other, since learners become aware of negative transfer and make efforts to get rid of it, which would result in facilitation of pragmatic development. Politeness as a crucial term in pragmatics is reviewed in the following section.

2. 2. 2   Politeness across cultures

Last section reviwed some key terms and conception concerning interlanguage pragmatics. Politeness is crucial to interpret pragmatic phenomenon in communication. This section illustrates some important theories of politeness, definition of politeness and the key role that politeness plays in communication, and it also demonstrates the different perception and production of politeness in Eastern and Western cultures.

2. 2. 2. 1   Politeness

Politeness is considered as a kind of pragmatic phenomenon when addressing the issues of pragmatics (Brown & Levinson, 1978; leech, 1983; Thomas, 1983) . Leech regards politeness as the key term to explain the indirectness in communication. His conversational-maxim is mainly derived from Gricean's Cooperative Principle, which is composed of Generosity, Tact, Modesty, Approbation, Agreement, and Sympathy maxims (leech, 1983) . Leech's model is criticized for its unrestrained number of maxims. However, it offers the ground for cross-cultural comparisons in terms of the perceptions of politeness and the use of pragmatic strategies.

Brownand Levinson's model of politeness (B&L) is viewed as the milestone on language and politeness. The core of this model is face-threatening acts (FAT). B&L provided a model of linguistic politeness illustrated in detail, which has attracted enormous criticisms. They argue that politeness could be divided into two types of politeness in terms of positive and negative face, positive politeness and negative politeness (Brown & Levinson, 1987, P 61).

Negative face: the basic claim to territories, personal preserves, rights to non-distraction-i. e. to freedom of action and freedom from imposition.

Positive face: the positive consistent self-image or " personality " (crucially including the desire that this self-image be appreciated and approved of) claimed by interactant.

Face originated in Chinese culture (mainzi, lian) bears different interpretations in B&L's model, which has remained a controversial issue. Some scholars argue that negative face only exists in western culture for its special emphasis on people's desires and right to freedom. Thus, it cannot be regarded as a universal theory to explain the politeness phenomenon across all languages and cultures (Leech, 2007). However, this model has paved the way for studies on speech acts from a cross-cultural perspective.

As mentioned above, these theories of politeness arefundamental to conduct research on speech acts. What is politeness? Watts (2003) defined: "politeness, like money, is one of the means by which we are able to adapt our behavior to that which is appropriate to the social interaction type in which we are involved. " He argues that politeness is socially and historically constituted, and it should form part of the linguistic resources that determine the discoursal patterns of social communications. Mills (2003, P 72) states:

> Politeness cannot be understood simply as a property of utterances, or even as a set of choices made solely by individuals, but rather as a set of practices or strategies which communities of practice develop, affirm, contest, and which individuals within these communities engage with in order to come to an assessment of their own and other's behavior and position within the group.

We can see that one of Mill's key terms that lay the ground of this definition is that of "community of practice". I chose to review these two definitions for some similar features which they share. First, politeness could be regarded as a set of linguistic forms or strategies that people from a certain community employ to achieve smooth interaction in order to maintain good interpersonal relations with others. Second, politeness is universal and particular, universal for some norms that all the social members should abide by, particular for some norms only belonging to a particular community or group. Third, Watts and Mills both take "appropriateness" as an important notion in relation to the judgment of politeness in utterances. This current study attempts to find out the perceptions of politeness from different cultures through exploring their linguistic forms and pragmatic strategies. Consequently, these definitions lay solid ground for this study.

Politeness is regarded as a crucial issue in communication. Politeness could be viewed as an implicit communicative strategy, which helps to establish or maintain pleasant relationship, save mutual face and get what we want in communication (Brown&Levinson, 1987; Levinson, 1983). Holmes (1995) argues that politeness is a type of behaviors, not only shows concern to others, but also refrains from distancing the interlocutors. As a result, politeness could be viewed as a type of very important strategy in shaping human relationships and achieving smooth communication.

As stated above, politeness is considered as a kind of communication strategy. We could use a set of certain linguistic forms to reflect this communication strategy. Holtgraves (2005) states that politeness, a theoretical concept, could be viewed as the overlapping part of sociocultural, individuals' cognitive and linguistic processes. He attempts to analyze politeness from social cognitive and psychological perspectives. And he stresses those language users as social beings carrying various beliefs, values and motives, which could be reflected in their conversation. According to Brown and Levinson (1987), face is the core notion in politeness model, which functions as a mediating construct that mediates between a number of social cognitive variables and language use. In another word, face-work can be achieved through politeness strategies, which could be interpreted as linguistic means. However, the perception of interpersonal relations, power and other factors influence the level of politeness (Holtgraves, 2005). He also states that people from various communities or cultures perceive these social variables in different ways, so acknowledgment of culturally conditioned expectation of politeness forms is crucial to eradicate the barriers in cross-cultural communication. In this study, my research attempted to find out the features of pragmatic strategies by making requests in Chinese between Asian and European students based on the different understanding of politeness. Thereby, politeness in Eastern and Western cultures will be review in the following passages.

2. 2. 2. 2   Politeness in Eastern and Western cultures

In 1987, Brown and Levinson offer an influential theoretical framework for studying politeness from cross-cultural and interlinguistic perspectives. However, serious debates are triggered for their overstress on individualistic and egalitarian motivation, which is embedded in Western culture, and neglect the group-centered hierarchy-based ethos of Eastern society. Although Brown and Levinson regarded the model of politeness as universal, they also admitted variations among diverse cultures and languages:

"The essential idea is this: interactional systematics is based largely on universal principles. But the application of the principles differs systematically across cultures, and within cultures across subcultures, categories and groups. "

Although there are different terms to symbolize politeness in various languages and cultures, neither absolute universalist position nor relativist position is tenable.

In 2004, Byon investigated the request speech act in terms of semantic formula and usage patterns between Koreans and Americans, and found out that Koreans tend to be more hierarchical, roundabout and collectivistic comparing with their American counterparts. In 1993, Spencer-Oatey argues that Chinese postgraduates show more respect to their tutors in regard to power but closer social distance than do their British counterparts. Koreans and Chinese both originated from Confucius philosophy, sharing similar perceptions of politeness. Americans and British are western countries sharing the same root of Socratic philosophy.

Although oriental cultures have the similar features, Chinese perception of politeness has its own particular characteristics. Social connection (Guanxi) works as a key word for better understanding politeness phenomenon in China. In fact, it is social network, the size of which is relied on the position or positions an individual wins or captures in the society. Guanxi and power symbolize capital, which is crucial to investigate politeness and impoliteness in Chinese (Xie, He, & Lin, 2005). In 1994, Mao suggests that politeness involves the communicative purpose in respect of the speaker, who may attempt to establish relationship, seek interpersonal connectedness to others in one's society. Since Chinese face is regarded as communal and interpersonal, politeness in Chinese, which is beneficial to both parties who engage in conversation with mutually shared orientation to negotiate, protect and elevate each other's fact (Zhang, 1995). Protecting other's face as well as helping others have a good reputation in their community is seen as polite actions in Chinese culture.

In this research, International students from different countries were chosen as participants for the cultural difference and different perception of politeness. Generally speaking, Asian students including Chinese have a similar sense of politeness, and European students tend to have different perception of politeness in contrast to Chinese. As a result, when they make requests in Chinese, they would employ different linguistic forms and semantic formulae to achieve politeness. Based on the pilot study, it was found that perception of politeness, the use of alerting or linguistic forms are changing among young people especially the 90's generation in China. However, these Chinese learners still expressed an "out-of-date" way in comparison to their native Chinese contemporaries.

2.2.3   Situational factors in requests

Numerous studies have been conducted to examine a variety of speech act performance in ILP in order to capture the variations of pragmatic strategies produced by people from different cultural and linguistic backgrounds, and to understand different communication styles across cultures (Beebe, Takahashi, & Weltz, 1990; House & Kasper, 1987). In 2011, Koc investigated the request strategies applied by Turkish learners of English and British native speakers of English. It systemized the various strategies used by Turkish learners, which were quite different from their British counterparts for cultural variations. Speech act theory was first raised by Austin (1962), and then criticized and developed by his student Searle (1976). This theory intends to illustrate how speakers convey intended meaning by using language as well as how hearers interpret the intended meanings embedded in the utterances produced by speakers. In 1982, Bruner, Roy, and Ratner indicate that focus is given to studies on speech act and politeness in ILP, and request speech act has remained as the priority for many researchers for being closest to the social interaction of the prototype.

Speaker benefits from the requests that he or she formulates by getting the hearer to do an act (Searle, 1979). Requests are made to get an object, assistance, or information, which is a basic and one of the most common speech acts in human interactions (Curl & Drew, 2008). And requests have always been associated with a special sensitivity because it imposes on the recipient to some extent (Brown & Levinson, 1987). As a result, request speech act would be the most appropriate for this study, which aims to examine learners' speech act realization from different L1 backgrounds.

Moreover, a request could be regarded as a face-threatening act (FTA), since both speakers and hearers' face would be affected: the hearer may feel imposed on by a request which embodies speakers' manifestation of power; the speaker may be afraid of offending the hearer for imposing something on him or her by producing a request act (Li, 2009). Consequently, speakers from various cultural backgrounds are prone to employ different pragmatic strategies and linguistic forms to satisfy hearers' negative face wants or speakers' own positive wants. In order to fulfill this purpose, when a speaker makes a request, she or he should consider the situational factors, such as power, social distance and imposition, which are viewed as the most influential factors in making speech acts (Lee, 2005). These situational variables will be addressed in the following section.

In 1987, Brown and Levinson argue that the evaluation of the degree of seriousness of an FTA including the following situational variables in almost all cultures: (1) social distance (D), the horizontal social dimension between the speaker and the hearer in front of the speech act. (2) Power (P), the vertical dimensions of status the speaker and the hearer hold. (3) Ranking of imposition (R), is culturally and situationally specific, by the degree to which the hearer is interfered with. Moreover, there is a formula to evaluate the degree of FTA, which have been changing, refining and challenging since then. In 1989, Blum-Kulka and House listed numerous other significant factors, and they grouped them into "context external" and "context internal" factors. The former includes social distance, power and interlocutors' rights and obligations, and the latter encompasses factors related to the requestive act directly, such as the purpose of request behavior, the ranking of imposition. However, social distance, power and imposition have remained as the most widely examined in request speech act (Economidou-Kogetsidis, 2010).

There are alternative terms for these three situational factors. For example, "status" and "dominance" are used in a great number of studies instead of "social power", but power remains the most common one (Economidou-Kogetsidis, 2010). This study adopts Brown and Gilman's (1972) definition of power, they state that power involves two parties: the speaker and the hearer, both of them cannot have power at the same time. There are many variables included in power: sex, age, strength, and their state in the family or wealth.

According to this, people who have power can control or exert influence on someone else. Moreover, power also involves the rights and obligations; for example, a customer has the right to complain, so the customer has a greater power than the waiter in this respect. Social power is viewed differently in various cultures. Social class and status might not be so important in an egalitarian culture as that in a culture that lays stress on vertical interpersonal relations. Japan is a typical culture emphasizing social class (Fukushima, 2000).

Regarding social distance, in 1996, Spencer-Oatey concludes that one or more of the following variables are involved when interpreting this factor: similarity or difference, frequency of contact, familiarity, positive or negative affection, sense of like-mindedness. This study follows Fukushima (2000) definition of social distance, he states it as follows: (1) similarity or difference between people, (2) the degree of familiarity, and (3) sense of likeness to each other. If they are friends, they know each other, but perhaps they don't like each other so well; if they are good friends, they are not only know each other very well, they like each other very much and establish a close relationship.

With regard to imposition, Thomas (1995) defined imposition as "how great the request you are making is," while Fukushima (2000) suggests that the following factors affect the ranking of imposition, such as time, efforts, financial and psychological burden that results from the requested acts. Goffman (1967) employs the concept of "free product" and "non-free product" to label the value of the outcome of requests.

Both situations and cultures affect the way that people perceive and assess these situational factors. In 1989, Blum-Kulka and House point out that people from various communities or cultures may differ from each other in their perception of social situations and in relative importance attributes to those three situational variables. This study examines the international students using Chinese to make requests, which eventually aims to capture the dynamic process of the changes of their perception of these variables in Chinese context. Consequently, we can assess whether these students' pragmatic competence developed or not, comparing their pragmatic strategies to that of their native Chinese counterparts' in the same scenarios designed based on those situational variables.

2. 3　Theoretical concepts

This section reviews two prominent theoretical approaches or perspectives evident in L2 pragmatic development and second language acquisition: (1) language socialization, (2) Dynamic systems theory, (3) the Intercultural Interaction Model.

2. 3. 1　Language socialization theory

Language acquisition does not touch on the subject of language socialization, which was derived from anthropological convictions that language facilicates children's development of social and cultural knowledge and sensibilities (Duranti, Ochs, & Schieffelin, 2012). Wood, Burner, and Ross (1976) states that language socialization derived from Vygotsky's notion termed "scaffolding" indicates that when instructors and more proficient peers offer support and guidance to less capable individuals, it helps to develop their competence in the process of learning. Other scholars echo their claim, and point out that sociocultural theory and activity theory laid solid ground for language socialization research (Duff, 2007; Duff&Talmay, 2011). Language socialization has not been widely applied in studies on language learning as it has in the areas of anthropology and sociology before (Wang, 2010). At an early stage, many studies on Language socialization focused on children's first language acquisition, which is viewed as L1 language socialization. In 1979, Ochs and Schieffelin claim that the study of child language learning includes developmental pragmatics, and the scope of pragmatics tends to involve "the context of situation", with an interest in speech acts, activities, stances, and etc.

Studies in second language acquisition from a language socialization perspective have become a hot zone attracting many scholars' attention in recent years (Bayley & Schecter, 2003; Duff, 2003; Duff & Talmay, 2011; Schieffelin & Ochs, 1986). In 2011, Duff argues that in the progression of L2 socialization, those who have higher proficiency level (teacher, tutors, peers) in the language will help those who have lower proficiency level (novices such as students and immigrants). He also states that second language (L2) socialization refers to a process of picking up the target language in order to participate in the practices of communities among newcomers or people returning to a community that they may once belong to, but lost linguistic competence. Duff (2007, P 310) defined language socialization as:

> ⋯the process by which novices or newcomers in a community or culture gain communicative competence, membership, and legitimacy in the group. It is a process that is mediated by language and whose goal is the mastery of linguistic conventions, pragmatics, the adoption of appropriate identities, stances (eg, epistemic or empathetic or ideologies, and other behaviors associated with the target group and its normative practices).

Language socialization research emphasizes how children and newcomers "are socialized through the use of language as well as how they are socialized to use language" (Ochs & Schieffelin, 1984). Based on above mentioned definition of language socialization, there are three features concerned: (1) newcomers or novices learn linguistic conventions, pragmatics, construction of new identities, stances through language learning process; (2) they acquire language gradually through social activities, such as, telling a story, attempting to solve a problem, playing a game and daily interactions etc. (3) language learning is a process of acquiring both linguistic and cultural knowledge. Language works as a medium,

through which interpretations and acquisition of sociocultural knowledge, ideolog-
ies, moral values, beliefs and knowledge structures can be achieved, in which
linguistic knowledge is embedded (Ochs, 1988). In current study, these Chinese
learners are newcomers, and they learn through social activities, in which ideology,
values and beliefs are embedded. Through learning Chinese, they tended to be
informed of Chinese cultural norms, and also through socializing in Chinese
communities, they picked up Chinese language. Consequently, this theory lays
solid ground for this study (see Figure 1).

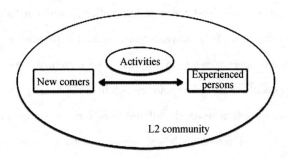

Figure 1   The second language socialization perspective

In 1997, Blum-Kulka defines that pragmatic socialization involves using
rules to regular conversation by novices, such as rules of turns taking and
politeness, modes of story telling and topic selection. Numerous studies on L2
socialization involve the teachers' instruction with explicit or implicit socialization purpose based on teachers' interaction with the students (Poole, 1992).
In 2001, Kasper suggests metapragmatic awareness of pragmatic practices is
reflected in explicit pragmatic socialization, which is prominent for the participants to induce the pragmatic norms. However, most socialization occurs implicitly, either through learning the pragmatic knowledge and strategies provided
by the more proficient participant, or through participants' repeated practices in

targeted communities.

Li (2000) states that most of the research adopts language socialization perspective to investigate interlanguage pragmatics according to a recent overview of studies on L2 pragmatic development. Moreover, language socialization or pragmatic development research is ethnographic in nature, because it tends to take a longitudinal approach for its emphasis on documenting the changing and dynamic process over a period of developmental time (Garrett & Baquedano-López, 2002). In 2011, Duff argues that most studies based on language socialization are ethnographies, which focus on the interactive routines that novices or newcomers must learn or internalize in order to adapt to a new sociocultural community. This current study aims to investigate international students' pragmatic development in China. Consequently, the longitudinal ethnographic approach is an appropriate research method.

Language socialization research differed from language acquisition research considerably for their different analytical focuses, it focuses on communication that help less experienced individuals in constructing knowledge, social behavior and affection rather than on more experienced individuals (Ochs, 2000). In 2002, Garrett and Baquedano-López argues that socializing routines regarded as the core of language socialization research has been close analysis of the mundane activities and interactions, which is contextually grounded and viewed as "habitus" in everyday life, allows researchers to probe into the hidden background knowledge that guides and organizes activities, which is seldom expressed explicitly. As a result, researchers collect data mainly targeted at activities undertaken by participants, such as, solving a problem, making a request, questioning, ordering and having an argument, etc. These activities provide more basic materials than empirical studies and serve as windows on hidden rules of organization and cultural conventions (Garrett & Baquedano-López, 2002).

With regard to this study, case study is employed to explore the international students' Chinese pragmatic development by focusing on request speech acts. International students in China are viewed as learners in SA context. The context of SA, in which an individual sojourns in new language communities, creates an ideal setting for the studies on second language socialization (Wang, 2010). It is assumed that learners in SA context should benefit from more contact with members of target language community. However, there is a scarce research that explores activity types that affect learners' pragmatic development. This research fills this gap by primarily relying on ethnographic interview and observation data to extract routine activities that aid or hinder pragmatic development. Furthermore, pragmatic development belongs to language development, so dynamic system theory could be used to explain the dynamic phenomenon, which is reviewed in the following section.

2.3.2 Dynamic systems theory

Dynamic Systems Theory (DST) synthesizes and derives from all the theories, which are used to explain language development (De Bot, Lowie, & Verspoor, 2007). In 2005, Thelen states that general principles of DST could be applicable to conceptualize changes at different levels and at various stages. This current study focuses on pragmatic development of international students, involving dynamic process of changes. Therefore, DST could be an appropriate theory to illustrate this complex and compelling process.

Language development is a complicated, intricate and even unpredictable non-linear process, which includes the numerous variables within the linguistic system and social community as well as the inner world of an individual (De Bot et al. , 2007). DST has become the science of complex system, which was viewed as a part of mathematics, and an equation was developed to explain such changing and complex trajectories. Thelen (2005) describes the characteristics of DST as a complexity, continuity and dynamic stability. As for complexity, human behavior, no matter whether psychological activities or overt, is produced by many different parts in different situations working together coherently. With continuity, it refers to the state of a system at a specific time, from its previous state and becomes the starting point for the next state. Concerning dynamic stability, generally speaking, human behavior is stable during a certain period of time, but new ones start to appear and old ones tend to disappear along with the progression of time. Dynamic stability is a tenet of DST, which means stability is discarded to transit to another stage (attractor states). However, De Bot et al. (2007) describes the major features of DST in respect to language development as follows: reliance on initial conditions, interconnectedness of subsystems, and advent of attractor states during the developmental process and variations in and among individuals. He also states that the initial state is very important, because minor variations at his beginning may result in dramatic differences in the long term. However, huge differences would not lead to limited effects, just as minor changes would not lead to significant effects. Systems are developed through interaction with both self and environment over a period of time. Temporary as attractor states are, they move on to another state because of the strength of the attraction and energy from the environment. At a certain time, small differences among individuals at the initial stage may end up with significant effects.

To sum up, according to Thelen's and De Bot et al.'s illustation, DST views that the language learning as a complex and dynamic systems composed of interrelated subsystems, and experiences different attractor states in the process of changing. All require energy to keep them moving onwards and developing in a non-linear way with individual varations for internal and external factors. Differences between individals at the initial stages might lead to various outcomes at the end (De Bot et al., 2007). As for this present study, cultural differences of the international students has been viewed as the main difference in the initial stage, whether the participants developed their pragmatic competence in different ways, and in what way they developed their pragmatic competence were targets to probe into. The DST is the proper theory to explain and analyze the complicated and dynamic process of their pragmatic development. However, L2 learners' motivation and acculturation attitudes in SA play an important role in L2 acquisition, which were not mentioned above. Thus, the following section focuses on a model, which illustrates the interrelationship between learners' motivation & acculturation attitudes and linguistic development.

2.3.3 The intercultural interaction model

This study targeted international students that studied in China (SA context) and were regarded as sojourners. Although they have been learning Chinese in SISU for one year, they have been viewed as newcomers in Chinese culture and experienced acculturation consciously or unconsciously. As a matter of fact, language and culture are two notions that are interwoven and insepa-rable, so the acquisition of L2, besides lexical and grammatical knowledge, is also the process of picking up a second culture (Brown, 1994). Culhane (2001) argues that learners connecting with native speakers acquire the target language "in a lifelike manner", and has been provided with more opportunities for friendship, social connections, and more profound linguistic and cultural input. However, Culhane (2004) shows that there is a kind of relationship between motivation for interaction with a target language group and the frequency of inter-group contact with native speakers, which means that acculturation attitudes have a significant influence on the acculturation and language learning process. The combination of motivation in SLA and accultur-ation attitudes of sojourners results in the emergence of Intercultural Interaction

Model (IIM), which offers an important perspective to view the international students' pragmatic development in this current study.

Culhane (2004) puts forward the Intercultural Interaction models (see Figure 2), which integrates motivation theories and acculturation, separates learners' motivation for SLA, and acculturation into three functional levels: instrumental, integrative, and psycho-social functioning. Instrumental functioning refers to individuals acquiring language and culture required for pragmatic objectives, such as meeting language levels for job-hunting, daily use in L2 context. Integrative functioning reflects on individuals that acquire target language and culture to replace their native ones, through integration into new sociocultural context. Psychosocial functioning shows that elements of target language and culture comes into the learners' everyday social and psychological use to the extent that they come to replace their first language and culture.

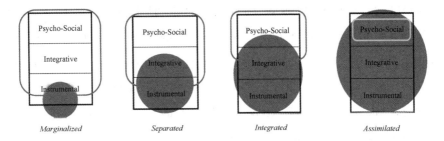

Figure 2   Intercultural interaction models (Culhane, 2004)

This model was established from the integration of SLA theories with the concepts from acculturation research, which implicates that learners' attitudes towards L2 speakers and culture play an important role in grabbing the chances for interaction with L2 speakers so as to acquire the cultural-based competence that is essential for proper use of target language and development of intercultural competence (Culhane, 2004). Learners acquire sufficient pragmatic knowledge based on understanding the culture norms, conventions, beliefs and values of the target language. As long as they acquire both pragmalinguistics and sociopragmatics, they know what to say in certain kinds of situations with a particular interlocutor. Consequently, those international students' motivation and acculturation attitudes towards L2 culture plays a crucial role in developing their pragmatic competence based on IIM.

2.4   Studies on interlanguage pragmatics

First, this section reviews empirical studies in study abroad for linguistic gains with a focus on L2 pragmatic learning and development. Second, studies on speech acts in second language are reviewed, and special attention is given to requests. Last but not least, studies on learning Chinese as L2 are reviewed as well. The limitations of the previous research are identified and research gaps are rationalized accordingly.

2.4.1   Pragmatic learning during study abroad

Many studies have shown great interests in comparing and contrasting the outcomes of the L2 learners who stayed in study abroad and their counterparts studying in their home country (Lafford, 1995; Matsumura, 2001; Rasouli Khorshidi, 2013). However, the outcomes of study abroad (SA) contradict with each other. Some studies point out that short-term stay has little impact on L2 learners' learning outcomes (Freed, 1990), while other studies found that even a few weeks' stay can impact L2 pragmatic development considerably (Matsumura, 2001; Rasouli Khorshidi, 2013). In 2010, Wang shows that SA setting alone could not guarantee language gains, and no single factor could be concluded as the influencing one on SLA for individual differences and a great number of variables within an individual making it even complicated. He suggests that a qualitative approach should be employed to understand the language socialization process though multiple data sources and in-depth description.

Research of study abroad programs has proved to help L2 learners develop oral proficiency (Lafford, 1995), grammar and writing skills (Isabelli & Nishida, 2005), listening response (Shively, 2015) and sociolinguistic competence (Evans, Alano, & Wong, 2001). In recent years, studies on the effects of SA on development of interlanguage pragmatic competence have witnessed considerable growth. As is known that pragmatics studies interactions between speakers and listeners in a meaningful way involving a socially and culturally constructed situation. In 2015, Taguchi suggests that L2 pragmatic competence is composed of linguistic knowledge and knowledge of social and cultural norms, and also includes how competently they apply the newly learned knowledge when performing linguistic functions in a specific situation. Learners in SA setting should be made aware of the linguistic or non-linguistic knowledge more directly and easily when immersed in such circum-stances. Consequently, numerous studies had been conducted to explore L2 pragmatic learning and development in SA settings.

In order to generalize research in a comprehensive way, and also provide an overall bird's eye of studies in this field. Cross-sectional and longitudinal studies are illustrated in sequence and then the research instruments applied are reviewed. Finally, the L2 language types involved are reviewed.

There are several cross-sectional studies concerning the SA experience and pragmatic gains by comparing the pragmatic growth of L2 learners in SA setting with those in their home country (Hassall, 2013; Matsumura, 2001; Xu, Case, & Wang, 2009). Félix-Brasdefer and Hasler-Barker's (2015) study investigates the effects of context on complimentary speech act produced by Learners of Spanish in SA context and at home. Although it was only an eight-week summer program in Mexico, all participants in SA produced compliments more native-like than their counterparts at home. However, this study also reveals that the quality and intensity of the input along with individual variation have impact on the outcomes of learners' pragmatic development. In 2001, a similar study conducted by Matsumura focused on Japanese students' perception of situational factors during the year they studied abroad in Canada through examining the pragmatic changes of offering advice. The results show that pragmatic growth of learners in SA setting was more effective than the ones stay at home.

In 2013, Hassall have examined Australians' change of Indonesian address terms in a short term SA setting. The result shows that the pragmatic competence of the participants developed substantially, and it also indicates that pragmatic transfer, lack of access to L2 pragmatic norms and maintaining their foreign identity all together impede learners' L2 pragmatic development.

Some interventions were applied to examine pragmatic development of L2 learners in SA context. In 2015, Alcón-Soler investigates how and to what degree pragmatic instruction and length of stay in SA affect learners' lexical and syntactical structures when making requests by e-mail. An experiment research method was employed to evaluate the outcomes of pragmatic development between learner in SA and at home. The findings show that length of stay interrelated with instruction, and played an important role in pragmatic change of learners' requests.

On the contrary, a few studies show opposite results involving SA and pragmatic development (Taguchi, 2008). He examined the relation between language contacts of L2 learners and pragmatic processing speed and pragmatic comprehension. In this study, participants stayed abroad for 4 months. The results revealed that language contact interrelated with comprehension speed, but does not correlate with accuracy of pragmatic comprehension.

To sum up, these cross-sectional studies yield contradictory results, and some of them suggest in-depth qualitative research should be conducted to explore the complicated phenomenon of learning process in SA context. Therefore, a number of longitudinal studies have been added to the literature. I selected the most frequently cited one here for further discussion.

Almost all of the longitudinal studies had applied both quantitative and qualitative method (Al-Gahtani & Roever, 2015; Iwasaki, 2008; Kinginger & Farrell, 2003; Rasouli Khorshidi, 2013; Regan, 1995; Warga & Schölmberger, 2007). Taking Kinginger and Farrell's (2003) study for example, they examine the potential effects of the SA context on pragmatic competence of 8 learners through employing pre-and post-test, biweekly journals and logbooks detailing language use. The findings show that changes of learners' sociolinguistic features did appear when they participated in a study abroad program.

Apart from the research method integrating pre- and post- text with interview or other qualitative data, Warga and Schölmberger (2007) elicited data at two-month intervals from L2 learners so as to examine the effect of a period of immersion on changes of learners' apologetic behavior. This study has yielded positive results and reported correlation between immersion and L2 pragmatic competence.

Bataller (2010) addressed the development of the request strategies of 31 nonnative speakers participating in four-month study abroad programs. He employed open role-play to capture the natural recordings of requests in service encounter scenarios made by L2 learners. The results revealed that learners' request production were improved after studying abroad, while other aspects remained unaffected.

In 2015, Taguchi points out that ethnographic studies should also be comprised of systematic and scheduled data collection in order to interpret learners' pragmatic change with supportive analysis of context and individuals. Though reviewing these longitudinal studies, we found that quantitative-descriptive studies incorporated with qualitative data were necessary to assess learners' access to pragmatic input and language contact at individual levels. Although those studies have reported the language contact or interaction with native speakers in SA context affect learners' pragmatic improvement, those factors, such as activity types, individuals' orientation, or attitudes towards host cultures etc. , have not been elaborated in detail, which would play a crucial role in L2 learners' pragmatic development. Thus, in response to the second research question of this present study, discourse completion test (DCT) data were collected at one-month intervals to figure out international students' pragmatic change, and interview data were followed up to analyze dynamic perception of politeness in Chinese culture. To answer the third research question, three case studies were applied to explore the complex phenomenon of achieving pragmatic growth.

With view to data collection instruments, among those studies concerning pragmatic learning and SA context, DCT was applied as the primary quantitative data collection instrument (Li, 2014; Rasouli Khorshidi, 2013; Warga & Schölmberger, 2007; Xu et al. , 2009), followed by multiple-choice questionnaires (Matsumura, 2001), audio-recorded naturalistic conversations (Bataller, 2010; Shively, 2015), pragmatic listening tasks (Taguchi, 2008), and language proficiency tests (Kinginger & Farrell, 2003). As for qualitative data collection method, language awareness interviews, observation and journals were mainly used (Kinginger & Farrell, 2003) . Concerning this research, DCT with twelve scenarios, natural audio-recordings, interview and observation/field notes were chosen for remedying each other's shortcomings.

Most of the second languages involved in this research domain are English, French, Spanish, Japanese and Korean (Cohen&R. L. Shively, 2007b; Iwasaki, 2008; Kinginger, 2008; Matsumura, 2001; Shively, 2015), a few studies focus on Chinese as second language in immersion program (Li, 2014).

This study investigates Chinese pragmatic development of international students in China, which fills the research gap and made contributions to learning Chinese as second language literature. Furthermore, examination of speech act strategies is applied to manifest learners' pragmatic competence. In this current study, request speech acts were chosen as the focus, which is reviewed in the following section.

2.4.2　Requests

In this section, empirical studies on request speech acts are reviewed to obtain general impressions of the strategies that subjects applied from different cultures. Inaddition, then requests in Chinese are examined as well.

2.4.2.1　Requests across cultures

Cross-Cultural Speech Act Realization Project (CCSARP) was the first influential and most well known study on speech acts, done by Blum-Kulka and Olshtain in 1984. CCSARP examined both request and apology speech act in eight languages. Discourse Completion Test (DCT) was employed as the primary data collection instrument, which was composed of sixteen situations involving both requests and apologies. The scenarios in DCT were designed in terms of situational factors such as power, social distance, imposition, rights and obligations. In 1984, Blum-Kulka and Olshtain found that the situational factors had significant impact on the selection of pragmatic strategies, and the perceptions of these factors yielded varied linguistic forms and strategies in different cultures.

The significant contributions that CCSARP have made were the establishment of an analytical framework for cross-cultural comparison of speech acts. Three levels of directness and nine substrategies were identified: (1) the most direct level includes Mood Derivable, Performatives, Locution Derivable, and Want Statement. (2) The conventionally indirect level comprises

Suggestive Formula and Query Preparatory strategy types. (3) The non-conventionally indirect level includes Strong Hint and Mild Hint strategy types. This analytical framework was adapted to this study to analyze politeness strategies of the international students from different cultures (Blum-Kulka & Olshtain, 1984).

Since then, numerous studies have been conducted to explore the request speech acts cross cultures (Blum-Kulka&House, 1989; Economidou-Kogetsidis, 2008, 2010; Fukushima, 2000; Hassall, 2003; Kahraman & Akkus, 2007; Koc, 2011; Kotorova, 2015; Lee, 2005; Lin, 2009; Rasouli Khorshidi, 2013; Rue & Zhang, 2008). In order to lay a solid ground for this study, I selected various studies in this field concerning requests compared across French, Russian, Korean and Chinese cultures.

In 1996, Mulken compared the politeness markers in requests between French and Dutch on the basis of a parallel corpus. Data was coded and analyzed based on a coding scheme developed by the CCSARP project. They stated that French and Dutch subjects tended to apply 'query preparatory' strategy as the primary head act requests, however, the French subjects applied far more supportive moves per head act than that of Dutch counterparts, and "grounder" is the most frequently used supportive move.

Kotorova (2015) investigated request strategies in Russian and German based on the contrastive research. They argue that face-threatening situations caused by requests are culturally related and differ in Russian and German culture. German culture is not likely to make requests, as they tend to deal with difficulties independently. However, Russians would ask for help from their neighbors for little things, such as, going to store. It is concluded that Russian culture stresses solidarity, while the German culture is more distant. Accordingly, requests produced by Russians are more direct using imperative as the most common means.

All the research reviewed above was involving the languages within western cultures. Some studies on requests in East Asian languages will also be reviewed in the following passage. In 2008, Rue and Zhang conducted a comparative analysis of requests in Mandarin Chinese and Korean, using naturally occurring conversational dialogue as the main data source. Adopting the coding scheme of CCSARP, they found that Chinese native speakers were more indirect than their Korean counterparts when producing requests, and the former prefer more indirect head acts such as interrogative and imperatives than the latter.

Apart from comparative studies on two languages all in Western cultures or all in Eastern cultures, studies on one language from Western cultures and the other one from Eastern cultures have also been carried out. Byon (2004) compared the realization patterns of requests in American English and Korean, made by Korean native speakers, American native speakers and American learners of Korean language. DCT was used to collect data and analyzed in terms of sociopragmatics and pragmalinguistics. Eventually, he concluded, "Korean are more indirect, collectivistic, hierarchical, and formalistic than Americans, whereas Americans are more direct, individualistic egalitarian, and pragmatic than Koreans".

2.4.2.2 Requests in Chinese

Although numerous studies have been carried out to examine requests in various languages and cultures, a few studies have investigated requests made by L2 learners focusing on Chinese language. Several studies were reviewed in this section for the sake of this study.

Hong (1996) examined the use of linguistic politeness of requests made by Chinese. A production questionnaire was applied to collect data. The findings revealed that the choice of politeness linguistic usage heavily depended on social distance and power relations between speakers and hearers. Lee-wong (1994) conducted a study to investigate requests made by Chinese native speakers from

Mainland China. Through adopting interview and questionnaire as data collection methods, the results show that Chinese native speakers prefer to use direct strategies and internal modifications to indirect ones and external modification, which reflects the phenomenon that Chinese culture attaches more importance to sincerity and solidarity. Moreover, it agreed on Hong's (1996) point of view that situational factors, such as social distance and power, affect the choice of strategies in making requests.

Huang (1996) examines request strategies between Taiwanese Mandarin and American English. According to the analysis of DCT, the study revealed that Taiwanese preferred direct strategies and used more alters and supportive moves than American English speakers. Gao (1999) discussed request types used by Chinese native speakers and stated that Chinese preferred to use imperatives to make a request rather than interrogative type, in comparison to American English.

To summarize, politeness strategies of requests differ from culture to culture. The participants in this current study selected are from both western and eastern cultures. Therefore, it could be safely concluded that their perceptions of politeness, the weight they put on situational factors, the strategy types and directness levels differ to a great extent. In this study, those international students studying Chinese in China for a short term varied the strategy of requests applied in Chinese from the initial stage. Through longitudinal exploration and scheduled data collection, this research aims to examine changes of request strategies among subjects from different countries, in comparison to that of Chinese native speakers. The results of the study could shed a new light on Chinese language learning and pragmatic development, an area that presently is rarely touched. The following section reviews the influencing factors that affect L2 pragmatic development.

2.4.3   Influencing factors on L2 pragmatic development

A number of studies have been conducted to explore variables affect pragmatic development. These studies could be categorized into two major groups in terms of factors from outside or inside: external factors and internal factors. Some of them focus on external variables such as explicit or implicit instructions (Abrams, 2014; Alcón Soler, 2005; Alcón-Soler, 2015; Eve&Josep, 2010; Glaser, 2013; Ifantidou, 2013; Koike&Pearson, 2005; Nguyen et al., 2012), length of stay (Felix-Brasdefer, 2004; Llanes & Muñoz, 2009; Lundell & Erman, 2012; Xu et al., 2009), intensity of interactions (Bella, 2011) and input treatment (Takimoto, 2009). And other studies examine the role of personal variables in learners' pragmatic development, including language proficiency level (Roever, Wang, & Brophy, 2014; Taguchi, 2011; Xu et al., 2009), cognitive processing ability (Taguchi, 2008), cultural distance (Rafieyan, et al. , 2014), and acculturation attitude (Culhane, 2004; Rafieyan, Behnammohammadian, & Orang, 2015). Figure 3 visualized the factors that affect pragmatic development.

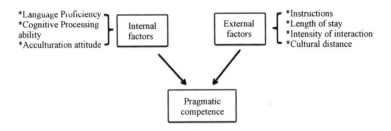

Figure 3   Language socialization theory

Concerning this current study, those case study subjects from France, Russia and Korea had studied in China for one year at an intermediate Chinese language proficiency level. Accordingly, those variables such as length of stay, language proficiency and input treatment could not yield the different personal trajectories of learners' pragmatic development. In other words, those factors, such as instructions, intensity of interactions, cognitive processing ability, cultural distance and acculturation would be the possible variables that make individual variations in developing L2 pragmatics. Several relevant empirical studies that shed light on this study have been chosen to review in the following passages.

Nguyen et al. (2012) examined explicit and implicit instructions on development of L2 pragmatic competence. Experiment research method was chosen to investigate the speech act produced by 69 Vietnamese learners of English. The results showed that both types of instructions accelerate pragmatic learning, whereas the explicit group outperformed significantly the implicit group in all aspects measured.

Bella (2011) investigated whether length of stay or interaction with the members of the target community has impact on learners' refusal speech act performance using role-plays. It revealed that the length of stay is not a effective factor, while the intensity of interaction can ensure pragmatic appropriateness and politeness. And this study advocates pedagogical intervention and meaningful chance for interaction that could enhance L2 pragmatic development.

Taguchi (2008) examined the correlation among language contact, cognitive processing ability and the development of pragmatic comprehension over a short-term immersion in target community. Forty and four Japanese learners in the United States were chosen as participants. In this study, the pragmatic listening and lexical assessment test and survey were employed to measure cognitive processing competence, pragmatic comprehension and amount of language contact. The findings showed that both cognitive processing ability and language contact affected the speed rather than the accuracy of comprehension.

In 2014, Rafieyan et al examined the relationship between the degrees of cultural distance between their L1 culture and L2 culture and pragmatic comprehension ability. English language learners from universities in Germany and South Korea were chosen respectively to compare their English pragmatic comprehension ability based on a pragmatic listening task testing. As German was close to British culturally, whereas South Korean culture and British culture have greater distance. The results indicated that German learners of English possessed better competence to understand the target language than their Korean counterparts.

Another study was carried out by Rafieyan et al. to understand the relationship between acculturation attitude and pragmatic comprehension in 2015. Eighty Iranian undergraduates learning English in Australia were selected as research participants. An attitude questionnaire and a comprehension test were employed to collect data. The findings showed that a strong positive correlation between acculturation attitude and comprehension ability has been found. The study argued that the amount of interaction with native speakers and familiarity with culture in the target community should be stressed during sojourns.

Although these studies reviewed aren't situated in Chinese context, they were chosen to provide different perspectives and a solid experiential ground upon which I attempt to conduct my research in a Chinese socio-cultural context. Those factors mentioned in previous studies helped me form a specific angle to look at my own research. However, I remain open minded to the emergence of new factors that facilitate or hinder learners' Chinese pragmatic development.

2. 5   Conceptual framework for this study

The review of key concepts, theoretical concepts and empirical studies related directly to this study provides a fertile ground for my research. The knowledge of interlanguage pragmatics, politeness and request can help to understand the inner relationship among them, and offer sufficient reasons for choosing request speech act as the means to examine subjects' pragmatic competence. As for the sociocultural theory, language socialization theory, dynamic systems theory and intercultural interaction model, they provide a theoretical lens to understanding the complicated phenomenon of L2 pragmatic development. Those empirical studies reviewed offered information concerning this topic, in the way researchers conducted those studies and where the limitations lie. My review of the emerging literature combined with my personal reflection on L2 pragmatic development provides a foundation for meaningful consideration on those international students' pragmatic changes and improvements in China.

The purpose of this study is to understand the pragmatic development in Chinese of international students for a short-term study in China. The review of three bodies of literature, along with my personal insights, contributed to a conceptual framework for conducting this study and analyzing the data. As for the developmental trajectories of individual learners from different cultural backgrounds, and the possible factors that aid or hinder learners' pragmatic development, the review of those empirical studies offered certain perspectives on them.

The sociocultural theory lays the ground for understanding the process of second language learning. Three primary constructs of the theory such as mediation, internationalization, and the zone of proximal development were reviewed to understand the dynamic cognitive process of perception of politeness. Dynamic systems theory illustrates the complex, dynamic and non-linear process of language acquisition. Language socialization developed from sociocultural theory is widely used to explore L2 pragmatic development with a focus on activities in study abroad context. And intercultural interaction model elaborates the interrelation among motivation, acculturation attitude and second language acquisition, which helps explain individual differences in pragmatic development and also offers insight into exploring the relationship between acculturation attitude and pragmatic development in abroad context. Therefore, I developed the conceptual framework (see Figure 4) based on those theories and models.

Studies on pragmatic development in SA were reviewed to determine the effect of sociocultural context on L2 pragmatic development. By reviewing the factors that affect L2 pragmatic development, two major categories emerged: internal factors and external factors. However, research about pragmatic development of international student from various backgrounds in China is rare, let alone the analysis of the influencing factors.

Although request speech act was frequently chosen to explore the development of pragmatic competence in a variety of studies, requests made in Chinese language by L2 learners were seldom touched upon. And the comparison of pragmatic strategies in requests in Chinese from the cross-cultural perspective was scarce. Moreover, few studies have been conducted longitudinally to examine L2 learners' pragmatic development in Chinese sociocultural context. As a result, this current study fills the research gap. The research questions are as follows:

(1) What are the features of pragmatic strategies in requests among Korean, French and Russian Students in SISU?

(2) In what way do their pragmatic strategies of requests change?

(3) What factors affect the changes of their pragmatic strategies?

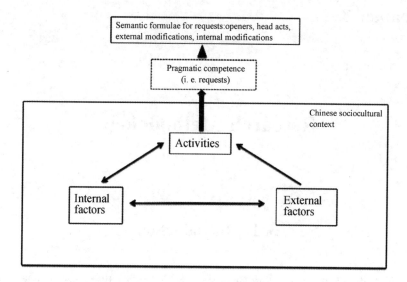

Figure 4   Conceptual framework

2. 6   Summary

This section reviewed the origin of interlanguage pragmatics, the definitions of politeness and request, different perceptions of politeness across cultures, and examined the situational variables that affect politeness strategies in making requests. Sociocultural theory, language socialization theory, dynamic systems theory and intercultural interaction models were reviewed to get a theoretical understanding of L2 pragmatic development. Three bodies of empirical studies were reviewed to further understand the possible factors that affect L2 pragmatic development, and the review of empirical studies on requests across cultures helped to form the analytical framework of this current study. The next section elaborates the research methodology in detail.

Chapter 3

Research Methodology

3.1 Introduction

In light of the preceding chapter, for example, literature review, key constructs, relevant theories and empirical studies on interlanguage pragmatics were illustrated clearly. This chapter attempts to describe, analyze and rationalize the research methodology, which is applied in terms of the research questions, showing the researcher's philosophical consideration of issues involved. Moreover, the criteria for selecting participants, data collection instruments and procedure, and data analysis protocol are demonstrated in detail as well.

This chapter first illustrates the rationale for the research method and then displays the general research design. The structure of this chapter is as follows: (1) Research questions of the study are put forward, along with the nature and interrelationship of each is described; (2) Rationale for the research method chosen is explained, especially the case study approach; (3) How to approach and select the participants of this study is elaborated; (4) Entry of the research site is stated; (5) Data collection method, such as discourse completion task (DCT), interview and observation is described and elucidated, and procedure of data collection is stated; (6) Methods for data analysis and analytic framework are presented; (7) Validity and reliability of the study are raised and discussed; (8) limitations of this study are pointed out; (9) Summary of this chapter and brief introduction of next chapter is offered at the end of this chapter.

3. 2　Research questions

The purpose of the study was to explore the developmental process of interlanguage pragmatic competence of international students in China, and dig out the factors that affect their pragmatic growth. The cultural background and the languages they spoke varied. In terms of the cultural background and the number of the international students in Shanghai International Studies University (SISU), Korean, Russian and French students were targeted and chosen as the tentative participants. The three-research questions are as follows:

(1) What are the features of pragmatic strategies in requests among Korean, French and Russian students in SISU?

(2) In what way do their pragmatic strategies of requests change?

(3) What factors affect the changes oftheir pragmatic strategies?

Among these three research questions, the first one is descriptive in nature, and is bound to describe the pragmatic strategies by making requests, which were produced by the participants from three different countries. Through comparing with the strategies employed by Chinese native speakers, the differences and similarities would be figured out accordingly. With view to previous studies, cross-cultural variations could be related to certain strategies that the participants choose. In light of the first question, three participants from these three different countries respectively were chosen to get longitudinal data to answer the second question. The second question is explorative and attempts to find out the individual developmental trajectories of pragmatic competence. The third question is also explorative, and aims to figure out the main factors that affect the developmental process of pragmatic competence individually. Logically speaking, these three questions are interrelated tightly to each other and go forward one by one. In view of the research questions, certain research method, data collection and data analysis method were chosen, which will be elaborated in detail in the following passages.

3. 3   Rationale for research design

The mixed research method is widely used, which is viewed as the third paradigm following the quantitative and qualitative method (Johnson & Onwuegbuzie, 2004). Tashakkori and Teddlie (2003) point out that more and more empirical studies in applied linguistics had employed mixed research method, which was also adopted in this study. Zheng and Ying (2015) point out that more and more empirical studies in applied linguistics employ mixed research method, which was also adopted in this study. Both cross-sectional and longitudinal data will be collected based on a survey and case study approach.

Before elaboration of the research method, some issues should be stated at first in terms of rationale for mixed research method, DCT, semi-structured interview andobservation in sequence.

3. 3. 1   Mixed research method

According to Tashakkori and Teddlie (2003), mixed research method is that the combination of quantitative and qualitative method occurs in the stage of research questions, research method, data collection and analysis. Therefore, the definition of quantitative and qualitative method should be given before elucidating the rationale for mixed method. Moreover, the nature of the research questions in the study are fundamental to choosing mixed research method, will be explained afterwards.

Qualitative method is that the researcher, regarded as kind of research instrument, interacts with the participants and collects diverse data through exploration of the phenomenon in the natural setting, which analyzes data inductively and generates theory eventually. Quantitative method is where certain features of the participants are tested quantitatively by adoption of proper data collection instruments, using statistics methods to find the relation among the variables so as to generalize the results (Creswell & Plano Clark, 2007). In 2006, Onwuegbuzie and Johnson stated that applying both quantitative and qualitative methods in a particular study could eventually help remedy the shortcomings and enhance the quality of the research.

Neither qualitative nor quantitative method itself elaborates under what kind of circumstances that they would be chosen. However, it is the research question but not the paradigm itself that determines the research method. In 2007, Creswell and Plano Clark point out that research questions in qualitative method are always explorative, and would be "what" or "how" questions, and these words appear frequently, such as "explore", "understand", " find out" etc. While research questions in quantitative method are always descriptive in nature, and would be "why" questions, and these words are employed to find the relationship among several variables, such as "influence", "determine" . Therefore, no matter what kind of research method you choose, it is the research questions that determine the type of method.

As stated above, the first research question: "What are the features of pragmatic strategies in requests among Korean, French and Russian students in SISU? ", attempted to figure out the difference of the pragmatic strategies among these three different cultures. The purpose of this question was to find out the general features of a community. As a result, a survey was the most appropriate instrument for it. The second question: "In what way do their pragmatic strategies of requests change?" and the third question: "What factors affect the changes of their pragmatic strategies?", both of which attempted to explore the dynamic process of pragmatic development. Accordingly, a few representatives of these three cultures were selected to find out the individual trajectories of pragmatic development in study abroad context. And the activities, personalities and attitudes of the participants towards Chinese culture were described in detail so as to dig out the factors that might aid or hinder the pragmatic development. As for these two research questions, case study was the most suitable instrument. Table 4 summarizes the research approaches.

Table 4 　　　　　　 **Research approaches responding to**

the features of research questions

Research Questions	Features	Data Collection Instrument	Research approach	Research Method
RQ1: What are the features of pragmatic strategies in requests among Korean, French and Russian Students?	Descriptive, description of features of pragmatic strategies in questing by international students from different cultures.	Elicitingques- tionnaire (DCT)	Survey	Mixed
RQ2: In what way their pragmatic strategies of requests change?	Explorative, exploration of the individual trajectories of pragmatic development.	DCT/ interview/ observation	Case study	Research
RQ3: What factors affect the changes of their pragmatic strategies?	Explanative, explanation of the factors influence on pragmatic development.	Interview/ observation	Case study	Method

The rationale for research instrument such as DCT, interview and observation will be explained in the following passages.

3. 3. 2 Quantitative method: Discourse Completion Test (DCT)

As stated above, quantitative method makes use of statistics to find out the relation among variables so as to generalize the results. In this study, DCT was applied as the main instrument for quantitative data collection, which will be justified in the following passages.

Discourse Completion Test (DCT) is used widely as adata-eliciting instrument in interlanguage pragmatic research. Participants are required to write their answers to specific scenarios, thereby providing the specific speech act for examination (Lin, 2009). DCT was firstly applied as data-eliciting tool in Cross-Cultural Speech Act Realization Project (CCSARP), in which researchers attempted to investigate the pragmatic strategies across diverse cultures, mainly focusing on request and apology speech acts. After that, DCT has gained big popularity and also received lots of criticism. As Wolfson states in 1989 that DCT was applied to collect data about what learners would like to say in a specific scenario, which was unable to get the actual responses in naturally setting. Although attacked by some researchers for its failing to capture learners' language performance in real context (Beebe & Takahashi, 1989), the DCT has been the most widely used data collection method in speech act research (Lin, 2009; Lundell & Erman, 2012). In recent years, DCT has been applied extensively in interlanguage pragmatic studies (Abolfathiasl & Abdullah, 2015; Félix-Brasdefer & Hasler-Barker, 2015; Ghanbari et al. , 2015; Lin, 2014; Rasouli Khorshidi, 2013; Seyyed & Mohammad, 2014; Yusefi et al. , 2015).

In 2005, AsHong has synthesized the shortcomings and advantages of DCT, and he listed its limitations as follows: lack for diversity of formulae and strategies, limited length of response and uncertainty of the actual occurrence rate of the speech act; and its advantages as follows: collecting large amount of data easily, controlling contextual variables efficiently, effective comparison among different languages and offering semantic formulae across cultures. Finally, Hong (2005) claims that as DCT is designed carefully, it is an effective way to examine speaker's pragmalinguistic knowledge of semantic formulae and pragmatic strategies they employed to perform the speech act, and their sociopragmatic knowledge of the cultural norms, particularly the situational factors embedded in a specific scenario. Blum-Kulka et al. (1989) and DeCapua (1998) has argued that DCT is viewed as an effective way to gain pragmatic strategies from various cultures, which offer the basis for cross-cultural comparison. This research intended to compare the features of pragmatic strategies in requesting by international students in China from three different cultures. Therefore, DCT turned out to be an appropriate instrument.

3.3.3　Qualitative method

As mentioned in 3.3.1, qualitative method is that the researcher interacts with the participants and collects diverse data in the natural setting, and analyzes data inductively. Moreover, this study was kind of ethnographic in nature, since it attempted to describe a culture of a group of people for a prolonged observation and interactions. Ethnography aims to understand native's life, his vision of the world through thick description.

Case study is used as the main approach, and ethnographic interview and participant observation as the major data collection instruments. Rationale for those will be illustrated in the following passages.

3.3.3.1　Case study approach

Utilizing case study in this study was primarily determined by the relationship between the purpose of this research and features of multiple case studies. This study intended to explore the pragmatic developmental process of Chinese learners from different countries, and to explain the interrelation among the factors that would affect language shift. An in-depth longitudinal investigation of individual learners served to satisfy this purpose. A case study provides a unique example of real people in real situations, enabling readers to understand ideas more clearly than simply by presenting them with abstract theories or principles (Cohen, Manion & Morrison, 2011). Creswell (1998) states that a case study targets to explore a "bounded system" or a case (or multiple cases) over time through detailed and in-depth description.

As a result, case study matched my researcher intent, with concentrating on capturing idiosyncrasies and complexities of human thoughts and behaviors. Moreover, more than one case was applied in this study, so multiple case studies stood out.

In 2008, Duff argues that although case studies are always related to qualitative research, cases could be analyzed quantitatively, e. g. in an experimental case study, a controlled group is comprised of several learners without intervention or treatment, and a experimental group consists of several learners receiving treatment. Both of them are tested at intervals during a period of time and data are analyzed and compared to evaluate the intervention. In this study, three participants from three different cultures were selected to test their pragmatic competence once a month during one semester. Therefore, the changes of pragmatic strategies and semantic formulae could be obtained, and the individual pragmatic developmental trajectories could be pined down.

Concerning the advantages of case studies, the researcher is allowed to focus on anindividual in a way that is hardly possible with a group of people, thereby the dynamic and complicated process of second language learning can be pined down for the rich description of each particular case (Li, 2009). In this study, multiple-case study was adopted to explore how all the complex factors behind pragmatic development interacted, which can also help explore in-depth the various cultural, pragmatic and individual reasons why Chinese learners experience language shift and pragmatic growth in a divergent or convergent way.

Since the characteristics of multi-case studies mentioned above, I strongly argued that case study was an appropriate research approach to address the second and third research question of this study. As is stated by Duff (2008), case study may employ interview, observation, documents such as primary data, while apply transcribed discourse and journal notes as secondary data. These different sources of data can triangulate each other to ensure trustworthiness. Interview and observation were chosen as the main data collection methods in the study, which will be described and justified in the subsequent passages.

3. 3. 3. 2   The ethnographic interviewing

In 1996, Kvale stated that with the emergence of interview as a research tool, humans were not simply regarded as manipulable subjects and data no longer viewed as somehow external to individuals, knowledge was generated through conversation between human beings. As mentioned, this study was ethnographic in nature, while there are mainly three sources to make interference in ethnographic research: (1) from what people speak; (2) from how people act; and (3) from the cultural tools people use (Spradley, 1979). Thereby, ethnographic interview is a crucial way to learn people's life history, experiences, cultural values and attitudes. In ethnographic interviewing, researchers may interview people without awareness, and have a casual and friendly conversation with them while introducing several ethnographic questions. Li (2009) states that the most common ethnographic interview consists of questions, which are always open ended. Ethnographic researchers should keep their mind open to new ideas, information and perspectives during the interview. Ethnographic interviews could be both formal ones, which are arranged beforehand with interview protocol, and informal conversations, which occur in coffee shops, lounge or dining hall without any preparations.

In 1998, Merriam shows that interviews can be divided into structured interview, semi-structured interview and open interview in light of research questions and the degree of formality. As semi-structured interview is explorative in nature, the researcher can be flexible and cope with the information instantly in the course of the interview. In this current study, semi-structured interview and ethnographic interview were not two different types of interviews, but they are named for different purposes. In this study, I applied ethnographic interview, which tended to be semi-structured. Since I was a new researcher, I was not confident enough to interview participants without any interview protocols.

Interviews were used for different purposes. After the participants complete DCT, I employed semi-structured interview to understand learners' cognitive process when they made a request. I would ask questions, such as, "What were you thinking when you use these words to make a request?" I also used ethnographic interviewing from time to time in the course of research to probe into participants' life stories, experiences and attitudes so as to explore the dynamic and complicated language learning process and the influencing factors that affected their pragmatic development.

One type of interviewing has gained a big popularity recently that is group interviewing. In 1987, Watt and Ebbutt have argued that group interviews can yield a wider spectrum of response than individual interviews. In this study, I employed group interview to pilot the study and get the holistic knowledge of the international students' Chinese pragmatic competence.

To sum up, interview and DCT were used as the primary data sources, with field notes or observation as the secondary source, which will be illustrated in the following passage.

3.3.3.3   Observation

There are two forms of observation, participant observation and nonparticipant observation. Participant observation in this study was applied. At first, I tried to observe the request behaviors that occurred in daily life in order to design DCT scenarios similar to these in real life. Secondly, I selected three participants from three different cultures for further in-depth observation. These participants' request behaviors made in real life were observed and recorded to compensate for the shortcomings of DCT. Thirdly, three of the participants from France, Russia and Korea were chosen in terms of their typical cultural characteristics they carried when making requests. Both classroom observation and observation of their daily life were conducted to find out their typical activities, their personalities and attitudes toward Chinese culture and native speakers, etc. Observation was also regarded as a triangulation method of the interview data.

In 1980, Spradley argues that there are two main purposes of participant observation in social science: (1) to be fully emerged in social activities in a particular situation; (2) to observe the social activities, individuals, and physical respects of the situation. In this study, I employed participant observation and took field notes for the following purpose. On the one hand, the features of the pragmatic strategies in requesting were detected by observing the participants' request behaviors in real life. On the other hand, the main and key activities were categorized to find the factors that caused their language shifts or the changes of their linguistic choices in requests.

3. 4 Research design

Within this section, entry of the research site, the criteria for selecting participants, techniques of data collection, detailed research procedure and data analysis protocol are reported. Justification for these issues will also be given when necessary.

3. 4. 1   The research site

The rationale for choosing Shanghai International Studies University (SISU) as the research site was based on the following considerations: Firstly, Shanghai, one of the biggest metropolitan cities in China, has gained big popularity for foreigners. According to the statistics of the number of the foreign students from Ministry of Education of the People's Republic of China in 2017, more than 442, 773 international students from all over world have studied in 829 different colleges or universities in China in 2016. The number of the international students in Shanghai ranked No. 2, just behind Beijing all around China.

Secondly, SISU is an internationally recognized academic institution with a high reputation, has already established partnership with more than 330 universities and institutions from 56 countries and regions, and nearly 4, 000 international students have been enrolled in SISU every year. There are four main types of international students in SISU, such as short-term/long-term language students, undergraduates, postgraduates and exchange students. Viewing these particular characteristics of SISU, I chose SISU as the general population.

Thirdly, as a doctoral student in SISU, it was more convenient for me to collect data for the study lasting nearly a year. And I could immerse in the research site to interview and observe the participants anytime.

When I talked to my supervisor about my idea of this research in September 2015, he was delighted and gave me some suggestions. He introduced Miss Li and gave me her Wechat, she was working in School of Chinese Studies and Exchange in SISU. Beyond my expectation, she was extremely helpful and kindly. Although there were lots of obstacles to find the proper participants for my study, after several small chats and meetings with her, she helped me to find the right ones with patience. I really appreciated what she had done for me.

3. 4. 2   Participants

This study employed random sampling for the DCT survey and purposive sampling for case study. In simple random sampling, each member has an equal chance of being selected from a list of the population, which is suitable for quantitative method. Purposive sampling is often applied in qualitative research, because researchers pick up the cases to be included in the study according to their evaluation of their typicality of the characteristics being explored (Cohen, Manion & Morrison, 2011).

In light of the purpose of this study, at first, 20 Koreans, 20 French, 20 Russians were chosen in Language Course Programs in SISU and 20 Chinese undergraduates in SISU were also chosen for baseline data, which can provide the tendency of the choice of pragmatic strategies and semantic formulae in making requests (see Table 5). These 60 international students had to pass Hanyu Shuiping Kaoshi (HSK) 3. Thus, the cross-sectional data were collected to compare the pragmatic strategies and linguistic forms with each other from cross-cultural perspective. The features of the pragmatic strategies were established for each culture. Moreover, three participants among the 60 students from these three cultures respectively were selected to explore the pragmatic developmental process after short-term studying in SA context. Those three participants had come to China in Sept 2015 without any experience of studying in China before. Moreover, the pragmatic strategies they employed should embody the features of their own culture. I started to collect data in October 2015. Because this study regarded acculturation attitudes as a very important variable as viewed in literature chapter (section 2. 3. 4). Accordingly, it attempted to find whether there is correlation between their acculturation attitudes and pragmatic development. In 1987, Berry, Kim, and Boski suggest that learners' acculturation attitudes become obvious after they stayed in the community of target language for about six months. As a result, I had to find the right participants who came to China in September and would stay one year. Finally, three of them were interviewed and observed frequently so as to find the factors that affect their pragmatic development (see Table 6).

Table 5　　　　　**Information of the 80 participants**

Sample	Number	Average age	Level
French learners (FCL)	20	21	Intermediate
Russian learners (RCL)	20	20.5	Intermediate
Korean learners (KCL)	20	20	Intermediate
Chinese native speakers	20	21	—

Table 6　　　　　**Information of the three case participants**

Anonymous Name	Country	Gender	Age	The duration of study Chinese	Level	The first time arrived in China
Eve	France	Female	20	3 years	Intermediate	2015.9
Amy	Russia	Female	21	4 years	Intermediate	2015.9
Joy	Korea	Female	21	2 years	Intermediate	2015.9

I approached Eve on 11th November, 2015. When I was going to talk with the teacher regarding classroom observation, I found her sitting in the classroom smiling at me. I treated her to a coffee and asked her to complete the DCT. After scanning her questionnaire, I decided to choose her as my case participant. Over the coffee, she accepted my invitation as my participant and we talked happily. As for Amy and Joy, Miss Li helped to find them. I invited Miss Li for a couple of coffees in Bella. After a brief introduction of my research, she was willing to help. I sent the requirement of participants' selection to her by e-mail. As the criteria was a bit strict, there were few of them to meet the standard. After reconsideration, I reconciled and adjusted the standard. For her great efforts, she sent me the information of several volunteer participants after a few weeks. I contacted them on the phone, and asked them to finish the DCT questionnaire. After data analysis and face-to-face interview, Amy and Joy turned out be the appropriate participants for the case study.

It was very hard to maintain rapport with these international students. As is known, this study was longitudinal and lasted nearly one year. Great efforts had been made to establish and maintain rapport. As for the cultural difference and personal variations, I treated them in a varied way. As for the Korean girl, Joy, she was quiet and submissive. She treated me as her friend at the very beginning. We hung out to have meals or coffee together, and we also went out for a walk sometimes. Concerning the French girl, Eve, she acted in a very polite way. She would stop eating, when I was talking to her over a meal. As you know, I was very talkative, so her food became cold and her meal lasted especially long. I sensed the distance between us. Sometimes, she postponed replying to my Wechat messages. Although we met several times in a month, she regarded me as a researcher more than a friend, which was not good for me to get the inner her feelings. As a young European girl, Eve is out going and open-minded. She told me that she was travelling around on weekends. So I invited Eve, Amy, Joy to visit me in Hangzhou. Joy had planned a trip to Hainan, so Eve, Amy and two their friends came to visit. I spent two whole days with them, not only showing them the scenic spots in Hangzhou, but also introducing Chinese culture—Teaism to them. They were extremely excited to see the Longjing tea garden and experience the special way of drinking tea. After that, they even took initiative to ask me to go out with them. And I felt the relationship was much closer than before.

Amy believed in Hinduism. She had some personal taboos. She was vegetarian, didn't eat any kind of meat. As a result, when we had a meal, I seldom ordered meat. Moreover, once I was having a coffee with several European girls including my Russian participant and chatting freely. We introduced a topic about the different ways the parents treated their children in western and eastern cultures. A European girl said that it was even written in law in her country that parents must support their children before they are 24 years old. The Russian girl was very quiet during the discussion and suddenly asked to leave. I was sitting there and figuring out what's going on. I recalled that she told me that her parents passed way a few years ago and she was living with her grandparents. She was sad and in a panic at that time, because she depended on her parents economically and emotionally. In order to support herself, she did some translations from Russian to Chinese and vice-verse. When we talked about issues between parents and children, I forgot her personal taboo. She still minded talking about this topic. I felt regretful of this incident and I did a lot to make up for this afterwards. I illustrated these stories that occurred to offer some useful experience of establishing and maintaining rapport with participants, international students in particular.

The reason why I selected Korean, French and Russian learners as participants lies in the following aspects. On the one hand, according to the statistics of international students, Asian and European students ranked No. 1 and No. 2 respectively in SISU (see Table 7). As at the national level, the number of the students from the following countries ranked top ten in 2015: Korea, Japan, Russia, Kazakhstan, Indonesia, Thailand, France, Spain, Italy and Ukraine (see Table 8). Byon (2004) has stated that the requests made by Korean speakers are prone to be more hierarchical and collective, while American speakers are inclined to be more individualistic and egalitarian. Therefore, it is likely that there are distinctions between those speakers from Eastern and Western cultures in requesting. Although Russia belongs to

Europe, it stretches across both Europe and Asia geographically. As a result, Russian culture is mixture of western and eastern culture. In 2015, Kotorova states that the request speech acts made by Russian and Germen speakers are quite different for cultural and linguistic elements in terms of sociopragmatics. Accordingly, Russian, French, Korean participants were chosen in this study. Some distinctive features of the pragmatic strategies could be found.

Table 7   The statistics of international students in SISU (Oct. 2015)

Area	Total number
Asia	381
Europe	145
America	46
Africa	18
Oceania	5

Table 8   The statistics of international students in SISU
on national level (Oct. 2015)

Rank	Country	Number	Percentage
1	Korea	119	18.8%
2	Japan	98	15.4%
3	Russia	46	7.2%
4	Kazakhstan	32	5.0%
5	Indonesia	42	6.6%
6	Thailand	33	5.2%
7	France	24	3.8%
8	Spain	24	3.8%
9	Italy	30	4.7%
10	Ukraine	13	2.0%

One the other hand, Korean culture and Chinese culture both belong to Asian cultures, which share similar features. For example, there are still some

Chinese characters in Korean. French is a representative of western culture and quite different from Chinese culture. And Russian culture is a combination of both Asian and Western culture. Therefore, it was supposed that the students from these three different cultures would develop their Chinese pragmatic competence in a varied way. The patterns of the pragmatic developmental process from these three cultures were supposed to be established, and individual trajectories would be found. Moreover, how the factors emerged and interacted with each other to affect their pragmatic competence will also be pined down.

3. 4. 3 Instruments

This section focuses on illustrating the design and administration of DCT, semi-structured interview and participant observation in detail.

3. 4. 3. 1 Design of Discourse Completion Test (DCT)

A written questionnaire, DCT, was designed based on the previous studies in this field (Blum-Kulka & Olshtain, 1984; Byon, 2004; Economidou-Kogetsidis, 2010; Halenko & Jones, 2011; Lin, 2009). There were both English and Chinese versions of the questionnaire. As mentioned in the literature review chapter, culture sheds light on people's thinking, value and behaviors to some extent, and Chinese culture helps construct the special interpersonal relationship. Some scholars have stated that Chinese tend to be more hierarchical, collective, indirect and formalistic in comparison to western people. With regard to request speech acts, requests between couples tend to be more direct than that between colleagues or professors and students (Zhang & Wang, 1997).

In 2010, Economidou-Kogetsidis suggested that the most widely examined and analyzed situational variables in request speech acts are social distance (D), power (P), and imposition (R). As Chinese culture gives weight to social status and social distance, which affect what you say in a particular scenario. Therefore, in this study imposition was controlled, with focusing on systemic variation of two social factors: social distance and power.

The social distance was treated as follows: familiar [D –] or unfamiliar [D +]. Power was treated as follows: speaker with higher status [P +]; interlocutors with equal status [P =] and speaker with lower status [P –]. Thus, there are six combinations: [D – , P +], [D – , P =], [D – , P +], [D + , P +], [D + , P =] and [D + , P –] (Byon, 2004) (see Table 9).

Table 9   **Social variables embedded in scenarios**

Social Distance	Referents in questionnaire	Relative social ranking with reference to speaker
Unfamiliar [+ D]	Administrator in SISU	Higher [P +]
	Stranger	Equal [P =]
	Group member	Lower [P –]
	Professor	Higher [P +]
Familiar [– D]	Good friend	Equal [P =]
	Roommate (goodfriends' younger sibling)	Lower [P –]

(Adapted fromByon, 2004)

Table 10 displays the scenarios in simple format, 12 scenarios were designed with two situations for each variable combination.

Table 10   **Scenario design and social variables**

Situation	Role Relationship	Social Distance	Power
1. Ask to get a new student Identity Card	Administrator-student	D +	P +
2. Consult the place of schooldormitory	Stranger-stranger	D +	P =
3. Ask to complete PPT	Stanger-stranger	D +	P –
4. Ask to copy PPT	Professor-student	D –	P +

续表

Situation	Role Relationship	Social Distance	Power
5.　Borrow sun cream	Friend-friend	D –	P =
6.　Borrow a laptop	Roommate-roommate	D –	P –
7.　Ask to change adormitory	Administrator-student	D +	P +
8.　Ask to take a photo	Stranger-stranger	D +	P =
9.　Ask to take notes	Stanger-stranger	D +	P –
10.　Ask forextension	Professor-student	D –	P +
11.　Ask to audio record	Friend-friend	D –	P =
12.　Borrow a pen	Roommate-roommate	D –	P –

When designing the scenarios, I took the following issues into account. Firstly, Scenario 1 and 7 were designed to understand how the students perceive their relationship with the administrators in the university in terms of the sociopragmatic aspect by making a request. Pan (2015) argues that the understanding and performance of politeness in public service are different among American and Japanese students. Accordingly, the request behavior of these two scenarios would turn out to be very interesting for the cultural difference.

Secondly, The scenarios should occur frequently in learners' daily life. Therefore, I designed a likert scale of these 12 scenarios to test possibility of the occurrence. Since I planned to use the DCT in October 2015, I had to finish all the things beforehand. As a result, I asked one of my friends to change the English version of the questionnaire into an electronic format, which would be much easier to approach the international students. The likert scale includes 5 choices of possibility, e. g.

You computer doesn't work, but you have to finish your homework tonight. So you want to borrow a laptop from your friend. (　　)

A. strongly impossible　　B. impossible　　C. not sure

D. possible   E. strongly possible

Twenty-six international students had completed the test, and the result showed that all the situations occurred frequently in learners' real life. More than 80% of participants chose scenario 1, 2, 5, 6, 8, 11, 12 as the most frequently occurred situation, and scenario 3, 4, 7, 9, 10 occurred less frequently but still possible. Therefore, these 12 scenarios are appropriate to elicit request behaviors.

Finally, in light of the literature review, the request behaviors produced by people from different countries and cultures differ from each other considerably. All the scenarios should be valid to grasp the difference and features of the pragmatic strategies among these three selected cultures. A small-scale survey was conducted before spreading to the tentative participants. 5 Koreans, 5 Russians and 5 Frenchmen were asked to complete the DCT. The result shows that all the scenarios were well designed to meet my requirements.

At the beginning of October 2015, I was allowed to enter the classroom for distribution of the questionnaires to the students enrolled in language course directly. All the learners were asked to write down the requests without hesitation, and had to complete the questionnaire in 30 minutes. After collecting, the finished questionnaires meeting the criteria for participants' selection were chosen to analyze. Data was analyzed instantly after data collection. The pragmatic strategies of the three cultures were found. As a result, I could select case participants based on it. Generally speaking, natural recording of requests and DCT completed by these three case participants embodied the features of those three different cultures respectively, which was one of the most important reasons that I selected them. And those three case participants were asked to finish the DCT at intervals of one month afterwards to find out the developmental trajectories of these learners.

3. 4. 3. 2　Administration of interviews

Interviews were conducted for two purposes: (1) to investigate what went through their mind when they use Chinese to make a request, to what extent they understand the Chinese culture and how they view themselves when using Chinese; (2). to explore their life stories, experiences, activities, motivation and acculturation attitudes, when they were studying in China. As for interview questions for examining motivation and acculturation attitudes, the scale for East Asian Acculturation Measure (EAAM) (Barry, 2001) were adapted in this study. The EAAM is composed of 29 items, which is outlined in four dimensions: "assimilation, separation, integration and marginalization". The prompts of the semi-structured interview were attached in Appendix C. Table 11 summarized the administration of semi-interviews and ethnographic interviews in this study.

Table 11　　　　　　　　**Administration of interviews**

Name	Time frame					
	Nov, 2015	Dec, 2015	Mar, 2016	April, 2016	May, 2016	June, 2016
Joy	30th, Easy Café	24th, Easy Café	15th, Bella Café; 23rd, Luxun Park	19th, Library	27th, 1#405	13th, Easy Café
Amy	16th, Bella Café; 26th, Bella Café	16th, Restaurant; 30th, Bella Café	15th, Easy Café; 30th, Library	9th – 11th, Hangzhou; 13th, Ciao Café; 26th, Online	30th, Online	11th, Icecream Store

续表

Name	Time frame					
	Nov, 2015	Dec, 2015	Mar, 2016	April, 2016	May, 2016	June, 2016
Eve	16th, Shanghai Hotel; 25th, Easy Café	7th, Bella Café	16th, Bella café; 28th, Easy café	9th – 11th, Hangzhou; 13th, Ciao Café; 21th, EasyCafé.	26th, Restaurant; 31th, Online	10th, Restaurant

Three case studies had been investigated for nearly eight months. Since January and February were winter holiday, I sometimes chatted with them on Wechat. At the beginning, interviews were administered more frequently for two reasons: (1) to get familiar with participants and establish rapport, (2) to attain useful background information of those participants. According to Table 11, interviews were mostly conducted through video chat in May 2016, because I fell and broke the bone in my right arm. Therefore, I took a break and stayed at home for nearly one month. Fortunately, those participants showed their concerns by sending E-mail or short messages to me, and they continued cooperating with me for my research.

3.4.3.3 Administration of participant observation

In order to get the information embedded in learner's mind, observation was conducted. Some scholars have claimed that instruction plays an important role in learners' pragmatic development (Mehmet, 1991; Pfingsthorn, 2012; Takimoto, 2009; Tan & Farashaiya, 2012). Therefore, I took two sessions of classroom observation in March and May respectively. Some significant elements emerged during participant observation, which will be discussed in the result chapter. In addition to that, I hung out with these three learners at least once a week. I observed how they made a request at service counters or other situations. Sometimes I recorded the naturally occurred request behaviors (I got permission from these learners in advance).

3. 4. 4   Data collection procedures

This section displays the general data collection procedures. Different types of data collection methods used in this study were aimed at triangulating so as to enhance the rigor of the study. I started with group interviews to pilot the study. Five international students from Turkey, Russia, Kazakhstan, Korea and Italy, volunteered to be interviewed on the first floor of the library in SISU. During the interview, I found that although they all passed HSK 3 or HSK 4, most of them were unconfident speaking Chinese and regarded the speaking and listening as the most difficult parts of learning Chinese. One of them told me that once one of her Chinese friends sent a gift to her as a birthday present and said that it was very cheap. She was confused why her Chinese friend sent a cheap gift to her and doubted their friendship between them. But the gift turned out to be a very expensive one and she understood that it didn't mean that the gift was cheap, but the utterance her friend delivered embodied with Chinese culture—modest. Therefore, I found that the pragmatic competence varies for the difference of their cultural background and length of stay in SA context among these international students, although their Chinese proficiency was at nearly the same level.

Secondly, I designed DCT in Chinese to elicit writing data of making requests, with manipulating the situational variables, such as social distance and power.

Thirdly, in order to understand the reasons why the participants chose particularlinguistic forms or why they changed the pragmatic strategies over one semester studying in China, I employed semi-structured interview to explore the cognitive processes that learners went through in their mind when they were completing the DCT. Moreover, ethnographic interview was used to know the factors that affect learner's language shift and pragmatic development.

Finally, I applied observation or field notes to triangulate the interview data, and also recorded naturally occurred request behaviors to remedy the shortcomings of DCT. Figure 5 visualizes the overall research procedures.

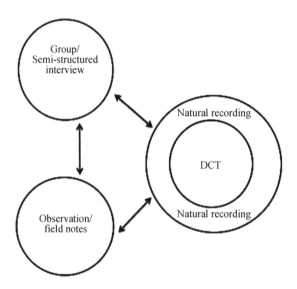

Figure 5   Overall data collection procedures

The time arrangement of the data collection was vital for the short retention of the international students in China. After their return, it was almost impossible to collect data. Therefore, I scheduled a detailed data collection timetable (see Table 12).

3. 4. 5   Data analysis

This section illustrates the analytical protocol of DCT (request speech act), field notes and interview in detail. Furthermore, the specific analytic procedures will be presented clearly as well.

Table 12　　　　　　　　　**Timetable for data collection**

Research approaches	Participants	Data collection methods		Time Frame
Survey	20Russians/ 20Frenchmen/ 20Koreans/20Chinese	DCT		Oct, 2015
Case studies	1Russian/1French/ 1Korean student	Semi-structured interview		Once in Nov, 2015
				Once in Dec, 2015
				Once in Mar, April, May, June, 2016
		Observation/ field notes	Classroom Observation	One week in Mar, 2016
			Observation	One week in May, 2016
			Observation	Nov, 2015—June, 2016

3. 4. 5. 1　Analysis of DCT data

As for the coding scheme of request acts, I consulted previous studies in English in 1989, primarily from Blum-Kulka et al. in CCSARP. According to this manual, a request speech act is composed of three moves: openers, head act (HA) and supportive moves (SM) or external modifications (EM). And the HA of a request is grouped as Direct (D), Conventional Indirect (CID) or Non-conventional Indirect (NCID), which are further grouped into 9 subcategories according to the degree of the directness (Lin, 2009) (Table 13). Some adjustment was made according to the data collected from native Chinese speakers, which will be demonstrated in Chapter 4. The semantic formulae were identified and tagged carefully with the help from my two fellow colleagues. The coding scheme of this study is illustrated and exemplified in Table 13.

Table 13   Request strategies based on their level of directness

Level of directness	Strategy	Example
Direct	Mood-derivable	Speak more slowly.
	Explicitperformative	I am telling you to shut up.
	Hedged performative	I would like to ask you to shut up.
	Obligation statement	You should come back later.
	Want statement	I wish you'd stop bothering me.
Conventionally Indirect	Suggestory formula	Let us play a game.
	Query-preparatory	Do you mind changing the seat?
Non-conventionally Indirect	Strong hint	Will you be going home now?
	Mild hint	You've been busy here, haven't you? (Getting the hearer to clean the kitchen)

(Blum-Kulka et al. , 1989; Byon, 2004; Cohen & Shively, 2007a)

As the part of head act, the internal modifications are subcategorized into lexical downgraders and lexical upgraders, which could be used to minimize or expand the illocutionary force. This study adopted the coding scheme of internal modifications generated by Rue and Zhang (2008), which is visualized in Table 14.

In addition to the strategies of HA, I also attempted to establish the semantic formulae for SM or EM. As stated by Byon (2004), supportive moves in request are illustrated in Table 15.

As for the openers, Rue and Zhang (2008) point out that most alerters serve to attract the hearer's attention and are mostly manifested in the form of address. They specified two kinds of alerters:

1) Openers with an upgrading function: Lin Zong (林总 ' general manager Lin' , surname + title)

Table 14   **Lexical modifications in Chinese requests**

Lexical modifications	Strategies	Examples
Lexical downgraders	Politeness marker	qing① （请 'please'）, laojia （劳驾 'excuse me'）, baituo （拜托 'please'）
	Downtoner	ne （呢）, le （了）, ba （吧）, Ma （嘛）
	Subjectivizer	juede （觉得 'feel'）, xiang （想 'think'）, renwei （认为 'believe'）
	Understater	yidianr （一点儿 'a little'）, yixie （一些 'some'）
	Appealer	…xingma? （…行吗? 'OK?'）, …keyima? （…可以吗? 'OK?'）, ... haoma? （…好吗? 'OK?'）
	Honorific	nin （您 'honorable you'）, gui （贵 'honorable/respectful'）
	Hesitation marker	zhege… （这个 'well…/uh…'）, nage… （那个 'well…/uh…'）
	Delimiter	zhiyou （只有 'only'）
	Hedge	dagai （大概 'perhaps'）, sihu （似乎 'seem'）, keneng （可能 'possibly/probably'）/youkeneng （有可能 'possibly'）
Lexical upgraders	Commitment indicator	yiding （一定 'definitely'）, kending （肯定 'surely'）
	Repetition of request	你过来! 你快点过来! ni guolai! ni kuaidianr guolai! 'Come here! Come here quickly!'
	Time intensifier	mashang （马上 'right now'）, ganjin （赶紧 'hurriedly'）

Adapted from （Rue & Zhang, 2008）

Table 15   **Supportive moves in requests by Byon （2004）**

Strategy	Meaning	Examples
Grounder	Reasons, justification	I forgot my notebook.

_____

① Chinese pinyin. All the Chinese characters were accompanied with Chinese pinyin in this study, which was displayed in phrases.

续表

Strategy	Meaning	Examples
Disarmer	Remove potential objections	I know you are very busy…?
Imposition minimizer	Reduce imposition	It shouldn't take long.
Preparator	Announcement of request, asking about the availability of something, permission of hearer (I'd like to ask you something).	I'd like to ask you something.
Getting a pre-commitment	Getting a promise from the hearer	Would you do me a favor?
Apology	Say sorry to someone	I'm sorry to bother you.
Gratitude	Say thanks to someone	Thanks for your work last week.

2) Openers with neutrals: hei/wei (嘿/喂 'Hey')

The requests made by the participants from native Chinese speakers were coded and some adjustment was made, which can be found illustrated in Chapter 4 with some examples directly extracted from the response collected in this study.

3.4.5.2　Analysis of interview and observation data

Case studies were analyzed mainly based on interview data and field notes. Interview data were transcribed, and then analyzed carefully using Nvivo software. Key categories and themes emerged unexpectedly. Ethnographic interview data were analyzed with different purpose. The interview data were analyzed to grasp the participants' perception of the language use and politeness in Chinese, and also to explore the factors causing their language shift and pragmatic development. Field notes served as the secondary supportive data to interview data.

3.4.5.3　Analytic procedures

This section elaborates the specific analytic procedures, and justifies the sequence when necessary. Three stages of data analysis and presentations are displayed in sequence.

At the first stage, requests made by Chinese were coded, distinctive semantic formulae of the head act and supportive moves were emerged, which served as the baseline data. Then, requests made by French, Korean and Russian students were coded and analyzed, which were listed comparing with that of Chinese correspondents. Both pragmalinguistic and sociopragmatic aspects of request speech acts were analyzed based on DCT responses collected. Considering language distance and cultural similarity among these four languages, some distinctive features of requests in Chinese were captured from French, Korean and Russian students.

At the second stage of analysis, three case participants were selected for further study (1French, 1 Russian and 1Korean). DCT were carried out at intervals of one month, and semi-structured interviews were conducted immediately after DCT each time. Pragmatic analysis of DCTs made by these three participants was conducted to design interview questions. And then, the interview data compensated the shortcomings of DCT to figure out the individual trajectories of pragmatic development. The divergences and convergences of the developmental process were synthesized. The same three participants were also explored to investigate the factors that affect the pragmatic developmental process. Ethnographic interview data and field notes were analyzed to find out the main factors that affect their language shifts.

At the last stage, all the findings were synthesized and theoretical and pedagogical implications were drawn. Figure 6 visualizes the flow of analytic procedures.

In this section, I described the coding scheme of request speech acts in Chinese, which was seldom found in the literature. Two experts were invited to check the coding process. And they gave some suggestions as well. Three stage analytic procedures were elaborated above, which interrelated with each other

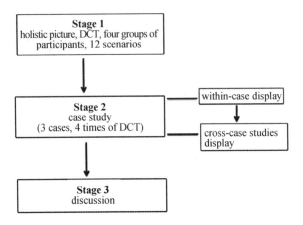

Figure 6   Procedures of data analysis

tightly and logically. Furthermore, in order to address the research questions in this study comprehensively, interviews were conducted before and/or after DCT data collection enabled me to understand the participants' experience, thoughts and perception of language use. Most studies in this area focus on the quantitative analysis to get the pragmatic features of second language learners, while this study attaches much importance on the developmental process based on qualitative analysis.

3.4.6   Validity and reliability

Validity and reliability are regarded as a vital element in the assessment the value of research. Validity is viewed as the most important issue in research methodology (Maxwell, 1996). Peer checks for my coding scheme and process were utilized. Constant discussions with my supervisor, experts in this area and my fellow colleagues about my research design were made to reduce subjectivity and personal biases to some extent. Apart from that, I have taken the following issues into consideration in my study.

Firstly, mixed research method was adopted. Quantitative data were collected to figure out the features of pragmatic strategies of these participants from different cultures. And qualitative data were used to explore the pragmatic developmental process of the participants. Different sources of data used in this study could address the research questions appropriately.

Secondly, purposeful sampling strategy was employed in this study. This study attempted to establish the cultural difference in pragmatic development, so participants from three countries were selected for their cultural differences. In light of the previous studies, Korean culture is similar to Chinese culture, French culture is quite different from Chinese culture and Russian culture would stand in the middle for the geographical and historical reasons. Language is tightly connected to the culture. Therefore, their request behaviors in Chinese were explored to find out the features of pragmatic strategies and their Chinese pragmatic developmental process. I am studying in SISU, which is international university with good reputation. As a result, I choose it as my research site. My familiarity with the contexts helped me to find proper participants, and also helped me to approach the participants easily whenever needed. The Chinese proficiency levels and length of study in China of these international students in SISU are quite different, so some criteria were set for the sample selection. As for the case studies, the participants who were representatives for each culture were selected in terms of their pragmatic strategies they applied in requests.

Thirdly, DCT as the main data collect instrument, was designed carefully. The twelve scenarios in DCT were designed in light of the previous studies and also checked and tested by twenty-six international students in SISU, which revealed that these scenarios occurred frequently. And fifteen international students completed the DCT as a pilot study, resulting in some revisions being made to enhance the inner validity of the DCT.

Fourthly, a triangulation strategy was applied to enhance the validity of the results (Merriam, 1998). Different sources of data were collected to triangulate the findings, and all the transcription of the interview data were checked by the participants themselves. Written DCT was used to investigate the participants' pragmatic growth or change by analyzing the semantic formulae they employed in DCT. As mentioned above, the shortcomings of DCT are that they are not natural data. Therefore, natural recordings and field notes were used to make up for this weakness. Moreover, the interview data enabled me to probe into participants' mental processes that would have resulted in their pragmatic change. As a result, triangulation was employed not only to ensure the validity, but also guarantee against interpretive bias by incorporating multiple data.

Finally, regarding the issue of reliability, the findings of this study can be replicated by other similar studies to a great extent. Qualitative research doesn't cover a broad range to provide the degree of reliability, which is required to allow for generalization of the findings. But the qualitative data were coded with two other colleagues to enhance the reliability of the findings. And for the quantitative part of this research, although the number of participants was not massive, the coding scheme of the pragmatic strategies of requests was carefully designed and checked by two experts in this area.

3.4.7　Ethical issues

In light of the ethics in qualitative research (Seidman, 2006), great efforts were made to ensure the confidentiality of the three informants. The measures were taken as follows: At first, permission was attained by explaining the purpose of this study, the role that the three participants would play, the detailed arrangement of the current research and the length of the study. I approached these informants through Miss Li's help, so I explained and discussed my research design with her several times. Some adjustments were made to further protect these international students' privacy.

Secondly, the confidentiality of the informants was kept by using anonymity in order to protect their privacy. Appointment was made with them beforehand via Wechat, and their suggestion was accepted in terms of the time and place of interviews. They were also told that they could withdraw from my research whenever and wherever they felt stressful or being harmed.

Thirdly, these informants were acknowledged of the arrangement and schedule of this research at the initial stage, and they could make some suggestions according to their curriculum and spare time. After transcribing the interview, the transcript was sent to them immediately, and they were asked to check and make revisions when necessary.

Fourthly, I kept good relationship with all the informants and offered help anytime. They were all international students in China to learn Chinese, so they were confronted with some difficulties in completing homework. I was delighted to help them solve the problems, whenever they came to me. Moreover, I often treated them to a meal or coffee after interviews and sent some small gifts to them at the festivals.

Atthe beginning, one of the informants was not willing to cooperate with me. I talked with her for several times and expressed my sincerity and the important role that she would play in my study. Finally, she changed her attitude towards my study. Although there were lots of obstacles, I tried my best to overcome. And I believed in the saying that nothing is impossible to a willing mind.

3.5   Summary

In this chapter, the research questions were formulated and rationalized why there search method is employed. Mixed research method was chosen for the nature of the research questions and the purpose of this study. The reason why DCT is applied as the main data collection instrument was also justified.

Semi-structured interview and field notes were used to explore the perception and thoughts of the participants when they used Chinese to make requests. These three data collection instruments were applied to achieve triangulation and remedy the methodological weakness.

There were four stages for data collection procedures. The procedures of data collection were illustrated in detail. From pilot study, design and administration of DCT to administration of interview and observation, the detailed timetables were given with explanation. As for the analytic protocol, the coding scheme of request speech acts was introduced and carefully specified. Moreover, analytic procedures were elaborated as well. Generally speaking, there were three steps for analyzing the data collected. Finally, validity and reliability were mentioned, and ethics of the study was also pointed out. In the following chapter, major findings are displayed accordingly.

Chapter 4

Features of Pragmatic Strategies

4. 1 Introduction

This chapter targets to address the first research question: what are the features of pragmatic strategies in requests among Korean, French and Russian students in SISU? In order to answer this question, features of pragmatic strategies in requests made by native Chinese speakers were identified first. twenty Chinese students in SISU were chosen to complete DCT with twlve scenarios, which provided a holistic representation of pragmatic strategies by analyzing semantic formulae of openers, HA (head act), IM (internal modifications) and external modifications (EM). 20 Korean, 20 French and 20 Russian students were selected randomly in SISU to complete the same DCT as their Chinese counterparts. With comparison, features of pragmatic strategies are illustrated for the cultural difference. This chapter provides with an overall background picture against which case study is conducted at later stages of this research.

The present chapter starts with general exploration of pragmatic strategies of request acts made by native Chinese (4. 2) , which is further categorized into semantic formulae of requests (4. 2. 1) , the most popular semantic formulae (4. 2. 2) and the effects of social constraints on semantic formulae (4. 2. 3). As a matter of fact, the identification and illustration of semantic formulae in requests could be viewed as the aspect of pragmalinguistics and elaboration of perceptions of social constraints reflected in different scenarios could be regarded as the aspect of sociopragmatics. Section 4. 3 compares the frequency of semantic formulae involving openers, HA, EM and IM in requests are made by these four cultural groups, and also identifie the effects of social constraints on semantic formulae as well. Section 4. 4 discusses the idiosyncrasies in request acts made by different cultural groups, which functions as the starting point to analyze the pragmatic development of those international students from different cultural backgrounds. It also rationalizes the necessity to conduct an in-depth case study via ethnographic research methods to explore the pragmatic developmental trajectories of those international students. Section 4. 5 summarizes the findings for the first research question.

This chapter attempts to display the quantitative data through a great number of tables, and then preliminary analysis of the data is conducted. However, the in-depth discussion is provided in general discussion (Chapter 6).

4. 2　Pragmatic strategies of request acts in Chinese

This section aims to identify the pragmatic strategies of requests in Chinese Language. First of all, as stated in section 3. 4, request speech acts could be divided into three moves: Openers, Head Act (HA) and External Medications (EM). And the HA of a request is categorized as Direct (D), Conventional Indirect (CID) or Non-conventional Indirect (NCID), which are further categorized into nine subcategories in terms of the level of the directness. The request acts made by twenty students in SISU were analyzed in terms of openers, HA and EM in sequence and semantic formulae for each move with examples demonstrated accordingly. And then the most popular semantic formulae were identified, along with rare occurrence of some special semantic formulae were listed as pragmatic features of requests in Chinese. Finally, perception of social constraints, namely power and social distance embedded in those twelve scenarios, was captured through quantitative and qualitative analysis as well.

4. 2. 1　Semantic formulae of request acts

The first goal of the analysis was to establish semantic formulae for request acts in Chinese language. I started out by using coding categories of requests in CCSARP (Blum-Kulka et al. , 1989), and the coding scheme identified by Rue and Zhang (2008). After extensive analysis of the data, categories emerged for openers, HA and EM respectively. Eventually, there are 7 types of semantic formulae for HA (Table 16).

Table 16　　　　　**Semantic formulae for the HA in Chinese**

Directness levels	Formulae	Description/example
Level 1: Direct strategies (Impositives)	Mood derivable	The grammatical mood of the head act determines its illocutionary force. For example, 借我拷一下课件! Jie wo Kaoyixia kejian! Lend the courseware to me!
	Performative	The speaker conveys the implied means by using a specific verb, making the request an order or a plea. For example, 我恳请您能同意延迟交作业的时间? Wo kenqing nin neng tongyi yanchi jiao zuoye de shijian. I beg you to agree on postponing the deadline of submission.
	Want statement	This formula reveals the speaker's desire, concern or want. For example, 我想换寝室。 Wo xiang huan qinshi. I want to change a dormitory.

续表

Directness levels	Formulae	Description/example
Level 2: Conventionally Indirect strategies	Suggestory formula	The speaker uses suggest conveying the illocutionary intent. That the answer to it is open. For example, 帮我们组做课件，怎么样？ Bang womenzu zuo kejian, zenmeyang? How about helping us make a courseware?
	Query preparatory (1)	The speaker requests the hearer by applying a preparatory question. For example, 1）你可以帮我取一下吗？ Ni keyi bang wo quyixia ma? Could you help me to fetch it? 2）能帮我们拍张照片吗？ Neng bang women pai zhang zhaopian ma? Can you take a photo for us? 3）请问宿舍区怎么走？ Qing wen sushequ zenme zou? Could you tell me how to get to location of the dormitory?
	Query preparatory (2)	The referential meaning of the utterance is the same as the query preparatory (1). However, its social meanings such as formality, politeness, power, and solidarity are differently encoded because of the different syntactic structure. The general syntactic structure is like "want statement/statement + short question formula", and the answer to it is closed. For example, PPT 由你来负责，好不好？ PPT you ni lai fuze, haobuhao? Could you take charge of PPT design? 想借你电脑一晚上，行吗？ Xiang jie ni diannao yiwanshang, xingma? Could I borrow the laptop from you for one night?

续表

Directness levels	Formulae	Description/example
Level 3: Non-conventionally Indirect strategies (Hints)	Strong hint	The intended meaning of the request is not formed explicitly. The speaker offers strong clues so as to make the hearer understood. For example, 有多余的笔吗? You duoyu de bi ma? Do you have an extra pen? (Intent: asking the hearer to lend a pen to the speaker.)

(Blum-Kulka & House, 1989; Byon, 2004; Rue & Zhang, 2008)

For this study, the level of directness was simplified into 6 HA formulae according to Table 16, such as mood derivable, performative, want statement, suggestory formula, query preparatory and strong hint. As for the limited room of the table, a few typical examples were presented above.

According to coding scheme of CSSARP, obligation statement and mild hint should be included. However, these two types of semantic formulae had not been found in this study. I state the reasons as follows: (1) The twelve scenarios were designed for the international students in SISU. As for obligation statement, speaker with higher status tends to convey illocutionary intent by stating obligation directly. In this study, the speaker with high status only occurred in the situation that the speaker happened to be the group leader. As a result, this type of formulae has not been seen. (2) DCT is a written test. Some spoken formulae would not be used in written questionnaire. "Ni mang ma?" (Are you busy?) is regarded as a mild hint in some situation, which is frequently used in spoken language. As a result, this might be the reason why the semantic formulae of mild hint have not been applied in this survey.

The internal modifications as the part of HA, play an important role in minimizing or maximizing the impositive force of a request by using various words or phrases to modify the head act. In this survey, only lexical downgraders have been found, which is presented in the following Table 17.

Table 17   Semantic formulae for internal modifications in Chinese

Formulae	Description/example
Politeness marker	Respectful and polite words are used before the head act in order to get the permission from the hearer. For example, qing (请 'please'), baituo (拜托 'please').
Downtoner	Particles are used at the end of the head act, which is meant to minimize the requestive force. For example, ne (呢), ma (嘛), bei (呗).
Understater	Adverbial modifiers are applied to minimize the illocutionary force. For example, yixia (一下), yidianr (一点儿 'a little').
Appealer	It is used to obtain the response from the hearer, which is usually put at the end of the sentence. For example, ···xing ma? (···行吗?), ···keyima? (···可以吗?), ···xingbuxing? (···行不行?).
Honorific	Respectful words are employed to covey politeness and deference. For example, nin (您 'honorable you'), gui (贵 'honorable/respectful').
Hedge	Vague utterance is used to avoid definiteness. For example, keneng (可能 'possibly/probably').

Adapted from (Rue & Zhang, 2008)

External modifications (supportive moves) are not part of the head act, often precede or follow the head act. They are applied to mitigate or aggravate a request act. There are thirteen types of semantic formulae for EM in Mandarin Chinese, which all function as mitigators of the requests. They are displayed in Table 18.

Table 18 **Semantic formulae for EM in Chinese**

Formulae		Description/example
Preparator		It is used before a request, speaker begin to use small chat before formulating a request. For example, 有件事情想拜托你。 You jian shiqing xiang baituo ni. I have something to trouble you.
Grounder	G + H	This is whena grounder (reasons, justifications for his or her request) is uttered, and then a request is made. 我校园卡丢了，想要补办一张。 Wo xiaoyuanka diu le. Xiang yao buban yizhang. I lost my student identity card. And I want to get a new one.
	H + G	This is when a request is made, and then a grounder is presented. 你能不能把上课的内容录音发我？今天我肚子痛没去上课。 Ni nengbuneng ba shangke de neirong luyin fa wo? Jintian wo duzi tong meiqu shangke. Could you send me the audio recorder of the course? My stomach aches, so I didn't go to the class.
Cost minimizer		The speaker makes the hearer feel that the request is not a heavy burden. 我做完作业马上还你。 Wo zuo wan zuoye mashang huan ni. I will return it to you as soon as I finish my homework.
Promiseof reward		The speaker promises to give the hearer a reward after the hearer carrying out the request. 好了，我请你吃饭。 Haole, wo qing ni chifan. I will invite you to a dinner after it finished.
Apology		The speaker apologizes for possible troubles caused by the request. 对不起。 Duibuqi. Sorry.

续表

Formulae	Description/example
Humbling oneself	The speaker lowers him/herself in order to get hearer's sympathy. 我对这方面不熟悉，就请你来做一下课件啦! Wo dui zhe fangmian bu shuxi, jiu qing ni lai zuoyixia kejian la! I am not familiar with this respect. You are requested to make the courseware.
Self-introduction	The speaker introduces him/herself. 我是 3 号楼 209 寝室的孙小琴。 Wo shi 3 haoluo 209 qinshi de sun xiaoqin. I am Sun xiaoqin from room 209, building No. 3.
Gratitude	The speaker expresses thanks to the hearer, which is mostly used at the end of the utterance. 谢谢! Xiexie! Thanks!
Begging for help	The speaker uses a plea to persuade the hearer to help him or her. 求求你。 Qiuqiu ni. I beg you.
Sweetener	The speaker compliments the hearer. 听说你电子技术超棒的。 Tingshuo ni dianzi jishu chao bang de. Itis said that you are good at information technology.
Disarmer	The speaker tries to eliminate any possible refusal from the hearer by expressing the possible difficulties that the hearer may confront with by the request. 我在周五之前一定交给你! Wo zai zhouwu zhiqian yiding jiaogei ni! I will submit it before Friday.

续表

Formulae		Description/example
Asking the hearer's opinion		The speaker asks the hearer's opinion so as to reduce the possibility of refusal from the hearer. 行不行? Xing bu xing? Is that OK?
Endingwords	Polite words	The speaker feels sorry that the possible burden the request would cause to the hearer by saying some polite words. 不好意思! Bu hao yisi! I am sorry! 辛苦你了! That's very kind of you!
	Modal particle	The speaker expresses the gratitude to the hearer by applying some fashionable new words, which often used among young generation. 么么哒! Memeda! Kiss you! 爱你哟! Ai ni you! Love you!

(Adapted from Blum-Kulka & House, 1989; Byon, 2004; Rue & Zhang, 2008)

Most of the semantic formulae had been found in English language, except the last type, ending words, which carry Chinese characteristics. In this study, I grouped them into two subcategories: polite words and modal particle. The Chinese people tend to use polite words ending the request to show their sincerity and appreciation of the help. As stated in chapter 3, these twenty participants were all post-90 students in SISU. The language they use carries the characteristics of young generation, which was quite different from the mid-aged or elder generation. The buzzwords found in this survey, such as "memeda"、 "ainiyou" at the end of the requests, were evolved from cyber or English language. Since all the undergraduate students in China are learning English as a foreign language, they pick up some conventionalized spoken English unconsciously and translate them into Chinese directly.

In addition to that, semantic formulae for openers were also analyzed in this study. In 2008, Rue and Zhang state that openers function to alert hearer's attention, and they are realized as terms of address in Chinese. Types of openers are shown in Table 19.

Table 19　　　　**Semantic formulae for openers in Chinese**

Formulae	Description/example
Title	In the form of "occupational title or role" which works as an addresser Laoshi (老师 'teacher'), tongxue (同学 'classmate'), jiaoshou (教授 'professor').
Name	In the form of 'surname or first name". Xiu Ming (秀明).
Greeting	In the form of "greeting" in social interaction. Ni hao! (你好! 'how are you?'), nin hao! (您好 'how are you?')
Attention-getter	In the form of "greeting" by using different formula. Heı (嘿 'hey'), buhaoyisi (不好意思 'excuse me!')
Kinship terminology	In the form of "kinship terminology". A yi (阿姨 'aunt'), xiongdi (兄弟 'brother')
Popular alerters	In the form of "popular alerter". Meinv (美女 'beauty'), shuaige (帅哥 'handsome man'), qinaide (亲爱的 'dear')

(Adapted from Blum-Kulka et al., 1989; Byon, 2004)

As illustrated in the above table, there are six types of semantic formulae for openers in Mandarin Chinese, with the last two types belonging to Chinese only. Zhang and Wang (1997) state that Chinese language possesses a very complicated address system, which is originated from "li" (礼 courtesy) in feudal society. The address system in Chinese can be grouped into two categories: kinship terminology and non-kinship terminology (Gu, 1992). Confucianism and agricultural civilization had impact on the formation of value and ideology of Chinese people, who are likely to be collectivism. They prefer to address people with kinship terminology to shorten the distance with the hearers. As a result, we found that "ayi" (阿姨, aunt), "xiongdi" (兄弟, brother) and "xuejie" (学姐, sister) have been used as openers in this survey.

After reform and opening-up policy, openers in Chinese had changed with the terms, such as "xiaojie" (小姐, madam) and "xiansheng" (先生, gentleman) becoming popular at that time (Zhang & Wang, 1997). However, the deterioration of connation for these terms resulted in their fading away in recent years. However, some popular terms, such as "meinv" (美女, beauty), "shuaige" (帅哥, handsome), "qinaide" (亲爱的, dear) and "baibeir" (宝贝儿, baby) become more and more popular among youngsters at present. The major reason would be that the western culture and English language have exerted influence on this new trend.

4.2.2   The most popular semantic formulae

This section aims to count the total numbers of the semantic formulae for openers, HA, EM and IM, and also identify the most frequently used semantic formulae for each move. Moreover, some semantic formulae with Chinese characteristics will be demonstrated. The number of semantic formulae for openers, HA, EM and IM are shown in the following Figure 7. The collected questionnaires were coded according to the coding scheme presented in Chapter 3.

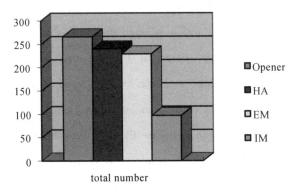

Figure 7   Total numbers of semantic formulae

Figure 8 visualized the total numbers of semantic formulae for opener, HA, EM and IM. It is evident that the Chinese users tend to use external modifications rather than internal modifications in request making performance. The number and frequency of semantic formulae for each move is demonstrated in the following tables.

Table 20   **Semantic formulae for openers①**

Move	Semantic formulae		Total number	Percentage (%)
Opener	Title	Title	81	30. 5
		Title + PM	32	12. 0
	Name		48	18. 0
	Greeting		60	22. 6
	Attention-getter		14	5. 3
	Kinship terminology		9	3. 4
	Popular alerters		22	8. 2
Total			266	100

Note: PM: politeness marker

---

① I first counted the total number of instances of each specific type of strategies (i. e. opener, HA, EM and IM) in requests. And then the number is divided by the total number.

As is shown in Table 20, the most frequent used semantic formulae for openers are "title" (30.5%), "greeting" (22.6%) and "name" (18%). The twelve scenarios were designed for campus life, and the hearers were often teachers, classmates, roommates and administrators. Accordingly, semantic formulae for title were prone to be "laoshi" (老师, teacher) and "tongxue" (同学, classmate) in this survey. We cannot find the equivalent for this category in English. In Chinese, we can use title or profession as openers to enhance respectfulness and formality in Chinese. In order to be more polite, politeness marker is often added to title, such as laoshi ninhao (老师您好, hello teacher) and tongxue nihao (同学你好, hello classmate). It was found that speakers tended to use "name" to address hearers when they are friends, classmates or roommates, and use "greeting" to alert stranger's attention. As mentioned above, "kinship terminology" (3.6%) with Chinese characteristics occurred often in some scenarios as well.

Table 21   **Semantic formulae for HA**

Move	Semantic formulae		Total number	Percentage (%)
HA	Mood derivable		44	18.3
	Performative		6	2.5
	Want statement		26	10.8
	Suggestory formula		5	2.1
	Query preparatory	QP (1)	118	49.2
		QP (2)	37	15.4
	Strong hint		4	1.7
Total			240	100

With view to semantic formulae for head acts in requests (see Table 21), "query preparatory" (64.6%) surpassed other types of strategies significantly.

Furthermore, Chinese users showed a greater tendency of use of the first subcategory of "query preparatory" (49.2%) when compared to the second type (15.4%). Most of them thought that query preparatory seemed more polite than other types of strategies for head act. Then "mood derivable" (18.3%) and "want statement" (10.8%) followed "query preparatory", which suggested that Chinese users preferred indirect strategy to direct strategy, which contradicted the previous findings conducted by Lee-wong (1994). He found that Chinese native speakers preferred to use direct strategies to indirect ones. Lee-wong's study was conducted more than twenty years ago, and language is dynamic and changing all the time. As a result, the findings in this survey were also reasonable.

Table 22   **Semantic formulae for EM**

Move	Semantic formulae		Total number	Percentage (%)
SM (External modifications)	Preparator		25	10.9
	Grounder	G + H	84	36.7
		H + G	43	18.8
	Cost minimizer		6	2.6
	Promise of reward		2	0.9
	Apology		4	1.7
	Humbling oneself		1	0.4
	Self introduction		2	0.9
	Gratitude		25	10.9
	Begging for help		4	1.7
	Sweetener		19	8.4
	Disarmer		1	0.4
	Asking for the hearer's opinion		1	0.4
	Ending words	Polite words	2	0.9
		Modal particle	10	4.4
Total			229	100

The most popular EM formulae consecutively for the Chinese native speaker (see Table 22) were "grounder + head act" (G + H) (36.7%), "header act + grounder" (H + G) (18.8%), "gratitude" (10.9%), "preparator" (10.9%) and "sweetener" (8.4%). Chinese users were prone to give reasons or justifications for requests, and they preferred to use reasons or justifications before making a request rather than after making a request. In 1997, Zhang and Wang stated that Chinese tend to be inductive in discourse. They preferred to talk about other things before coming to the point, which was viewed as a courteous way in social interaction. Consequently, they would use "preparator" to start a conversation, which is a very natural move in conversation among Chinese interlocutors. Moreover, Chinese users often applied "gratitude" to express their sincerity and loyalty in requests. Furthermore, "sweetener" sometimes was employed to mitigate the requests and maintain good relations with others.

Regarding the IM, the frequency of the types of semantic formulae is displayed in the following Table 23.

Table 23   **Semantic formulae for IM**

	Semantic formulae	Total number	Percentage (%)
Lexical modifications	Politeness marker	25	25.8
	Downtoner	26	26.8
	Understater	6	6.2
	Appealer	28	28.9
	Honorific	11	11.3
	Hedge	1	1.0
Total		97	100

As is shown in Table 23, Chinese speakers often used "appealer" (28.9%), "downtoner" (26.8%) and "politeness marker" (25.8%) as IM when making requests. They would like to soften the impositive force of the requests by applying the downgraders. "Appealer" was often used at the end of the head act to ask for permission by showing respectfulness to the hearer, namely, ···xingma? (···行吗? Is that OK?), ···keyima? (···可以吗? Is that OK?), and ···haobuhao? (···好不好? Is that OK?). Viewing to this type of strategies, want statement or statement was uttered first, and then "appealer" was followed. Such syntactic structure is convenient to be made in spoken language and usually used among acquaintances. "Downtoner", such as ba (吧), ne (呢), ma (嘛), bei (呗) and la (啦), was popular among young Chinese people. Moreover, "politeness marker", such as qing (请, please), baituo (拜托, please), mafan (麻烦, sorry for causing troubles) and buhaoyisi (不好意思, sorry) occurred in requests frequently as well.

4.3   Effects of cross-cultural differences on pragmatic production

As stated in Chapter 2, literature review, interlanguage pragmatics (ILP) targets to study L2 learners' performance and development of pragmatic competence in a language that is totally new to them (Byon, 2004). Moreover, according to Cross-cultural Speech Act Realization Project (CCSARP) (Blum-Kulka & House, 1989), learners with cross-cultural and cross-linguistic background tended to produce diverse strategies in request speech acts. Consequently, this section attempts to identify the features of pragmatic strategies produced by international students from Korea, France and Russia through comparing semantic formulae in requests by learners with that of Chinese native speakers.

4.3.1   Comparison of semantic formulae across cultures

In this section, the collected questionnaires of DCT were marked sentence by sentence on the basis of semantic formulae used by Chinese native speakers, which were presented in the tables in the section 4. 2. Comparison is made in the respect of semantic formulae for openers, HA, EM or IM in sequence in the following passages. SPSS was used to examine the significant difference between those three cultural groups and Chinese group.

4. 3. 1. 1　Openers

Openers could be regarded as a part of the requests, which are used to attract the hearer's attention to the particular speech act (Blum-Kulka & House, 1989). In this study, openers were divided into six categories in accordance with their secondary functions: title, name, greeting, attention-getter, kinship terminology and popular alerters. All the categories were covered by learners, except for popular alterters by French learners of Chinese language.

As presented in Table 24, all four groups differed in terms of the most commonly used formulae for openers. The total number of semantic formulae for openers by learners was less than that of Chinese native speakers. The three most popular formulae for openers of CNS were "title" (30. 5%), "greeting" (22. 6%) and "name" (18. 0%). As for KCL, the three most favored formulae were as follows: "title" (24. 6%), "attention-getter" (22. 9%) and "greeting" (18. 9%). Those for RCL were "title" (26. 5%), "greeting" (25. 5%), "name" (11. 7%) and "kinship terminology" (11. 7%). And those for FCL were "greeting" (38. 7%), "attention-getter" (22. 0%) and "title" (17. 9%).

Chinese language, FCL: French learners of Chinese language.

Concerning Chinese native speakers, features of semantic formulae had been identified and analyzed in section 4. 2. They were prone to use "title", e. g. "tongxue" (同学, classmate) or "laoshi" (老师, teacher), "greeting", e. g. "ni hao" (你好, how are you?) or "nin hao" (您好, how are you?) and "name".

Table 24   Semantic formulae for openers by four cultural groups

		CNS	KCL	RCL	FCL
Title	Title	(30. 5) 81	(24. 6) 43	(26. 5) 54	(17. 9) 30
	Title + PM	(12. 0) 32	(5. 1) 9	(11. 3) 23	(10. 1) 17
Name		(18. 0) 48	(13. 1) 23	(11. 7) 24	(5. 3) 9
Greeting		(22. 6) 60	(18. 9) 33	(25. 5) 52	(38. 7) 65
Attention-getter		(5. 3) 14	(22. 9) 40	(11. 3) 23	(22. 0) 37
Kinship terminology		(3. 4) 9	(11. 4) 20	(11. 7) 24	(6. 0) 10
Popular alerters		(8. 2) 22	(4. 0) 7	(2. 0) 4	0
Total		(100) 266	(100) 175	(100) 204	(100) 168

Note: CNS: Chinese native speakers, KCL: Korean learners of Chinese language, RCL: Russian learners.

Table 25   Log-likelihood ratio of formulae for openers

		CNS-KCL		CNS-RCL		CNS-FCL	
		LL	P	LL	P	LL	P
Title	Title	0. 180	0. 671	1. 822	0. 177	5. 139	*0. 023
	Title + PM	31. 611	*0. 000	13. 956	*0. 000	19. 649	*0. 000
Name		2. 872	0. 090	0. 423	0. 515	21. 555	*0. 000
Greeting		10. 318	*0. 001	0. 354	0. 552	0. 124	0. 724
Attention-getter		0. 462	*0. 497	1. 550	0. 213	12. 123	*0. 000
Kinship terminology		3. 483	0. 062	6. 332	*0. 012	0. 280	0. 597
Popular alerters		7. 284	*0. 007	13. 210	*0. 000	29. 928	*0. 000

(Note: $P < 0.05$ means significantly different. "LL" means log-likelihood, " * " marks significant different between two groups.)

In order to analyze in-depth the different use of semantic formulae for openers between other cultural groups and Chinese group, I used SPSS to examine the significant difference by log-likelihood ratio. As shown in Table 25, horizontally speaking, all the three cultural groups differed from Chinese group in "titel + PM" and "popular alters" . Along with the statistics in Table

24, different use of semantic formulae were identified and illustrated in the following passage.

With regard to KCL, the Korean subjects tended to use "title" like their Chinese counterparts. And followed by "attention-getter", namely, "buhaoyisi" (不好意思, excuse me), "duibuqi" (对不起, sorry) and "daraoyixia" (打扰一下, excuse me). They also preferred to employ "greeting", such as "nihao" and "ninhao", while the former one far more used based on qualitative analysis of the content of the questionnaire.

Viewing to RCL, "title" and "greeting" were the first and second most popular addresser among Russian participants, just as their Chinese counterparts. However, "name" (11.7%) and "kinship terminology" (11.7%) were used at the same percentage. And there was a significant difference for "kinship terminology" ($P = 0.012 < 0.05$). Those Russian users tended to use "kinship terminology", such as "didi" (弟弟, brother), "meimei" (妹妹, sister), "xiongdi" (兄弟, brother) and "pengyou" (朋友, friend). Chinese native speakers seldom used those formulae. It was assumed that the L1 transfer influenced RCL to some extent.

Concerning FCL, they were quite different from Chinese native speakers in the use of formulae for openers. As shown in Table 33, use of formulae by French subjects differed from that of Chinese most significantly, since 5 indicators differed significantly. As is known that French and Chinese differed considerably in language forms and usage. In this survey, "greeting" was used as the most frequent formula, since French people tended to use "comment va tu?" (How are you?). Followed by attention-getter, namely "hei" (嘿, hey), "duibuqi" (对不起, pardon) and "buhaoyisi" (不好意思, excuse me). They rarely used "title", "title + PM" to address teachers. It could be safely concluded that formulae for openers by FCL were strongly affected by their L1.

4.3.1.2　Head acts

Head act is the core part of request speech act. Types of semantic formulae had been divided into seven subcategories in this part, although no "mild hint" was found in Chinese native speakers' request speech acts. As displayed in Table 34, all four groups differed in terms of the most commonly used formulae for head acts. The total number of semantic formulae for head acts by learners was more than that of Chinese native speakers. There were total twelve scenarios and twenty participants, so there would be two hundred and forty head acts. However, learners produced more than two hundred and forty even some of them misunderstood some scenarios or didn't complete a few scenarios. One reason would be explained by "reduplication" which was further explained in the following section about IM. Learners were prone to use two or more head acts in one scenario for clarifications or confirmation of understanding. Warga and Schölmberger (2007) point out that L2 learners overused some types of strategies for L1 transfer and their desire of making themselves understood correctly.

Table 26   Semantic formulae for HA by four cultural groups

		CNS	KCL	RCL	FCL
Mood derivable		(18.3) 44	(21.6) 56	(11.5) 28	(8.3) 20
Performative		(2.5) 6	(1.2) 3	(17.7) 43	(4.6) 11
Want statement		(10.8) 26	(8.9) 23	(8.2) 20	(7.1) 17
Suggestory formula		(2.1) 5	0	0	(2.5) 6
Query preparatory	QP (1)	(49.2) 118	(50.2) 130	(52.7) 128	(67.2) 162
	QP (2)	(15.4) 37	(15.4) 40	(8.7) 21	(6.2) 15
Strong hint		(1.7) 4	(1.9) 5	(1.2) 3	(3.3) 8
Mild hint		0	(0.8) 2	0	(0.8) 2
		(100) 240	(100) 259	(100) 243	(100) 241

According to Table 26, the three most popular formulae for HA of CNS were "query preparatory (1)" (49.2%), "mood drivable" (18.3%) and "query preparatory (2)" (15.4%). As for KCL, the three most favored formulae were the same as those Chinese subjects, although the proportion differed: "query preparatory (1)" (50.2%), "mood drivable" (21.6%) and "query preparatory (2)" (18.9%). Those for RCL were "query preparatory (1)" (52.7%), "performative" (17.7%) and "mood derivable" (11.5%). And those for FCL were "query preparatory (1)" (67.2%), "mood drivable" (8.3%) and "want statement" (7.1%).

The patterns of head acts produced by KCL were almost similar to those of Chinese native speakers. As displayed in Table 27, only two indicators showed a significant difference between Korean group and Chinese group. Moreover, although those three cultural groups all preferred "query preparatory", they were all distinct from Chinese group for "query preparatory (2)" (see Table 27). Learners might be unfamiliar with this type of query. In addition to "query preparatory", Russian subjects were more likely to use "performative" rather than "mood derivable". French users tended to be the most indirect in comparison to that of the other three groups. They preferred to employ "query preparatory" in most scenarios.

To sum up, French participants tended to be more indirect and preferred "query preparatory", which confirmed the previous findings (Mulken, 1996). Russians were more likely to ask for help and consider it a very natural behavior (Kotorova, 2015), that's why they preferred "performative" in this survey.

Table 27   **Log-likelihood ratio of formulae for HA**

		CNS-KCL		CNS-RCL		CNS-FCL	
		LL	P	LL	P	LL	P
Mood derivable		1. 022	0. 312	3. 064	0. 080	5. 197	*0. 023
Performative		1. 468	0. 226	25. 874	*0. 000	2. 087	0. 149
Want statement		0. 311	0. 577	0. 063	0. 802	5. 583	*0. 018
Suggestory formula		7. 080	*0. 008	7. 080	*0. 008	0. 287	0. 592
Query	QP (1)	0. 005	0. 946	0. 003	0. 954	0. 050	0. 842
preparatory	QP (2)	8. 679	*0. 003	3. 962	*0. 046	10. 091	*0. 001
Strong hint		0. 020	0. 889	0. 174	0. 677	1. 646	0. 200
Mild hint		0. 421	0. 517	0. 000	1. 000	0. 421	0. 517

4. 3. 1. 3   External modifications

As mentioned above, external modifications (supportive moves) are employed to mitigate or aggravate a request act, which often precede or follow the head act.

As shown in Table 28, the most popular formulae among the four cultural groups were as follows: " grounder ", " preparator ", " gratitude " and "sweetener". As for "grounder", French subjects unlike Chinese native speakers, tended to use H + G formulae (37. 6%). Byon (2004) states that in written DCT, speakers or writers are more likely to make a request before a grounder so as to express their intended meaning as clear as possible. Based on the data, it is inferred that Chinese speakers tended to provide a grounder before making request for saving face. Moreover, the types of formulae Chinese native speakers and Korean subjects used were more diverse, while RCL and FCL tended to be monotonous. Some types of formulae had not been covered by RCL and FCL, such as promise of "reward", "disarmer" and "ending words".

Table 28   Semantic formulae for EM by four cultural groups

		CNS	KCL	RCL	FCL
Preparator		(10. 9) 25	(13. 4) 32	(15. 6) 30	(12. 7) 27
Grounder	G + H	(36. 7) 84	(43. 1) 103	(44. 6) 86	(22. 5) 48
	H + G	(18. 8) 43	(12. 1) 29	(13. 5) 26	(37. 6) 80
Cost minimizer		(2. 6) 6	(2. 5) 6	(1. 0) 2	(0. 5) 1
Promise of reward		(0. 9) 2	(4. 2) 10	0	0
Apology		(1. 7) 4	(0. 4) 1	0	(4. 2) 9
Humbling oneself		(0. 4) 1	(0. 4) 1	(0. 5) 1	0
Self introduction		(0. 9) 2	(4. 6) 11	(2. 1) 4	(1. 4) 3
Gratitude		(10. 9) 25	(6. 7) 16	(11. 4) 22	(12. 2) 26
Begging for help		(1. 7) 4	(0. 4) 1	0	(0. 9) 2
Sweetener		(8. 4) 19	(7. 1) 17	(10. 3) 20	(4. 7) 10
Disarmer		(0. 4) 1	0	0	0
Asking for the hearer's opinion		(0. 4) 1	(0. 8) 2	(1. 0) 2	(3. 3) 7
Ending words	Polite words	(0. 9) 2	(3. 9) 9	0	0
	Modal particle	(4. 4) 10	(0. 4) 1	0	0
		(100) 229	(100) 239	(100) 193	(100) 213

Apart from the five most popular formulae, Korean subjects tended to overuse "promise of reward". There was a significant difference between Korean and Chinese in terms of "promise of reward" ($P = 0.028 < 0.05$). As it is presented in Table 29, comparing with the formulae for EM used by Chinese users, Korean had six indicators with significant difference, followed by French with five. Based on those two tables, Korean subjects tended to overuse those formulae in requests making, which resulted in the significant difference of some types of formulae, while French subjects were prone to use less, which caused the significant difference in respect of some formulae. Korean subjects were still more familiar with those semantic formulae than other two cultural groups. The reason might be that they attempted to show off their language proficiency, which resulted in overuse of formulae.

Table 29   **Log-likelihood ratio of formulae for EM**

		CNS-KCL		CNS-RCL		CNS-FCL	
		LL	P	LL	P	LL	P
Preparator		0. 891	0. 345	1. 412	0. 235	0. 480	0. 489
Grounder	G + H	1	0. 886	0. 000	0. 987	10. 134	*0. 001
	H + G	4. 120	*0. 042	2. 725	0. 099	0. 021	0. 885
Cost minimizer		0. 081	0. 776	2. 594	0. 107	4. 723	*0. 030
Promise of reward		4. 804	*0. 028	2. 878	0. 090	2. 878	0. 090
Apology		2. 185	0. 139	5. 991	*0. 014	2. 189	0. 139
Humbling oneself		0. 000	1. 000	0. 000	1. 000	1. 412	0. 235
Self introduction		6. 348	*0. 012	0. 797	0. 372	0. 230	0. 632
Gratitude		4. 953	*0. 026	1. 073	0. 300	0. 136	0. 712
Begging for help		2. 014	0. 156	2. 014	0. 156	0. 684	0. 408
Sweetener		0. 789	0. 374	0. 137	0. 711	5. 723	*0. 017
Disarmer		0. 000	1. 000	0. 000	1. 000	0. 000	1. 000
Asking for the hearer's opinion		0. 367	0. 545	0. 367	0. 545	6. 194	*0. 013
Ending words	Polite words	4. 379	*0. 036	2. 878	0. 090	2. 878	0. 090
	Modal particle	8. 944	*0. 003	14. 563	*0. 000	14. 563	*0. 000

Those "ending words", such as polite words, namely "xinkule" (辛苦了, thanks), "mafale" (麻烦了, sorry for causing troubles) and "baituole" (拜托了, please) had not been found in previous studies in request acts. Korean subjects were prone to overuse this type of formulae (3.9%, P =0. 036 <0. 05), while Russian speakers and French speakers hadn't employ this type of formulae. Moreover, "modal particle" was popular among youngster with close relationship, which was not witnessed in the requests made by Russian and French subjects. All the three cultural groups differed from Chinese group significantly in "modal particle" (see Table 29), which is described as the formulae with Chinese characteristics in last section.

4. 3. 1. 4 Internal modifications

As mentioned in section 4. 2, internal modifications as the part of HA, are employed to minimize or maximize the impositive force of a request. In this survey, only lexical downgraders had been found in requests made by Chinese native speakers. However, syntactic downgraders appeared in learners' requests (see Table 30).

According to Table 38, there are several features shared by all learners in general. First, "politeness marker" was overused by Korean subjects (31. 1%), Russian subjects (61. 7%) and French subjects (48. 6%), in comparison to Chinese native speakers (25. 8%). It could be explained that learners attempted to use more "politeness marker", such as "qing" (请, please), to show their respect and deference to the hearer. Since they were not familiar with Chinese sociocultural context and applied this type of formulae excessively. Second, it seems that Chinese users tended to use "downtoner" (26. 8%) to minimize the impositive force, but all the learners rarely used this strategy. Since they were not familiar with this type of formulae. Third, "reduplication" emerged in learners' requests but not in Chinese counterparts. This phenomenon was explained further by Table 39, the examination of log-likelihood ratio of formulae for IM. We found that all the three cultural groups differed from Chinese group in the respect of "downtoner" and "reduplication" .

Based on Table 30 and Table 31, some distinction and features of formulae used by those three cultural groups were found and described in thefollowing passage.

As far as Korean subjects concerned, the total number of formulae for IM was much more than that of Chinese users. Apart from overuse of "politeness marker" (33. 1%), "reduplication" (12. 6%) was overused to repeat the head act in a request speech act, which had a significant difference with

Chinese users (P = 0. 000 < 0. 05). There was one example extracted from the data collected in this study.

Table 30   Semantic formulae for IM by four cultural groups

	Semantic formulae	CNS	KCL	RCL	FCL
	Politeness marker	(25. 8) 25	(33. 1) 42	(61. 7) 74	(48. 6) 52
	Downtoner	(26. 8) 26	(7. 1) 9	(0. 8) 1	0
Lexical	Understater	(6. 2) 6	(10. 2) 13	(7. 5) 9	(5. 6) 6
downgraders	Appealer	(28. 9) 28	(23. 6) 30	(17. 5) 21	(11. 2) 12
	Honorific	(11. 3) 11	(6. 3) 8	(5. 8) 7	(20. 6) 22
	Hedge	(1. 0) 1	(0. 8) 1	(0. 8) 1	0
Syntactic	Conditional	0	(6. 3) 8	(1. 7) 2	(6. 5) 7
downgraders	Reduplication	0	(12. 6) 16	(4. 2) 5	(7. 5) 8
	Total	(100) 97	(100) 127	(100) 120	(100) 107

Table 31   Log-likelihood ratio of formulae for IM

		CNS-KCL		CNS-RCL		CNS-FCL	
		LL	P	LL	P	LL	P
	Politeness marker	1. 864	0. 174	6. 042	*0. 014	2. 714	0. 099
Lexical downgraders	Downtoner	9. 200	*0. 002	31. 408	*0. 000	39. 349	*0. 000
	Understater	3. 101	0. 078	0. 546	0. 460	0. 038	0. 845
	Appealer	0. 015	0. 903	0. 853	0. 356	4. 170	*0. 041
	Honorific	0. 426	0. 514	0. 276	0. 600	5. 093	*0. 024
	Hedge	0. 000	1. 000	0. 000	1. 000	1. 412	0. 235
Syntactic downgraders	Conditional	11. 598	*0. 001	2. 878	0. 090	10. 744	*0. 001
	Reduplication	21. 232	*0. 000	7. 648	*0. 006	13. 112	*0. 000

eg. "Jin Xiuming, bang wo na ge kuaidi. Wo zai waimian. Ni neng bang wo na kuaidi ma?"

　　Please help me fetch the parcel, Jin Xiuming. I was not in here. Could you help me to get the parcel?

　　With regard to Russian subjects, "politeness marker" was excessively employed with high percentage (61.7%), which was distinct from Chinese users significantly ($P = 0.014 < 0.05$). One reason was that they were more likely to use "performative" as head acts. "Politeness marker" was always accompanied with performaitve strategy.

　　Viewing to French subjects, they had more indicators (5 types of formulae) that showed significant difference from Chinese users in comparison to other two cultural groups, which proved the conclusion made above that there was further linguistic and cultural distance between Frenchmen and Chinese. Moreover, they tended to apply "honorific" (20.6%, $P = 0.024 < 0.05$) in head act. It might relate to the effect of L1 transfer. As is known, there are two terms for "you" in French, namely "tu" and "vous", just as "ni" and "nin" in Chinese. But the use of those two words is cultural specific. The French preferred to use "nin" (您, you) in requests to show respect to strangers and teacher (D + or P +).

　　To sum up, the semantic formulae for openers, HA, EM and IM vary among those four cultural groups when they made requests in Chinese. Those types of formulae produced by those three cultural groups differed from Chinese group significantly: "title + PM" and "popular alter" for openers, "query preparatory (2)" for HA, "modal particle" for "EM" and "downtoner" and "reduplication" for IM. The difference results not only from the effect of their first language and cultural background, but also from uncertainty and unfamiliarity with the frequent formulae in specific context. The following passage attempted to make clear their understanding of Chinese socio-cultural situations that they confronted with.

4.3.2　Perceptions of situational variables across cultures

　　As stated in Chapter 2 section 2.2.3, when a speaker makes a request, he or she should take the situational factors into account, such as social distance, power, etc. , which are viewed as the most important factors in formulating request speech acts (Lee, 2005). Blum-Kulka and House (1989) stresses that people from various countries or cultural backgrounds might have different interpretations of social situations and different relative importance associated with the situational factors. Since Chinese attach more importance to interpersonal relations, which play a crucial role in getting capital in the society. The scenarios in this survey were designed in terms of two situational variables: power and social distance, which were regarded as the most influential factors that affect the types of formulae speakers apply in Chinese. Accordingly, this section attempts to examine the types of semantic formulae that international students employed in requests in Chinese, which eventually aims to capture their understanding and perception of these variables in Chinese context, and based on which helps to know their sociopragmatic competence as well.

4.3.2.1   Power

All the participants from Korea, Russia and France were at intermediate level in Chinese language. Accordingly, the effects of language proficiency level on the use of semantic formulae could be ignored. However, the cultural background, L1 transfer could cause the difference in the use of formulae (Blum-Kulka & House, 1989; Byon, 2004; Lee, 2005). This section aims to identify the variations of perception of power in requests made by those three cultural groups.

As is shown in Table 40 and Table 41, power did affect the use of semantic formulae for openers, HA, EM and IM to some extent. However, those three cultural groups differed from each other in the number of formulae and types of formulae they employed.

The formulae for openers, HA, EM and IM used by Korean subjects, tended to be the most similar as that of Chinese native speakers among those three cultural groups. As the formulae for openers, Korean subjects were prone to use "title", "title + PM" and "greeting" in the S < H situations, use "attention-getter" and "name" in the S = H situations and "greeting" in the S > H situations. Although there differed in the S = H and S > H situations, Korean students used more polite words to address the hearer with higher status. It is known that Korean and Chinese are all belong to eastern culture. As a result, power plays an important role in the use of formulae. According to the number of formulae for HA, Korean subjects were likely to be more direct than Chinese users. Although the most frequent types of formulae Korean subjects employed were almost similar to that of Chinese subjects, the former was inclined to use more direct strategies in all respects. When Korean subjects made requests to the hearer with high status, they tended to use "grounder" to mitigate the impositive force. But except for grounders, they preferred to use "sweetener" to the hearer with lower status to show their power and friendliness, which was the same as Chinese users. This phenomenon is also regarded as virtue in China, "zun lao ai you" (尊老爱幼, respect the old and cherish the young).

Russian subjects tended to use "title", "greeting" and "title + PM" to address the hearers with high status, but were prone to use "greeting", "name", "attention-getter" in the S = H. It seemed that power affected the use of formulae in terms of openers. However, the most frequent formulae, for the S > H and S < H situations were query preparatory (47.6% for S > H, 41.8% for S < H) and performative (21.9% for S > H, 21.5% for S < H). Moreover, the total number of the formulae for EM in [S < H], [S = H] and [S > H] situations was as follows: 76, 32 and 63. It shows that power didn't affect the use of formulae by Russian users. They tended to use "grounder" and "gratitude" in the S > H and S = H situations, while they preferred "grounder" and "sweetener" in the S < H situations. As for the formulae for IM, the total number of "politeness marker" for the S = H situations would be the highest among those three situations. Consequently, we could conclude that power had exerted some influence on the use of semantic formulae, but the effects were not so obvious and systematic as their Korean counterparts.

"Greeting" turned out to be favored by French users regardless of the status of the hearers. As is known, "bonjour" (good morning) and "bonsoir" (good evening) are used as common terms for openers in French. However, they were prone to use "title" and "greeting" as the most frequent formulae in the S < H situations, and tended to use "greeting" and "attention getter" in the S = H and S > H situations. Comparing to other three cultural groups, French subjects were the most indirect in making requests. "Query preparatory (1)" (61.7% S < H, 76.5% S = H, 61.7% S < H) was the most frequent formulae for HA regardless of the situations. Furthermore, they preferred "grounder" just like other cultural groups, but they tended to use "H + G" more frequent in almost all the three situations. The study conducted by Byon in 2004 shows that American English native speakers inclined to utter a request before a grounder, since they wanted to make themselves understood as clear as possible unconsciously and also for the 'written discourse style'. French culture belongs to western culture, which has the similar features as English speakers. Moreover, according to the interview data, those European participants were almost multilingual and they could speak English at a very young age. Concerning the formulae for IM, French subjects tended to use "politeness marker" regardless of situations, and they used it most in the S = H situations but not the S < H situations. To sum up, power is very significant variable in the use of formulae for different situations, but it works in the S < H situations, but hard to find the difference between S = H and S > H situations. French people are more egalitarian and individualistic, which conforms the previous studies (Cohen & Shively, 2007b; Warga & Schölmberger, 2007).

Table 32

Distribution of semantic formulae for openers and HA by power

		S<H (P+)				S=H (P=)				S>H (P−)			
		CNS	KCL	RCL	FCL	CNS	KCL	RCL	FCL	CNS	KCL	RCL	FCL
Title	Title	(44.5) 40	(56.7) 34	(40) 28	(38.2) 26	(7.4) 6	(8.6) 6	(8.9) 7	(1.7) 1	(18.0) 11	(7.4) 2	(34.5) 19	(10) 3
	Title + PM	(33.3) 30	(15) 9	(18.6) 13	(10.3) 7	(34.5) 28	0	(10.1) 8	(10) 6	(13.1) 8	0	(3.6) 2	(13.3) 4
Name		0	(1.7) 1	(1.4) 1	0	(27.2) 22	(24.3) 17	(21.5) 17	(6.6) 4	(39.4) 24	(18.5) 5	(10.9) 6	(16.7) 5
Greeting		(14.4) 13	(16.7) 10	(30) 21	(39.7) 27	(3.7) 3	(17.1) 12	(35.4) 28	(56.7) 34	(3.3) 2	(40.8) 11	(5.5) 3	(13.3) 4
Attention-getter		(3.3) 3	(8.2) 5	(7.1) 5	(11.8) 8	(9.9) 8	(40) 28	(15.2) 12	(25) 15	(4.9) 3	(25.9) 7	(10.9) 6	(46.7) 14
Kinship terminology		(4.5) 4	(1.7) 1	(2.9) 2	0	(3.7) 3	(4.3) 3	(7.6) 6	0	(3.3) 2	0	(29.1) 16	0
Popular alerters		0	0	0	0	(13.6) 11	(5.7) 4	(1.3) 1	0	(18.0) 11	(7.4) 2	(5.5) 3	0
Total (openers)		(100) 90	(100) 60	(100) 70	(100) 68	(100) 81	(100) 70	(100) 79	(100) 60	(100) 61	(100) 27	(100) 55	(100) 30
Mood derivable		(6.1) 5	(12) 11	0	(4.9) 4	(13.2) 10	(24) 19	(20.7) 17	(12.4) 10	(29.4) 25	(30.2) 26	(13.9) 11	(7.4) 6
Performative		(4.9) 4	(1.1) 1	(21.9) 18	(3.7) 3	(1.3) 1	(1.2) 1	(9.8) 8	(2.5) 2	(2.4) 2	0	(21.5) 17	(7.4) 6
Want statement		(18.3) 15	(22.8) 21	(19.5) 16	(16.1) 13	(1.3) 1	(1.2) 1	0	(4.9) 4	(1.2) 1	(1.2) 1	(5.1) 4	0
Suggestory formula		(1.2) 1	0	0	0	0	0	0	0	(7.0) 6	0	0	(7.4) 6
Query preparatory	QP1	(58.5) 48	(50) 46	(47.6) 39	(61.8) 50	(52.6) 40	(55) 44	(63.4) 52	(76.5) 62	(36.5) 31	(46.5) 40	(41.8) 33	(61.7) 50
	QP2	(9.8) 8	(13) 12	(11) 9	(8.6) 7	(30.3) 23	(18.6) 15	(6.1) 5	(3.7) 3	(18.8) 16	(15.1) 13	(13.9) 11	(6.2) 5
Strong hint		(1.2) 1	(1.1) 1	0	(4.9) 4	(1.3) 1	0	0	0	(4.7) 4	(4.7) 4	(2.5) 2	(7.4) 6
Mild hint		0	0	0	0	0	0	0	0	0	(2.3) 2	(1.3) 1	(2.5) 2
Total (HA)		(100) 82	(100) 92	(100) 82	(100) 81	(100) 76	(100) 80	(100) 82	(100) 81	(100) 85	(100) 86	(100) 79	(100) 81

Table 33

Distribution of semantic formulae for EM and IM by power

		S < HP +				S = H P =				S > H P -			
		CNS	KCL	RCL	FCL	CNS	KCL	RCL	FCL	CNS	KCL	RCL	FCL
Preparator		(6.7) 6	(8.7) 7	(10.5) 8	(7.8) 5	(6.9) 5	(13.2) 10	0	(18) 12	(18.4) 16	(18.3) 15	0	(12.2) 10
Grounder	G + H	(50.0) 45	(65.5) 53	(51.4) 39	(34.3) 22	(27.8) 20	(38.2) 29	(65.6) 21	(13.4) 9	(25.3) 22	(25.6) 21	(41.3) 26	(20.7) 17
	H + G	(17.8) 16	(13.6) 11	(22.4) 17	(32.8) 21	(22.2) 16	(9.2) 7	(9.4) 3	(52.2) 35	(18.4) 16	(13.4) 11	(9.5) 6	(29.3) 24
Cost minimizer		(4.4) 4	(1.2) 1	0	(1.6) 1	(1.4) 1	0	0	0	(3.4) 3	(6.1) 5	(3.2) 2	0
Promise of reward		0	0	0	0	(5.6) 4	(11.8) 9	0	0	(1.2) 1	(1.2) 1	0	0
Apology		(2.2) 2	0	0	(9.4) 6	0	(1.3) 1	0	0	0	0	0	(3.7) 3
Humbling oneself		0	0	0	0	0	0	0	0	0	(1.2) 1	(1.5) 1	0
Self introduction		(5.6) 5	(1.2) 1	(2.6) 2	(1.6) 1	0	(6.6) 5	0	0	0	(6.1) 5	(3.2) 2	(2.4) 2
Gratitude		(6.7) 6	(1.2) 1	(11.8) 9	(7.8) 5	(20.8) 15	(14.5) 11	(25) 8	(13.4) 9	(5.7) 5 0	(4.9) 4	(7.9) 5	(14.6) 12
Begging for help		(1.1) 1	(1.2) 1	0	0	0	0	0	(3) 2	0	0	0	0
Sweetener		(2.2) 2	(2.5) 2	(1.3) 1	(1.6) 1	(2.8) 2	0	0	0	(21.8) 19	(18.3) 15	(30.2) 19	(11) 9
Disarmer		(1.1) 1	0	0	0	0	0	0	0	0	0	0	0
Asking for the hearer's opinion		0	(1.2) 1	0	(3.1) 2	0	0	0	0	0	(1.2) 1	(3.2) 2	(6.1) 5

续表

		S<HP+				S=H P=				S>H P−			
		CNS	KCL	RCL	FCL	CNS	KCL	RCL	FCL	CNS	KCL	RCL	FCL
Ending words	Polite words	(2.2) 2	(3.7) 3	0	0	(5.6) 4	(3.9) 3	0	0	(1.2) 1	(3.7) 3	0	0
	Modal particle	0	0	0	0	(6.9) 5	(1.3) 1	0	0	(4.6) 4	0	0	0
Total (EM)		(100) 90	(100) 81	(100) 76	(100) 64	(100) 72	(100) 76	(100) 32	(100) 67	(100) 87	(100) 82	(100) 63	(100) 82
Politeness marker		(41.2) 21	(32.1) 9	(56.8) 21	(33.3) 15	(32.6) 15	(47.9) 23	(75) 33	(84.8) 28	(30.2) 13	(38.5) 10	(64.5) 20	(64.3) 9
Downtoner		(2.0) 1	0	0	0	(17.4) 8	(14.5) 7	(2.3) 1	0	(16.3) 7	(7.7) 2	0	0
Understater		(9.8) 5	(14.3) 4	(10.8) 4	(4.5) 2	(34.8) 16	(6.3) 3	(6.8) 3	(6.1) 2	(34.9) 15	(23) 6	(6.5) 2	(14.3) 2
Appealer		(7.8) 4	(35.7) 10	(13.5) 5	(13.3) 6	(13.0) 6	(25) 12	(15.9) 7	(9.1) 3	(18.6) 8	(30.8) 8	(29) 9	(21.4) 3
Honorific		(37.2) 19	(17.9) 5	(18.9) 7	(48.9) 22	(2.2) 1	(6.3) 3	0	0	0	0	0	0
Hedge		(2.0) 1	0	0	0	0	0	0	0	0	0	0	0
Total (IM)		(100) 51	(100) 28	(100) 37	(100) 45	(100) 46	(100) 48	(100) 44	(100) 33	(100) 43	( ) 26	(100) 31	(100) 14

In conclusion, power affected the use of semantic formulae for openers, HA, EM and IM, but the effects on those three cultural groups varied. The formulae of requests differed in some respects. Formulae used by Korean subjects were similar to that of Chinese, but difference still existed. Russian and French subjects showed deference and respectfulness to "teachers" and "administrators" in this survey, while they treated the hearers with equal or lower status in an equal way. Moreover, French subjects were prone to be most indirect regardless of the situations.

4.3.2.2   Social distance

It was stated that power had exerted influence on the use of semantic formulae. Another situational variable, social distance, had played an important role in choosing semantic formulae as well.

As is shown in the following Table 34, 35, 36, 37, Korean subjects acted in the similar way as Chinese users in this survey. They tended to use "greeting" to address the hearer in the [D+] situations, and employ "name" or "kinship terminology" to address the persons in the [D-] situations. However, they were prone to apply "title" and "title + PM" to alert the teachers' attention, while they chose "greeting" and "attention getter" to address the administrators. It indicated that Korean subjects were more likely to regard requests as the obligations of the administrators whose work was to provide service in the university. This interpretation could be confirmed by the use of formulae for HA. They tended to use "query preparatory" (37.0%) or "want "statement" (32.6%), when hearers were administrators, while they preferred "query preparatory (1)" and "query preparatory (2)", when hearers were professors.

As for the formulae for EM, Korean subjects were inclined to use more formulae in the [D-] situations with the preference of "grounder". However, the total number of "grounder" was highest in the teachers' and administrators' situations. It could be concluded that power was a more significant variable in the requests rather than social distance among Korean users.

Moreover, they tended to use "politeness marker" in strangers' situations rather than that in teachers' or administrators' situations. It could be thought to remedy the absence of external modifications in the strangers' situations. They chose the internal modification "politeness marker" to mitigate the impositive force in requests. There was the same phenomenon among Chinese users.

Russian subjects were inclined to use "greeting" in administrators' and strangers' situations, while they were prone to use "title" to address teachers and group members. Moreover, although the hearers, such as administrators and group members were all strangers to them, they address hearers in different ways. Concerning formulae for HA, Russian participants tended to be more direct than their Chinese counterparts. Russian subjects were prone to use "performative" (43.6%) and "query preparatory" (25.6%) in group members' situations [D +], and to use "query preparatory" (47.6%) and "mood derivable" (40.5%) in the good friends' situations [D –]. According to the statistics in the following tables, they were likely to be the most direct among those three cultural groups. However, they mainly employed "query reparatory" (71.8%) in the teachers' situations. It implicates that Russians tended to value power over social distance in some sense.

As for formulae for EM, they were prone to use "grounder" (G + H > H + G) in the [D +] situations. And they preferred to "preparator" before making requests in the strangers' (45.5%) and good friends' situations (27.8%). It shows that Russians preferred to use small talk to lay the grounder for the requests. Like Chinese and Korean subjects, Russian speakers were also prone to use "sweetener" to the hearer with lower status in the group members' situations. With view to the internal modifications, "politeness marker" was the most popular formulae for Russian participants. The total number of "politeness marker" was higher in the [D +] situations. And "honorific", eg. nin (您, you), was also applied in the administrators' and teachers' situations.

Russian culture is combination of Eastern and Western Culture, as for the openers, they acted in the western style, but concerning the formulae for HA, SM and EM, they were inclined to lay more emphasis on power in comparison to social distance.

French subjects were prone to use " greeting " and " attention getter " in the most situations, but they preferred to use " title " and " title + PM " in the teachers' situation. It was affected by their L1, which had already been illustrated in last section. They tended to use " query preparatory " in all these six situations. And they employed " performative " and " suggestive formula " sometimes in group members' situations. French tended to be indirect in request making. As for EM, they tended to employ " grounder ", but they preferred to use " grounder " before making requests in the [P -] situations, such as strangers, good friends' and roommates' situations, while other cultural groups tended to use " grounder " to the hearers with high status. Concerning internal modifications, those French subjects just like Russian participants favored " politeness marker " . However, the total number of " politeness marker " was higher in the [D +] situations, particularly high in the strangers' situation. And "honorific", eg. nin (您, you), was also applied frequently in the administrators' and teachers' situations. It seemed that power and social distance exerted the similar influence on the use of formulae by French subjects. French was found to be egalitarian as other westeners (Byon, 2004; Mulken, 1996).

Table 34　　**Distribution of semantic formulae for openers and HA by social distance (1)**

		Administrator (D+)				Stranger (D+)				Group member (D+)			
		CNS	KCL	RCL	FCL	CNS	KCL	RCL	FCL	CNS	KCL	RCL	FCL
Title	Title	(7.7) 3	(20) 4	(6.3) 2	0	(12.2) 5	(8.6) 3	(11.1) 4	0	(33.3) 12	(15) 3	(67.9) 19	(11.1) 2
	Title + PM	(43.6) 17	0	(9.4) 3	(3.1) 1	(68.3) 28	0	(16.7) 6	0	(27.8) 10	0	(7.1) 2	(22.2) 4
Name		0	(5) 1	0	0	0	0	0	0	(22.2) 8	(15) 3	(3.6) 1	(11.1) 2
Greeting		(35.9) 14	(45) 9	(62.5) 20	(84.4) 27	(4.9) 2	(25.6) 9	(47.2) 17	(72.4) 21	(5.6) 2	(45) 9	(7.1) 2	(22.2) 4
Attention-getter		(5.1) 2	(25) 5	(15.5) 5	(12.5) 4	(7.3) 3	(62.9) 22	(25) 9	(27.6) 8	(8.3) 3	(5) 1	0	(33.4) 6
Kinship terminology		(7.7) 3	(5) 1	(6.3) 2	0	(2.4) 1	0	0	0	(2.8) 1	(15) 3	(14.3) 4	0
Popular alerters		0	0	0	0	(4.9) 2	(2.9) 1	0	0	0	(5) 1	0	0
Total (openers)		(100) 39	(100) 20	(100) 32	(100) 32	(100) 41	(100) 35	(100) 36	(100) 29	(100) 36	(100) 20	(100) 28	(100) 18
Mood derivable		(12.5) 5	(21.7) 10	0	(10) 4	(2.5) 1	(6.8) 3	0	(2.6) 1	(25) 10	(23.3) 10	(7.7) 3	(7.9) 3
Performative		(2.5) 1	(2.2) 1	(29.3) 12	(7.5) 3	0	(2.3) 1	(15) 6	0	(5.0) 2	0	(43.6) 17	(15.8) 6
Want statement		(42.5) 17	(32.6) 15	(34.1) 14	(22.5) 9	(2.5) 1	(2.3) 1	0	(7.6) 3	0	(2.3) 1	(10.4) 4	0
Suggestory formula		(2.5) 1	0	0	0	0	0	0	0	(10) 4	0	0	(15.8) 6
Query preparatory	QP (1)	(32.5) 13	(37.0) 17	(26.8) 11	(40) 16	(87.5) 35	(72.7) 32	(80) 32	(87.2) 34	(30) 12	(41.9) 18	(25.6) 10	(39.5) 15
	QP (2)	(7.5) 3	(6.5) 3	(9.8) 4	(15) 6	(7.5) 3	(15.9) 7	(5) 2	(2.6) 1	(27.5) 11	(18.6) 8	(10.4) 4	(10.5) 4
Strong hint		0	0	0	(5) 2	0	0	0	0	(2.5) 1	(9.3) 4	(2.3) 1	(10.5) 4
Mild hint		0	0	0	0	0	0	0	0	0	(4.6) 2	0	0
Total (HA)		(100) 40	(100) 46	(100) 41	(100) 40	(100) 40	(100) 44	(100) 40	(100) 39	(100) 40	(100) 43	(100) 39	(100) 38

Table 35 Distribution of semantic formulae for openers and HA by social distance (2)

		Professor (D –) (D) (D+)				Good friend (D –) (D+)				Roommate (D –) ( )			
		CNS	KCL	RCL	FCL	CNS	KCL	RCL	FCL	CNS	KCL	RCL	FCL
Title	Title	(85.7) 36	(75) 30	(68.4) 26	(72.2) 26	(5.3) 2	(8.5) 3	(7) 3	(2.8) 1	0	0	0	(5.9) 1
	Title + PM	(9.5) 4	(22.5) 9	(26.4) 10	(16.7) 6	0	0	(4.7) 2	(16.7) 6	0	0	0	0
Name		0	0	(2.6) 1	0	(57.9) 22	(48.6) 17	(39.5) 17	(11.1) 4	(50.0) 13	(8) 2	(18.6) 5	(17.6) 3
Greeting		0	(2.5) 1	(2.6) 1	0	0	(8.6) 3	(25.6) 11	(36.1) 13	0	(8) 2	(3.7) 1	0
Attention-getter		(4.8) 2	0	0	(11.1) 4	(7.8) 3	(17.1) 6	(7) 3	(19.4) 7	(3.8) 1	(24) 6	(22.2) 6	(47.1) 8
Kinship terminology		0	0	0	0	(5.3) 2	(8.6) 3	(14) 6	(13.9) 5	(11.6) 3	(52) 13	(44.4) 12	(29.4) 5
Popular alerters		0	0	0	0	(23.7) 9	(8.6) 3	(2.2) 1	0	(34.6) 9	(8) 2	(11.1) 3	0
Total (openers)		(100) 42	(100) 40	(100) 38	(100) 36	(100) 38	(100) 35	(100) 43	(100) 36	(100) 26	(100) 25	(100) 27	(100) 17
Mood derivable		(2.5) 1	(2.2) 1	0	0	(23.7) 9	(43.3) 16	(40.5) 17	(21.4) 9	(41.9) 18	(37.2) 16	(20) 8	(7.3) 3
Performative		0	0	(15.4) 6	0	(2.6) 1	(2.7) 1	(4.8) 2	(4.8) 2	0	0	0	0
Want statement		(2.5) 1	(13) 6	0	(9.8) 4	0	0	0	(2.4) 1	0	0	0	0
Suggestory formula		0	0	0	0	0	0	0	0	0	0	0	0
Query	QP (1)	(70) 28	(63) 29	(71.8) 28	(82.9) 34	(63.2) 24	(32.4) 12	(47.6) 20	(66.7) 28	(39.5) 17	(51.2) 22	(57.5) 23	(85.4) 35
preparatory	QP (2)	(22.5) 9	(19.6) 9	(12.8) 5	(2.4) 1	(7.9) 3	(21.6) 8	(7.1) 3	(4.7) 2	(9.3) 4	(11.6) 5	(17.5) 7	(2.4) 1

续表

	Professor (D－) (D) (D+)				Good friend (D－) (D+)				Roommate (D－) ()			
	CNS	KCL	RCL	FCL	CNS	KCL	RCL	FCL	CNS	KCL	RCL	FCL
Strong hint	(2.5) 1	(2.2) 1	0	(4.9) 2	(2.6) 1	0	0	0	(9.3) 4	0	(5) 2	0
Mild hint	0	0	0	0	0	0	0	0	0	0	0	(4.9) 2
Total (HA)	(100) 40	(100) 46	(100) 39	(100) 41	(100) 38	(100) 37	(100) 42	(100) 42	(100) 43	(100) 43	(100) 40	(100) 41

Table 36　Distribution of semantic formulae for EM and IM by social distance (1)

		Administrator (D+)				Stranger (D+)				Group member (D+)			
		CNS	KCL	RCL	FCL	CNS	KCL	RCL	FCL	CNS	KCL	RCL	FCL
Preparator		(9.5) 4	(2.8) 1	(4.5) 2	(21.7) 5	(6.25) 1	(15.4) 2	(45.5) 5	(11.1) 2	(29.8) 11	(33.3) 14	(17.7) 6	(16.7) 7
Grounder	G+H	(64.2) 27	(82.9) 29	(59.1) 26	(30.5) 7	(6.25) 1	(38.5) 5	(18.1) 2	(22.2) 4	(13.5) 5	(4.8) 2	(2.9) 1	(11.9) 5
	H+G	(16.7) 7	(14.3) 5	(20.5) 9	(30.5) 7	(6.25) 1	(7.7) 1	0	(38.9) 7	0	(2.4) 1	0	(11.9) 5
Cost minimizer		0	0	0	0	(6.25) 1	0	0	0	0	(2.4) 1	0	0
Promise of reward		0	0	0	0	(6.25) 1	0	0	0	0	0	0	0
Apology		0	0	0	0	0	0	0	0	0	0	0	0
Humbling oneself		0	0	0	0	0	0	0	0	0	(2.4) 1	(2.9) 1	0

续表

		Administrator (D+)				Stranger (D+)				Group member (D+)			
		CNS	KCL	RCL	FCL	CNS	KCL	RCL	FCL	CNS	KCL	RCL	FCL
Self introduction		(2.4) 1	0	(4.5) 2	(4.3) 1	0	0	0	0	(5.4) 2	(9.5) 4	(5.9) 2	(4.8) 2
Gratitude		(4.8) 2	0	(11.4) 5	(13) 3	(62.5) 10	(15.4) 2	(36.4) 4	(16.7) 3	(5.4) 2	(2.4) 1	(8.8) 3	(21.4) 9
Begging for help		0	0	0	0	0	(23) 3	0	(11.1) 2	0	0	0	0
Sweetener		0	0	0	0	0	0	0	0	(45.9) 17	(33.3) 14	(55.9) 19	(21.4) 9
Disarmer		0	0	0	0	0	0	0	0	0	0	0	0
Asking for the hearer's opinion		0	0	0	0	0	0	0	0	0	(2.4) 1	(5.9) 2	(11.9) 5
Ending words	Polite words	(2.4) 1	0	0	0	(6.25) 1	0	0	0	0	(7.1) 3	0	0
	Modal particle	0	0	0	0	0	0	0	0	0	0	0	0
Total (EM)		(100) 42	(100) 35	(100) 44	(100) 23	(100) 16	(100) 13	(100) 11	(100) 18	(100) 37	(100) 42	(100) 34	(100) 42
Politeness marker		(26.1) 6	5	12	9	(69.7) 23	17	21	19	(31.4) 11	() 4	13	5
Downtoner		0	0	0	0	(3.0) 1	0	0	0	(11.5) 4	() 1	0	0
Understater		(8.7) 2	0	2	0	(21.3) 7	0	0	0	(31.4) 11	() 2	0	0
Appealer		(8.7) 2	5	3	6	(3.0) 1	6	2	1	(25.7) 9	() 7	0	2
Honorific		(56.5) 13	1	4	11	(3.0) 1	3	0	0	0	0	0	0
Hedge		0	0	0	0	0	0	0	0	0	0	0	0

续表

	Administrator (D+)				Stranger (D+)				Group member (D+)			
	CNS	KCL	RCL	FCL	CNS	KCL	RCL	FCL	CNS	KCL	RCL	FCL
Conditional	0	0	0	2	0	0	0	0	0	( ) 3	0	1
reduplication	0	5	1	0	0	0	0	0	0	( ) 6	0	1
Total (IM)	(100) 23	16	21	28	(100) 33	26	24	20	(100) 35	( ) 23	13	9

Table 37　Distribution of semantic formulae for EM and IM by social distance (2)

	Professor (D-)				Good friend (D-)				Roommate (D-)			
	CNS	KCL	RCL	FCL	CNS	KCL	RCL	FCL	CNS	KCL	RCL	FCL
Preparator	(5.0) 2	(13) 6	(18.8) 6	0	(11.1) 7	(12.7) 8	(27.8) 10	(20.4) 10	(12.5) 6	(2.5) 1	(2.8) 1	(7.5) 3
Grounder	(45) 18	(52.2) 24	(40.6) 13	(36.6) 15	(36.5) 23	(38) 24	(52.8) 19	(10.2) 5	(29.2) 14	(47.5) 19	(69.4) 25	(30) 12
	(15) 6	(13) 6	(25) 8	(34.2) 14	(22.3) 14	(9.5) 6	(8.3) 3	(57.1) 28	(37.5) 18	(25) 10	(16.6) 6	(47.5) 19
Cost minimizer	(7.5) 3	(2.2) 1	0	(2.4) 1	0	0	0	0	(4.2) 2	(10) 4	(5.6) 2	0
Promise of reward	0	0	0	0	0	(14.3) 9	0	0	(2.1) 1	(2.5) 1	0	0
Apology	(2.5) 1	0	0	(14.6) 6	0	(1.6) 1	0	0	0	0	0	(7.5) 3
Humbling oneself	0	0	0	0	0	0	0	0	0	0	0	0
Self introduction	(5.0) 2	(2.2) 1	0	0	(1.6) 1	(4.8) 3	0	0	0	(2.5) 1	0	0
Gratitude	(5.0) 2	(2.2) 1	(12.5) 4	(4.9) 2	(7.9) 5	(12.7) 8	0	(12.2) 6	(6.2) 3	(7.5) 3	(5.6) 2	(7.5) 3

续表

	Professor (D -)				Good friend (D -)				oommate (D -)			
	CNS	KCL	RCL	FCL	CNS	KCL	RCL	FCL	CNS	KCL	RCL	FCL
Begging for help	(2.5) 1	(2.2) 1	0	0	0	0	(11.1) 4	0	0	0	0	0
Sweetener	(5.0) 2	(4.3) 2	(3.1) 1	(2.4) 1	0	0	0	0	(2.5) 1	0	0	0
Disarmer	(2.5) 1	0	0	0	(1.6) 1	0	0	0	0	0	0	0
Asking for the hearer's opinion	0	(2.2) 1	0	(4.9) 2	0	0	0	0	0	0	0	0
Ending words — Polite words	(5.0) 2	(6.5) 3	0	0	(9.5) 6	(4.8) 3	0	0	(2.1) 1	0	0	0
Ending words — Modal particle	0	0	0	0	(9.5) 6	(1.6) 1	0	0	(6.2) 3	0	0	0
Total (EM)	(100) 40	(100) 46	(100) 32	( ) 41	(100) 63	(100) 63	(100) 36	(100) 49	(100) 48	(100) 40	(100) 36	(100) 40
Politeness marker	(24.1) 7	(19) 4	(50) 9	(25) 6	(9.1) 2	(24) 6	(48) 12	(52.9) 9	0	(37.5) 6	(46.7) 7	(44.4) 4
Downtoner	0	0	0	0	(31.8) 7	(28) 7	(4) 1	0	(38.5) 5	(6.2) 1	0	0
Understater	(44.8) 13	(19) 4	(11.1) 2	(8.4) 2	(50.0) 11	(12) 3	(12) 3	(11.8) 2	(53.8) 7	0	(13.3) 2	(22.3) 2
Appealer	(13.8) 4	(23.9) 5	(11.1) 2	0	(9.1) 2	(24) 6	(20) 5	(11.8) 2	(7.7) 1	(25) 4	(33.3) 5	(11.1) 1
Honorific	(17.3) 5	(19) 4	(16.6) 3	(45.8) 11	0	0	0	0	0	(6.3) 1	0	0
Hedge	0	(4.8) 1	(5.6) 1	0	0	0	0	0	0	0	0	0
Conditional	0	(4.8) 1	0	(8.3) 2	0	(8) 2	(8) 2	(5.9) 1	0	(12.5) 2	0	(11.1) 1
reduplication	0	(9.5) 2	(5.6) 1	(12.5) 3	0	(4) 1	(8) 2	(17.6) 3	0	(12.5) 2	(6.7) 1	(11.1) 1
Total (IM)	(100) 29	(100) 21	(100) 18	(100) 24	(100) 22	(100) 25	(100) 25	(100) 17	(100) 13	(100) 16	(100) 15	(100) 9

4. 4   Features of pragmatic strategies across cultures

As stated above, learners from different cultural and linguistic backgrounds employed various types of strategies in requests making. The features of pragmatic strategies will be identified in terms of the most frequently used formulae as well as difference between other cultural groups and Chinese cultural group.

As is shown in Table 38, the most popular formulae for openers, HA, EM and IM varied among those four cultural groups. Chinese native speakers tended to use "title", "greeting" and "name" as formulae for openers, preferred indirect strategies with high percentage of "query preparatory", favored to use reasons or justifications before or after making requests, and were prone to employ "downtoner" as formulae for IM between friends or intimate relations. Along with the findings stated in section 4. 2, it indicates that power and social distance played a crucial role in choosing of the formulae, and power works more intensive than social distance. Moreover, although some formulae, such as "kinship terminology", "popular alerters", "politeness word" and "modal particle", were not extensively used, they were characterized as special terms with Chinese characteristics. French subjects seldom or didn't use them at all.

According to Table 38, types of formulae and strategies Korean subjects employed were the most similar to that of Chinese native speakers among the three foreign cultural groups. However, differences still existed. They preferred to choose "attention-getter" to alter hearers' attention, use "politeness marker" to mitigate impositive force and apply "duplication" to make themselves understood as much as possible. As mentioned in section 4. 3, the effects of power were more systematic and significant than that of social distance, which was quite similar to that of Chinese.

Table 38 **The most popular semantic formulae**

for the four culturfal groups

	Ranking	CNS	KCL	RCL	FCL
Openers	1st	Title	Title	Title	Greeting
	2nd	Greeting	Attention-getter	Greeting	Attention-getter
	3rd	Name	Greeting	Name/ Kinship terminology	Title
Head acts	1st	QP (1)	QP (1)	QP (1)	QP (1)
	2nd	Mood derivable	Mood derivable	Performative	Mood derivable
	3rd	QP (2)	QP (2)	Mood derivable	Want statement
External Modifications	1st	G + H	G + H	G + H	H + G
	H + G	Preparator	Preparator	G + H	
	3rd	Preparator/ Gratitude	H + G	H + G	Preparator
Internal Modifications	1st	Appealer	Politeness marker	Politeness marker	Politeness marker
	2nd	Downtoner	Appealer	Appealer	Honorific
	3rd	Politeness marker	Reduplication	Understater	Appealer

Formulae for openers used by Russian subjects were similar to that of Chinese native speakers, but Russian subjects preferred to use "kinship terminology". But the formulae for "kinship terminology", such as "xiongdi" (兄弟, brother), "meimei" (妹妹, sister) and "pengyou" (朋友, friend), were rarely used as addressed by Chinese native speakers. Moreover, the findings in section 4.3 show that Russian turned out to be the most direct among those four cultural groups, when they made requests in Chinese. And they tended to use "politeness marker" to show respect to the hearers. Power and social distance worked equally on the use of formulae in requests made by Russian subjects, which was quite different from that of Chinese or Korean counterparts.

According to Table 38, French subjects' language and culture were totally different from Chinese, which was embodied in the requests French subjects made in this survey. As for the formulae for opener, they tended to choose "greeting" and "attention-getter", which could be regarded as the effects of L1 transfer. Although "query preparatory (1)", "mood derivable" and "want statement" were most popular formulae for HA, the percentage of "query preparatory (1)" (67. 2%) was particularly high. It was likely that French subjects were the most indirect among those four cultural groups. It confirmed the previous studies conducted by Mulken (1996) who stated that French people preferred to use "query preparatory" as the primary strategy for head act in making request performance. Like Korean and Russian subjects, French subjects preferred to use "politeness marker" . This phenomenon could be viewed as the common situations for Chinese language learners. They attempted to be more polite by using "politeness marker" . Moreover, French subjects tended to use "honorific", which could be explained by the difference between "tu" and "vous" (Ismail, Aladdin, & Ramli, 2014).

In conclusion, the description of Chinese and Korean as being more hierarchical, collectivistic, roundabout in comparison to French counterparts. In 2004, Byon pointed out that Korean tended to be more hierarchical, collective than Americans. Frenchmen and Americans belonged to western cultures; while Chinese and Korean all originated from Confucius culture, and belonged to eastern cultures. Consequently, the patterns or pragmatic features of those four cultural groups found in this study were reasonable.

4. 5   Summary

In order to answer the first research question, which tends to find out the features of pragmatic strategies in requests among Korean, French and Russian students, this chapter applied analyzed data to yield the findings in terms of semantic formulae for openers, HA, EM and IM.

Features of pragmatic strategies of Chinese native speakers were identified first, which was used as a baseline data for later comparison. The formulae that Korean students employed were similar to that of Chinese, while French differed from Chinese native speakers most and Russian students stood in the middle. Furthermore, it was found in LL examination that the formulae, such as "title + PM" and "popular alter" for openers, "query preparatory (2)" for HA, "modal particle" for EM and "downtoner" and "reduplication" for IM, produced by those three cultural groups had significant difference from that of Chinese native speakers.

The effects of power and social distance on the use of formulae were examined, which could represent learners' sociopragmatic competence. Korean subjects tended to be indirect, showed deference to the hearer with higher status, and used casual terms to address friends or roommates. Russian students were regarded as the most direct in comparison to Chinese, Korean and French counterparts for the high percentage of "performative" and "mood derivable" . French subjects were more likely to employ "query preparatory" in most of the situations and considered as the most indirect ones. Social distance exerted influence on the use of the formulae in requests but not as significant as power. The features of pragmatic strategies among those cultural groups primarily resulted from L1 transfer and perception of politeness embedded in their cognition.

This chapter laid the ground for exploration of international students' pragmatic development trajectories, offered a holistic picture of the pragmatic features of those international students from Korea, France and Russia, and provided with sufficient information for the design of semi-structured interview questions tracking their pragmatic changes based on DCT data. Moreover, in order to investigate in-depth, the pragmatic development of learners from different cultural backgrounds in study abroad context and probe into the reasons behind their different trajectories of pragmatic development, three participants chosen from Korea, Russia and France respectively are described and analyzed in detail in the following chapter. Those three participants were representatives of each culture in the initial reading of their data. The following chapter is featured by quantitative data embedded in qualitative data within a case study, along with a cross-case display afterwards.

Chapter 5

Pragmatic Development

5. 1 Introduction

Chapter 4 analyzed the idiosyncratic nature of pragmatic strategies in requests produced by learners from Korea, Russia and France, which provided a general picture of pragmatic features of those three cultural groups. The previous chapter lays the solid ground of this chapter, which attempts to explore in-depth the trajectories of pragmatic development of those learners and the factors that aid or hinder the development process qualitatively primarily. Therefore, the purpose of this chapter is to answer the following two research questions: In what way do their pragmatic strategies of requests change, and what factors affect the changes of their pragmatic strategies?

In chapter 4, the most popular formulae employed by learners from Korea, Russia and France, and the categories of formulae for opener, HA, EM and IM that had a significant difference from Chinese groups and most popular formulae were identified based on the quantitative analysis. When learners made requests in Chinese, those categories varied from culture to culture. In order to investigate the pragmatic development, three learners representing Korean, Russian and French cultures in some sense were selected among the 60 informants. Those three participants were required to finish the questionnaire (DCT) every month from March to June 2016. As a result, they were tested four times in one semester. In order to get rid of the negative effects of repetitive test of the same DCT questionnaire, the order of 12 scenarios are rearranged each time. Focus was given to the categories of most frequently used formulae produced by the three case participants. The development trajectories of cultural difference were found based on analysis of qualitative data. And interview data were added to explain changes of the use of formulae, and which also helped to understand changes of the perception of politeness among those participants.

Those three case participants were also longitudinally investigated to dig out the factors that might aid or hindertheir pragmatic development. A description is provided concerning their background information, including language-learning experience, socializing style, perception of various constructs. Such a description helps readers to understand why international students acted in a certain way in SISU. Moreover, a detailed description of participants' cultural background, motivation and acculturation attitude, activities and contextual factors is also provided to give the reader a clear illustration of the three participants. These four aspects were generated based on literature review and original data collected, such as interview and field notes. The goal of the illustration is to capture any possible factors that might have either facilitated or constrained their development of pragmatic competence.

Structurally, this chapter is comprised of the following sections. Section 5. 2, 5. 3, 5. 4 are targeted to analyze the pragmatic developmental trajectories of Korean participant, Russian participant and French participant respectively, and factors that affect their pragmatic development are also described in details. As for pragmatic trajectories of those three cases, the analysis takes into account the categories of most frequently used formulae at four times test and their changes of perceptions of situational variables. Section 5. 5 discusses the findings across those three cases. Convergences and divergences of factors that impact their pragmatic development are discussed.

5. 2   Joy-a Korean student: shy, unsociable and practice-oriented

Joy was selected for its typicality of characteristics of pragmatic strategies in requests in Chinese. This section attempts to explore how a Korean student, Joy developed her pragmatic competence and understand the reasons leading to such outcomes. Shy and unsociable as she was, she didn't like to take initiative to make friends. Thereby, she didn't make any Chinese friends during sojourn. However, she regarded classroom instruction as the most effective way to learn Chinese language. This section was arranged in the following sequence: introduction of Joy's background, analysis of her pragmatic development trajectory, and description of her cultural background, motivation and acculturation attitude, social activities and contextual factors that might aid or hinder her pragmatic development.

5. 2. 1   Joy's Profile

The first case participant is Joy (pseudonym used for the sake of confidentiality), a 21-year-old female student. At the time of data collection, she was an exchange student at SISU in the intermediate language course. She finished her first year studying at Andong University in Korea as a Chinese language major. She arrived at Shanghai, China in September 2015. She volunteered to be a participant when she heard of my research from her Chinese teacher. Therefore, she was willing to frequently spend time going out and chatting. In the application to this exchange program at the university, her Chinese language proficiency should be at intermediate level. Although she passed HSK 3 (hanyu shuiping kaoshi), she was unable to communicate appropriately in Chinese in a fluent manner.

Her hometown is Daegu, which is located in the southeast Korea. She is the only child of a quite well off family. Her family was regarded as a up-middle class according to the socio-economic status, as her father ran a company producing and exporting machine parts for TV sets and her mother is a housewife. Her tuition fee and living expenses were mainly dependent on her family. She had a good sense of fashion and always dressed in fashionable clothes. She had long curly hair, which was dyed in light brown and she always wore makeup whenever I met her. However, she was quiet and introverted in nature. She told me that she was not good at communicating with others, particularly strangers. She told me that her family was very traditional. The oldest person had to eat first when they were having a meal together. She was told to behave herself at a very young age, and always followed her parents' suggestions. She wore big smiles when I met her at the first time according to my field notes. She made efforts to make some Chinese friends to practice her speaking and listening. But she wasn't successful, and always hung out with Korean friends.

She learned English as a foreign language when she was in the elementary school, however her English was poor. We met for the first time in November. When I tried to speak Chinese to her, she couldn't understand. I attempted to use English to introduce my research purpose, but she still couldn't follow me. Her Chinese was better than her English, although she had only studied Chinese for almost two years. She explained that she had to learn English, because it was an obligatory subject in school, but didn't have much interest in it. She chose to learn Chinese out of her curiosity and interests. As mentioned above, her father was in charge of a company, who traded with Chinese businessmen, and wanted Joy to learn Chinese so that she could help him sometimes. So she developed an early interest in Chinese language. She found it easy to learn Chinese, because many characters or sounds in Chinese are the same as in

Korean.

I observed and interacted with Joy on various occasions in different places on campus and off campus. Over the course of this research, she was not aware of my research, but regarded me as a friend. I treated her frequently to meals or coffees for her cooperation and help. She always felt uncomfortable and insisted to pay by herself. She went back to Korea in February for winter vacation, and she brought me a bottle of facial moisturizing cream for a gift after her returning in March. She described this as her philosophy—"courtesy demands reciprocity" (the same as "li shang wang lai" in Chinese culture). Based on interview data and occasional informal talks, I was able to record our communication in the form of field notes and interview transcription over a period of nine months. In the following sections, I describe Joy's pragmatic features at the beginning, her pragmatic development trajectory, and the factors that might affect her pragmatic development.

5.2.2　Joy's pragmatic features of requests

Based on Table 47, at the verybeginning, the most frequently used formulae by Joy were as follows: "attention getter", "title" and "kinship terminology" for openers; "QP (1)", "performative" and "QP (2)" for HA; "G + H", "preparator" and "H + G" for EM and "politeness marker" and "appealer" for IM. It was evident that the most furequently used formulae applied by Joy were similar to that of the ones used by the most of Korean subjects based on Table 39.

Furthermore, some naturally occurring data of requests made by Joy were recorded for triangulation. In Mar 23 [rd], 2016, Joy and I went for a walk in the park, she asked a strange student to take a photo for us.

Table 39   **Most frequently used formulae by Joy**

	Ranking	Joy	KCL
Openers	1st	Attention-getter (n=5)	Title
	2nd	Title (n=5)	Attention-getter
	3rd	Kinship terminology (n=2)	Greeting
Head acts	1st	QP (1) (n=5)	QP (1)
	2nd	Performative (n=3)	Mood derivable
	3rd	QP (2)	QP (2)
External Modifications	1st	G + H (n=5)	G + H
	2nd	H + G (n=3)	Preparator
	3rd	Preparator (n=2)	H + G
Internal Modifications	1st	Politeness marker (n=5)	Politeness marker
	2nd	Appealer (n=3)	Appealer
	3rd		Reduplication

#Natural recording#

Qing ni pai zhang zhaopian! (nodding her head)

Please take a photo for us!

This scenario is similar to scenario 8 in DCT (ask to take a photo). She preferred to use "performative" for HA, "politeness marker" for IM. She was nodding her head when making the requests. She told me that people acted in this way to show respect for others. Thus, generally speaking, Joy could be viewed as a typical case for Korean subjects in this sense.

5.2.3 Joy's development trajectory

As mentioned in Chapter 2, i. e. literature review, pragmatic competence could be divided into two aspects: pragmalinguistic competence and sociopragmatic competence. Pragmalinguistic competence focuses on linguistic structures for utterances in a language, and describes how we must use them in a language in a correct way. In this study, analysis of semantic formulae for openers, HA, EM and IM could be regarded as the aspects of pragamlinguistic competence. Sociopragmatic competence lays stress on the sociocultural aspects of social interaction, and emphasizes the situational variables. (leech, 1983; Thomas, 1983). Qualitative analysis of requests made by learners is applied to evaluate the development of Joy's sociopragmatic competence in this study.

5.2.3.1 Pragmalinguistic development

This section aims to track Joy's pragmalinguistic development trajectory. In comparison to the most frequent formulae used by Chinese students, Joy's changes of formulae within one semester in China will be illustrated. Joy tended to use "attention-getter" such as "qingwen" (请问, excuse me), "buhaoyisi" (不好意思, sorry), and "wei" (喂, hey) in various situations from T1 to T4 regardless of the situational factors. However, Chinese students seldom used this type of formulae. Moreover, Joy was prone to employ "meimei" (妹妹, younger sister) to address her roommate in the DCT test (see Table 40). Joy preferred to use "laoshi" (老师, teacher) and "tongxue" (同学, classmate) to address professors, administrators and unfamiliar students on the campus. It was obvious that the formulae for openers had not changed much from T1 to T2.

As displayed in Table 41, the formulae for head acts used by Joy had changed from T1 to T4. Compared with her Chinese counterparts, her pragmatic strategies changed towards a native like way. However, her changes of formulae displayed in a "U" shape way. Joy tended to use "QP (2)" rather than "QP (1)" in T2, it seemed that her pragmalinguistic competence declined. She preferred to use the syntactic structure such as " ···, keyima?" (···, 可以吗?, could I ···?), because she memorized this formulae from a dialogue in the textbook, and it seemed that this type of syntactic structure was easier to use in requests.

Table 40   Most frequently used formulae for openers by Joy

	T1 (n = 12)	T2 (n = 12)	T3 (n = 12)	T4 (n = 12)	CNS
Opener	Title (n = 5)	Greeting (n = 5)	Title (n = 6)	Title (n = 4)	Title
	Attention-getter (n = 3)	Attention-getter (n = 3)	Attention-getter (n = 3)	Attention-getter (n = 3)	Greeting
	Kinship terminology (n = 2)	Name (n = 2)	Kinship terminology (n = 2)	Kinship terminology (n = 2)	Name

Note: T1: the first time, T2: the second time, T3: the third time, and T4: the forth time.

I think that " ···, keyima?" is easier to formulate a request, and which could be used in various situations. My friends or classmates instructed me in this way. Furthermore, I observed that native speakers ask for help in this way as well. As a result, I preferred to use it in requests.

However, she didn't use this type of formulae in T3 and T4, it was because she thought that it was administrators' obligation to offer service for the students. And she changed to use "want statement" in administrators' situations. The following examples were extracted from the data collected:

T3: Qingwen wode shiyou gen wode shenghuo xiguan buyiyang, wo yao huan ge fangjian, qing ni bangzhu wo.

Excuse me, I and my roommate have different living habits, so I want to change a room. Please help me!

T4: Buhaoyisi, wo yao huan fangjian, yinwei wo gen shiyou shenghuo xiguan buyiyang. Mafannile.

Excuse me, I want to change a room, because my roommate and I have different living habits. Sorry to trouble you.

Table 41   Most frequently used formulae for HA by Joy

	T1 (n=12)	T2 (n=12)	T3 (n=12)	T4 (n=12)	CNS
Head acts	QP (1) (n=5)	QP (2) (n=5)	QP (1) (n=4)	QP (1) (n=5)	QP (1)
	Performative (n=3)	QP (1) (n=3)	Want statement (n=3)	Want statement (n=3)	Mood derivable
	QP (2) (n=3)	Want statement (n=2)	Performative (n=2)	QP (2) (n=2)	QP (2)

And Joy changed "performative" to "QP (2)" in T4 in unfamiliar equals' situations. She asked an unfamiliar student to take a photo for her on campus. According to interview data, Joy regarded "qing" as the way to show her respect to the stranger in T3, but she realized that "QP" would be more polite based on her observation of the requests made by native speakers. For example:

T3: Tongxue, qing ni bang women pai zhang zhaopian. Xiexie.

Classmate, please take a photo for us! Many thanks!

T4: Tonxue, bang women paizhang zhaopian, keyima?

Classmate, could youtake a photo for us?

On the whole, Joy didn't use "mood devriable" much from the beginning to the end. As described in last chapter, Chinese students tend to use direct strategy by employing "mood devriable" to maintain the intimate relationship among friends. However, Joy didn't use it in friends' or roommates' situations consistently in a single DCT questionnaire. As a result, Joy developed her pragmalinguistic competence to some extent, but still had a long way to go.

According to Table 42, Joy tended to use "grounder" before making requests from T1 to T4. However, the use of grounder after making requests decreased from T2 to T4 and the use of "preparator" and "gratitude" increased significantly. It seemed that Joy changed her external formulae towards the opposite direction from Chinese. Concerning the formulae for internal modifications, Joy preferred to employ "politeness marker" from T1 to T4. She began to use "downtoner" such as "ba" (吧) in T3 and T4. However, Chinese students tend to use "appealer" most frequently rather than "politeness marker".

Table 42   Most frequently used formulae for EM and IM by Joy

	T1 (n = 12)	T2 (n = 12)	T3 (n = 12)	T4 (n = 12)	CNS
EM	G + H (n = 5)	G + H (n = 7)	G + H (n = 7)	G + H (n = 5)	G + H
	H + G (n = 3)	Gratitude (n = 3)	Preparator (n = 3)	Preparator (n = 3)	H + G
	Preparator (n = 2)	Preparator (n = 2)	Gratitude (n = 2)	Gratitude (n = 2)	Preparator/ Gratitude
IM	Politeness marker (n = 5)	Politeness marker (n = 7)	Politeness marker (n = 3)	Politeness marker (n = 5)	Appealer
	Appealer (n = 3)	Appealer (n = 3)	Downtoner (n = 1)	Appealer (n = 2)	Downtoner
		Understate (n = 2)		Downtoner (n = 1)	Politeness marker

To sum up, Joy did develop her pragmalinguistic competence to some extent in term of the changes of the use of semantic formulae for openers, HA, EM and IM. However, the outcome of her pragmatic development was not dramatic.

5. 2. 3. 2 Sociopragmatic development

As mentioned above, sociopragmatic competence lays stress on the sociocultural respect of interaction. Accordingly, learners' perception of politeness in diverse situations could reflect their sociopragmatic competence. The twelve scenarios in this survey were designed in terms of two situational variables: power and social distance, which were regarded as the most important factors that affect the types of formulae that speakers use in Chinese. This section attempts to analyze the changes of Joy's perceptions of these two variables from T1 to T4 mainly through qualitative analysis.

＊Changes of perception of power

Overview of the data, I found that the types of formulae and formulae sequence used by Joy in the scenarios with same variables were similar in every single DCT questionnaire. With view to power, there are three major types of situations: [P +], [P =] and [P -]. Examples will be extracted according to power so as to understand the development of her sociopragmatic competence. Data were extracted and analyzed as follows:

(1) Situation: ask to get a new student identity card [D + , P +]

T1: Buhaoyisi, wo meiyou xiaoyuan yikatong. Wo yao banxinde, ni keyi bangzhu wo ma?

Sorry, I don't have student identity card. I need to get a new one. Could you help me?

T2: Nihao, qingwen wo de xiaoyuan yikatong diaole, suoyi wo yao xinde.

Hello, I lost my student identity card. So I need a new one.

T3: Qingwen, wo diaole wode ka, wo yao xinde. Qing ni bangzhu wo.

I lost my student identity card. I need a new one. Could you help me.

T4: Qingwen, buhaoyisi, wo diaole xiaoyuan yikatong. Wo yao xin de.

Sorry to disturb you. I lost my student identity card. I need a new one.

Taking a close look at the requests made by Joy from T1 to T4, slight changes had been made. As for alerters, she employed "attention getter", such as " buhaoyisi" and "qingwen" or "greeting", such as "nihao" to address administrators in the university. Chinese native speakers preferred to address their "teacher" in this situation. Moreover, Joy was direct in request making by employing "want statement" from T1 to T4. As mentioned above, it was administrator's obligation to offer service to staff and students. As a result, she had neither employed "title" or "title + PM" for alerters, nor used "honorific" for internal modifications.

We would like to ask administrators for help directly in Korea, because it is their obligation. I think it is the same in China. As a result, I translate the expression from Korean to Chinese directly. (Joy, T3)

(2) Situation: ask to copy PPT [D – , P +]

T1: Laoshi, wo xiang kaobei zhemen ke de kejian, keyima? Mafannile.

Teacher, I want to copy the PPT of this course, is it OK? Sorry to trouble you.

T2: Nihao, wo yao zhemen ke de kejian. Ni zhidao zhege zai naer?

Hello, I want PPT of this course. Do you know where it is?

T3: Laoshi, wo yao kao zheke de kejian, mafannile.

Teacher, I want to copy PPT of this course. Sorry to trouble you.

T4: Qingwen, wo yao zhemen ke de kejian, keyima? Buhaoyisi.

Hi, I want PPT of this course, is it OK? Sorry.

Joy employed "title", "attention getter" and "greeting" to alert hearers' attention in this situation. It was impolite to address a professor like this in the university in China. Moreover, she preferred "QP (2)" or "want statement" as head act. As mentioned in section 4, QP (2) was not as polite as QP (1), since its social meanings such as formality, politeness, power, and solidarity are differently encoded. From the linguistic form, it seemed that Joy didn't perceive the teacher as a person to whom she should show deference. However, she explained it as follows:

Teachers or professors enjoy high prestige in the university in Korea, and I think this is the same situation. But I haven't confronted with this kind of situation here, so I don't know how to make a request in a very polite way. (Joy, T3)

Accordingly, Joy's perception of power remained stable from T1 to T4, which was similar to Chinese native speakers. However, her pragmalinguistic competence didn't develop to match her soicopragmatic competence. As a result, it seemed that Joy didn't show enough respect to professors or teachers.

(3) Situation: consult the place of schooldormitory [D + , P =]

T1: Nihao, wo xianzai quxuexiao sushequ, zhege difang zai naer? Wo zhaobudao.

Hello, I want to go to the location of dormitories. Where is it? I can't find it.

T2: Nihao, qingwen xuexiao sushequ zainaer?

Hello, could I ask you where the location of dormitories is?

T3: Tongxue, qingwen, wo yao qusushe. Sushequ zai naer?

Classmate, I want to go to the location of dormitories. Where is it?

T4: Nihao, tongxue, xuexiao sushequ zai naer? Wo zhaobudao.

Hello, classmate. Where is the location of dormitories? I can't find it.

When Joy interacted with strangers on the campus, she used "greeting", such as "nihao" in T1 and T2, but she changed to use "tongxue" in T3 and "nihao, tongxue" in T4. Chinese subjects would use "tongxue" before "nihao". The reversed sequence of alerters would be her unfamiliarity with frequent formulae in Chinese.

I didn't know how to address strange student, when I first arrived at SISU. I heard some classmates or Chinese students address stranger students "tongxue" quite often. And I began to use it in this situation. (Joy T3)

According to Joy, she changed the way ofaddressing stranger students by learning from others. Moreover, she applied "QP (1)" from T1 to T4, which was similar to that of Chinese native speakers.

(4) Situation: ask to take notes [D + , P -]

T1: Wo qing ni ba women taolun de neirong jilu xialai, keyima? Ma fan ni le.

I ask you to take notes of the content of our discussion, is it ok? Sorry to trouble you.

T2: Nihao, womenzu xuyao jilu taolun de neirong. Qing ni jiluyixia, keyima?

How are you? Our group needs to take notes of the content of our discussion. Could you help me to take notes?

T3: Tongxue, qingwen women xuyao yigeren jilu taolun neirong, qing ni jilu yixia. Xiexieni.

Classmate, we need one person to take notes of the content of our discussion. Could you take notes? Thank you!

T4: Tongxue, womenzu xuyao ren jilu taolun neirong, qing ni fuze. Mafannile, buhaoyisi.

Classmate, our group needs one person to take notes of the content of our discussion. Could you take charge of it? Sorry to trouble you. Sorry.

As for alerters, Joy employed "greeting" in T2 and "tongxue" in T3 and T4. She preferred to be indirect by using "QP (2)" in T1 and T2, but changed to be direct by employing "performative" in T3 and T4. Joy was the group leader in this situation, and she had the power to arrange the tasks of other group members.

I am the group leader, and I am entitled to arrange the tasks for other group members. In order to be more effective and efficient, I would make requests as direct and simple as possible. And nobody would regard me as impolite. (Joy T3)

To sum up, Joy's pragmalinguistic competence developed to some extent based on the qualitative analysis, which triangulates the quantitative data in the last subsection. However, her perception of power remained stable. She was indirect toward the hearers with higher status, and direct to the hearers with lower status. Although Koreans tended to be the most similar to that of Chinese native speakers based on section 4.3.2.1, Joy was not as polite as Chinese native speakers when the hearers were administrators. It would be the slight different school cultures between Korea and China.

∗ Changes of perception ofsocial distance

This section aims to explore Joy's understanding of another situational variable, social distance, and also present the changes of the perception of social distance based on qualitative analysis. In this study, concerning the variable—social distance, DCT questionnaire was designed based on [D +] (unfamiliar) and [D –] (familiar). As stated in the last section, administrator with higher status but unfamiliar [D + , P +] and professor with higher power but familiar to speakers [D – , P +], Joy respected professor more than administrators, and she regarded administrators as someone offering service for staff and students in the university. Consequently, social distance was not so significant as power. Some other examples are extracted from the data collected to further discuss Joy's perception of social distance.

(1) Situation A: ask to take a photo [D + , P =]

T1: Tongxue, qing ni paizhang women lianggeren de zhaopian.

Classmate, please take a photo of us.

T2: Nihao! Qing ni paizhao, keyima?

Hello, could you take a photo?

T3: Tongxue, qing ni gei women paizhao. Xiexie!

Classmate, please take a photo of us, thanks!

T4: Tongxue, qing ni pai yixia zhao.

Classmate, please take a photo.

(2) Situation B: borrow a pen [D – , P –]

T1: Meimei wo wang dai bile. Ni jieyixia.

Sisiter, I forgot to bring a pen. Lend one to me.

T2: Wode bi wangdaile. Ni jie wo, keyima?

I forgot to bring a pen. Could you lend one to me?

T3: Meimei, jiezhibi, xiexie.

Sister, Lend a pen to me. Thanks.

T4: Meimei, wo wangdai bile. Jie wo ba!

Sister, I forgot to bring a pen. Lend it to me!

As for the scenario A, speaker asking a stranger student to take a photo,

Joy became more direct in T3 and T4 by using "performative" as head act. However, Chinese native speakers tended to use "query preparatory" in this situation. Moreover, when Joy asked to borrow a pen from a roommate, she tended to be more direct by using "mood derivable" in T1, T3 and T4, which was similar to those of Chinese subjects in this study. She preferred to use "meimei" in scenario B, which sounds strange to Chinese native speakers. Chinese subjects were prone to use "name" or "popular alerter" to address someone that was close to them. In terms of the linguistic forms, we could find the different formulae for openers and head acts in those two scenarios. Therefore, Joy sensed the difference between stranger and acquaintance, but the development of her pragmalinguistic competence dragged behind that of her sociopragmatic competence.

The hearer is stranger, but to take a photo is not a big favor. As a result, I think it is OK to ask for help directly. As for my roommate, we are close to each other, and borrowing a pen is small favor. If I asked her in a very polite way, she would think I want to keep distance from her. (Joy, T3)

The findings reinforced the argument that the development of pragmalinguistic competence and sociopragmatic competence was not at the same speed. As for Korean participant, Joy's perception of social distance was similar to those of Chinese subjects. But her linguistic forms produced the illusion that she didn't understand the difference.

5.2.3.3 Subsection summary

Regarding the developmental trajectory of Joy's pragmatic competence, the findings show that Joy, as a representative of Korean subjects, employed formulae that were highly similar to that of Chinese subjects in various occasions at the beginning. However, her pragmatic competence didn't change much during the course of this research. Although Joy's perception of situational factors remained stable and was similar to that of Chinese subjects, the development of her pragmalinguistic competence didn't follow up for frequent improper use of linguistic forms · in diverse situations. Her sociopragmatic competence was not as well developed as her pragamalinguistic competence.

5. 2. 4   Joy's cultural background

Although Korean and Chinese don't belong to the same language family, there are some Chinese characters in Korean.

There are many Chinese characters in media, such as news on TV and formal situations. So I think Chinese is not difficult for us to learn. I have studied it only for two years and passed HSK 3.

Moreover, Korean culture and Chinese culture originated from Confucianism (Rue & Zhang, 2008). As a result, they had a similar perception of politeness. Gu (1990) states that Confucius was dedicated to restore "li", which is mainly concerned with social order of the slavery system of the Zhou Dynasty and hierarchy. However, social hierarchical relations have faded away in modern China, which still has impact on the perception of politeness of modern Chinese. There are four basic elements included in Chinese perception of politeness: respectfulness, modesty, refinement and attitudinal warmth. Joy sensed similarity and difference between Chinese and Korean cultures.

If you watch news on TV in Korea, you would see lots of Chinese characters in it. I think Korean and Chinese cultures are similar.

Geographically, these two countries are located next to each other, and communications between them would be intensive culturally, economically or politically. Historically, both Korean culture and Chinese culture belong to Eastern culture. I had learned Chinese history, economy and literature in the university in my country. Thus, I knew something about it.

She regarded age and social status as the most important variable that would affect her use of formulae. And she was vague about the types of formulae for diverse situations in Chinese.

I think I should be more polite to professors and the aged, and there are some politeness markers in Korean to show special respect to them. When we have meals with aged people, we use "식사해요" (meok jja[①], please have meal) to show our deference. But we use "먹자" (sik ssa hae yo^5, lets eat) to our friends before starting a meal. We are friends, so we needn't be too polite. Anyway, I am still very vague about the polite expressions in Chinese. And I think "nin" and "qing" are politeness markers in Chinese.

According to Joy, her perception of situational factors was similar to that of Chinese native speakers. The distance between language learner's culture and the culture of the target language community serves as an important factor that determines the level of pragmatic comprehension (Rafieyan et al. , 2014). That's why her sociopragmatic competence was similar to Chinese native speakers for shorter cultural distance between Korean and Chinese culture, and her pragmalinguistic competence surpassed the other two case participants in the

---

① 5 Rome pronunciation.

first test. However, her development of pragmalinguistic competence was slow, and her use of linguistic forms under various circumstances was still in its infancy.

5. 2. 5   Joy's motivation and acculturation attitude

Motivation consists of instrumental and integrative motivation, which is essential to learn a foreign or second language (Gardner, 1979). According to Garner, instrumental motivation means that learners aim at gaining linguistic growth, showing no interests in interaction or socializing with members of the target language; while integrative motivation refers to learners' willingness and interests in learning a second or foreign language through communication with native speakers. Concerning Joy, she was interested in Chinese language and culture, and wanted to get a job related to Chinese after graduation.

One of my friends was quite interested in Chinese, and she often talked about Chinese food, Chinese people, and Chinese culture to me. I became interested in it gradually under her influence. Furthermore, China's economy is developing at a surprising speed, and more and more Korean people learn Chinese. As for my major, quite a lot of my classmates told me that it would be easier to get a job with immersion experience in China. So I am here.

Moreover, she said that Chinese was widely used nowadays in Korea for business, travelling and education. Joy came to China to get learning experience and linguistic growth. According to her, she could make progress whether she made Chinese friends or not, because there were sufficient language courses and diverse occasions to interact in Chinese.

I don't think it important to make Chinese friends and socializing with them. You know there are 4 – 5 periods of Chinese classes every weekday. Teachers speak Chinese only in classes. Sometimes I have to speak Chinese, if I want to buy a coffee or open my account in the bank.

In short, Joy was mainly motivated to learn Chinese in China for job-hunting after graduation. Moreover, she didn't regard it important to integrate herself in Chinese culture to achieve linguistic growth. Thus, Joy's motivation was a mainly instrumental one. Her general impression of Chinese could be as follows:

I think Chinese people are generous and passionate. Chinese food is amazing, but a little bit oily. What's more, although it was very quiet in small cities in China just like in Korea, it was a bit noisy here in Shanghai. Moreover, I see lots of Chinese spit around here. Anyway, Chinese culture is broad and profound. I would like to know more about it. However, I found that lots of Chinese young people have become more westernized, because they prefer to eat KFC and Pizza, watch Hollywood movies, and celebrate western festivals.

Joy had one Chinese friend— Alice in SISU. They knew each other in Korea. She felt happy to stay with her, but Alice was too busy to meet her. As a result, she turned to her Korean friends, when she felt upset.

When I feel unhappy, I'd like to talk to my good friends in Korea on the Internet or Korean friends here. I feel close to them. Since I am not good at speaking Chinese, they could not understand me well. I miss Korean food, my parents and friends, so I went back to Korea for one month in February.

According to Berry's four distinct acculturation patterns: integration, separation, assimilation and marginalization (as stated in Chapter 2), Joy was grouped into separation. The reason was that she showed greater interests in maintaining Korean culture over Chinese culture. This factor seemingly hindered her pragmatic development, as the level of acculturation attitude plays an important role in pragmatic comprehension (Rafieyan et al. , 2015).

I put motivation and acculturation attitude together to evaluate Joy's functional level of motivation for Chinese language learning and acculturation attitude towards Chinese culture in terms of Intercultural Interaction Model (Berry et al. , 1987; Gardner, 1979). This model was illustrated in Chapter 2, which integrates Garner's instrumental and integrative motivation with Berry's four distinct acculturation patterns into an orientation toward learning a new culture and language. This model was divided into three functional levels: instrumental, integrative, and psychosocial functioning. In light of analysis and discussion, Joy was at instrumental functioning level.

5. 2. 6 Joy's social activities

International students are regarded as new comers in China, who learn linguistic conventions, pragmatics to communicate with native speakers throughsocial activities in light of language socialization theory. In order to adapt to the new sociocultural context, they also have to struggle to construct their new identities in this community. This subsection attempts to demonstrate the most important routinized activities that Joy took part in to shed light on her development of pragmatic competence.

5. 2. 6. 1 Classroom learning

As for international students at intermediate level, there are 4 main subjects, such as "intensive reading", "viewing, listening and speaking", "listening and speaking" and "reading and writing" . They have 4 periods (around three-hour classroom learning) each weekday. I observed Joy's classroom learning twice during the research. She was an active learner in the classroom, who responded to the teachers from time to time. Joy regarded classroom learning as the most important opportunity for her linguistic growth.

I have classes every day except weekend. I like to have classes here, all the subjects are taught by Chinese teachers. It is very important that Chinese teachers know what is right and wrong. They are the authority regarding the use of Chinese language. Since all the classes are taught in Chinese, my listening improved a lot. Moreover, I could get feedback from my Chinese teacher immediately.

Chinese culture was integrated into some subjects, which could help international students know Chinese sociocultural context to some extent.

One of my subjects is called "listening and speaking", which is very interesting and useful. It introduces the famous places, table manners, how to ask direction, and festivals. I was acknowledged with Chinese culture in this subject. Moreover, our teacher would extend the topic and discuss the differences between Chinese culture and other cultures. I like "viewing, listening and speaking" as well. Our teacher introduced some Chinese movies to us. I learned some expressions from the movie.

As for Joy, classroom learning was an effective and efficient way to make progress. Many studies show that language proficiency has impact on pragmatic competence (Allami & Naeimi, 2011; Li, 2014) . However, classroom learning unlike daily interaction outside the classroom, learners could not gain pragmatic development directly unless the content is designed for its sake.

5. 2. 6. 2 Travelling around China

As previously mentioned, Joy was born into a well off but traditional Korean family. Her personality and socializing style was affected by her family education to a great extent. She was passive, and seldom took initiative to seek opportunities for making friends:

> I believe in fate. We might become friends since we were in the same class, or living in the same dorm. I know you because of your research. My Chinese teacher came to me and told me that a doctoral student was looking for a Korean participant. I volunteered to be your participant and make friends as well. But I don't like to say "hello" to strangers or take initiative to seek opportunities of making friends. What's more? My parents told me that girls should act in a way to show her elegance and self-respect.

As a matter of fact, there were only graduate students and doctoral students on Hongkou campus in SISU, who were always busy studying. Few of those Chinese students would like to spend time making foreign friends. Thus, Joy had not made many Chinese friends in China. Moreover, as a submissive and quiet girl, she didn't communicate in Chinese frequently.

> When I went to Chinese restaurant for a meal, my friends always had idea of what to eat. I don't like to make decision, because I am afraid that my friend would not like the dishes that I ordered. I like to make friends with someone who is talkative. As you know I don't like to talk too much, and I prefer to listen to others.

As a result, Joy didn't have many opportunities to practice her Chinese, which might result in her show development of pragmatic competence. However, Joy would interact with native speakers when she was travelling around China.

Most international students are fond of travelling while studying abroad. Traveling could bring good time to them, which could also help them acknowledge with local customs and practices. Joy had been to many cities during one year in China, such as Beijing, Hangzhou, Suzhou, Nanjing, Yunnan, Hainan, Neimenggu, Wuhan and Haerbin. She was extremely excited, when she chatted with me about the places that she had been to. She didn't have economic burden when studying in China. She regarded traveling around China as an effective way to make linguistic progress.

I enjoy travelling around China, and indulge myself in this kind of activities. Sometimes I found it was time consuming to make plans for the tour, so I took part in various types of tour groups in China. They provide with good services at quite low prices. Moreover, I could make friends with lots of the members of tour groups. We chatted with each other in Chinese mostly, because they could not speak Korean.

She told me about many interesting stories during her tours. The following incident could be viewed as turning point to her in respect of pragmatic development.

I went to Hainan by myself, and booked a room through an app called Airbnb. The landlady was in her 50s. I called her "dama", which I read on the textbook long time ago. She felt unhappy, but she realized that I was a foreigner. As a result, she told me that it was impolite to call her "dama" nowadays. And she asked me to call her "ayi". I was confused,

I learned in the class that "ayi" was my mother' sister. I talked to my only Chinese friend through Wechat to make clear of this term. Since then I was quite careful to address varies types of people.

Joy told me that she preferred to take taxi to go out, because some drivers would like to chat with her through the journey. According to my field notes:

[*Field notes*: 19th, *April.*]

Joy reacted to me faster than before, when I talked to her in Chinese. Furthermore, she spoke Chinese much more fluent and could use some four-character idioms, such as "minsikuxiang" (冥思苦想, with careful consideration). But she employed it in an improper context. I asked her when she would go back to Korea. She replied, "wo mingsikuxiang le henjiu, dasuan daizai zheli." (I think for a long time and I am going to stay.)

Travel was an important external factor for Joy in terms of the data collected. However, her development of pragmatic competence was not significant, because travelling could not replace normal socializations with friends that took place much more frequently. The topics were more diverse among friends, which could be small talk, academic problems, language learning, rapport establishing, making requests etc.

5. 2. 6. 3   Activities on electronic platform

With the emergence of advanced electronic technology, the products of new information technology make our lives moreconvenient. The electronic technology provides the platform with free entrance and sufficient information. Joy stated that she had learned Chinese through the new technology platform.

I chatted with my classmate or friends in Chinese through Wechat and watched Chinese movies through software named "youku". Recently, I have been absorbed in an entertainment program called "shijie qinnian shuo" (世界青年说, youth talk all around the world). The program is very interesting and easy to understand, so I could catch up. When I felt upset, I would listen to Chinese songs through the app named "QQ music". Moreover, I prefer to buy stuff through "taobao". I have to chat with the seller through the communicative tool before making the deal. My Chinese improved a lot. It is weird that the seller addressed me "qing" (亲, dear), I felt uncomfortable. I don't like this term.

According to Joy's narration, we found that she used Chinese through technology tools. She noticed the pragmatic strategies through communicating with sellers on "taobao", but she refused to change her use of openers.

5.2.7 Contextual factors

5.2.7.1 School culture

As for the administration mode, all international students were arranged in school dormitories in SISU with two foreign students sharing a room. People around Joy were foreigners in the classroom or in the place where she lived. Personally speaking, I had studied in the UK for one year doing my masters program, so I could apply for any type of apartment that I would like, or I could arrange accommodations for myself. I took advantage of this school policy by renting a house with three foreign students, who were from Spain, UK and Japan. Therefore, I could practice my oral English and familiarize myself with various cultures. Joy complained about the school accommodations a bit.

I think if I lived with some Chinese people, I could have more chance to practice Chinese and get familiar with phrases that frequently used in daily interactions. Only in this way, I could know Chinese culture well.

Moreover, dependent as Joy was, she felt disappointed that there was no official program for searching language partners on the campus. She was dependent on school's administration for her experience in Korea.

You know I have a Chinese friend in SISU who I met and knew in Korea. I knew her through school program. Everyone could apply for a language partner in my university. I submitted my application, and school notified me the people who would be my language partner. I know Alice in this way. We had lots of things in common, so we get along very well with each other. We could find the proper language partner easily, because we need to write down our personality, hobbies and description of ideal language partner in the application forms.

I had the same experience, I found my language partner in the language center in the university, when I was in the UK. We became good friends and still got in touch with each other. Pragmatic improvement is closely related to the use of targeted language based on language socialization theory. As a result, it would be a good idea that some programs are officially organized to help foreign students find language partners, which would be beneficial to Chinese native speakers as well.

* Textbook content

As described above, Joy had very limited chance to interact with native speakers daily. Her language input mainly depended on textbook and classes. I found that Joy overuse those formulae in the questionnaire, such as " … keyima?" (可以吗, is it ok?), "qing ni bangzhu wo" (请你帮助我, help me please) and "qingwen…." (请问, could you tell me). She explained:

> I learned those formulae in the textbook both in Korea and China. My teachers asked me to memorize those formulae, so I can use them freely in daily life. And gradually, I used to employ those formulae for convenience. Moreover, I found "kebukeyi" is simpler than "nengbuneng".

Joy considered the textbook as "bible", and memorized the expression carefully in case she would use them in interactions.

> The contents in the textbook are authoritative and trustworthy. Sometimes I can't get the right words or expressions during interaction with friends in Chinese. As a result, I tried very hard to memorize some frequently used phrases that appeared in the similar occasions written in the textbook. At least, I needn't be afraid of making mistakes.

Textbooks are always old fashioned and updated very slow. Nowadays, under the influence of Internet, lots of cyber words became popular among youngsters in communication, such as formulae for openers: "qing" (亲, dear), "qingaide" (亲爱的, dear), "baobao" (宝宝, baby) and etc. I can't find those popular formulae used by Joy in questionnaires from T1 to T4. In addition, as previously stated, Joy was uncomfortable and did not like being referred to a "qing" by seller on "Taobao". Therefore, the formulae in textbook could be an important factor that constrained her pragmatic development.

5.2.7.2 Host members' attitudes

Host members' attitudes referred to the attitudes that the majority of Chinese held towards the international students in this current study. The number of Chinese learners of Korean language is quite small in China, in comparison to that of English language. Joy was not so welcomed as her European classmates, who felt frustrated in making Chinese friends.

A great number of Chinese are learning English, and some of them eager to find a native speaker or western person to practice their oral English. My British classmate told me that some Chinese on the road frequently stopped her for practicing English. But I never ran into this kind of situation. I saw many Korean restaurants in Shanghai, and cosmetics made in Korea are popular, but few Chinese people would like to speak Korean to me. I left my name and phone number in Bella (a café in SISU), and attempted to get a language partner. But the result turned out to be very disappointing.

Chinese people had stereo typical impression of Koreans. In recent years, many Chinese women had gone to Korea for cosmetic surgery. Some Chinese thought that most Korean women had been received cosmetic surgery, because the technique in Korea was very well known.

If I got the chance to chat with Chinese native speakers, they would ask me about cosmetic surgery. For instance, "did you get a cosmetic surgery?" As a matter of fact, quite a small number of Koreans choose to get surgery. And second, Chinese would like to consult which brand of cosmetics made in Korea is popular. To be honest, I was sometimes annoyed and didn't to want to continue the conversation. It seems that Chinese relate Korea with cosmetic surgery and cosmetics in their mind.

Joy had to explain to Chinese each time about this topic, so she had unpleasant communication experience with Chinese native speakers. She didn't make any Chinese friends throughout the whole course of my research. The reason might be that she unconsciously tried to avoid the unpleasant topic. Host members' attitudes affected the extent to which learners make efforts to socialize with native speakers. It is very difficult to achieve pragmatic improvement without interaction in the targeted language.

5. 2. 8 Section summary

This section analyzed and discussed Joy's pragmatic development trajectory and the factors that might facilitate or constrain Joy's pragmatic development based on both quantitative and qualitative data. Joy's pragmatic competence had developed in a slow and uneven way. Her pragmalinguistic competence did improve but not in a prominent way. However, Joy's perception of the situational factors was similar to that of Chinese according to qualitative analysis of DCT data and interview data. Therefore, it was safe to conclude that the development of Joy's sociopragmatic competence preceded her pragmalinguistic competence.

Moreover, this chapter probed into the factors that shaped Joy's pragmatic development trajectory. The findings discussed above suggested that the main factors that affected Joy's pragmatic development could be grouped into following categories: cultural background, motivation and acculturation attitude, social activities and contextual factors.

Through reviewing the interview data, cultural background had played a crucial role in shaping Joy's perception of situational variables. Joy was informed of Chinese culture through school or family education. Her perception of power and social distance was similar to that of Chinese. As a result, her sociopragmatic competence remained stable through her studying in China. Moreover, Joy was mainly motivated by job-hunting to learn Chinese. She was shy and didn't make much effort to interact with native speakers or integrate herself into Chinese culture. Accordingly, Joy's motivation and acculturation attitude hindered her pragmatic development to some degree. Submissive and unsociable as Joy was, she didn't take initiative to make friends. It was apparent that the limitation of natural interaction with native speakers constrained Joy's pragmatic development.

According to the qualitative data, Joy was practice-oriented girl. She was fond of travelling around China. She spared every possible opportunity to practice her Chinese when travelling around various cities in China. Moreover, classroom learning was described as the most effective activity involving her acquisition of Chinese language. Entertainment activities on electronic technology platform also offered her some chance to communicate in Chinese. All those activities facilitated her progress in respect of Chinese pragmatic competence.

However, based on the analyzed data, school culture and host members' attitude, had not played a positive role in Joy's pragmatic development. Chinese native speakers' stereotypical impression of Korean people annoyed Joy sometimes, which made her refrain from chatting with Chinese people. Furthermore, the formulae or expressions she memorized from the textbook made the use of formulae in her requests monotonous and out-of-date. In Addition, lack of an officially organized program for language partners made her feel more separated. It seems that these factors might hinder her from developing pragmatic competence.

In conclusion, the reason that Joy's pragmalinguistic development remained slow could be that ravelling and classroom learning could not replace natural interaction or socialization with Chinese native speakers, which involves diverse topics and more complicated variables in conversations.

5. 3 Amy-a Russian student: open-minded, sociable and interaction-oriented

Amy was selected for its representative for Russian subjects in terms of pragmatic strategies in requests in Chinese. This section attempts to explore how Amy develop her pragmatic competence and understand the reasons leading to such outcomes. Open-minded and sociable as she was, her pragmatic learning tended to be interaction-oriented. She spared every possible opportunity to interact with Chinese native speakers, and regarded use of the target language was the effective way to pick up the language. It was arranged in the following sequence: introduction of Amy's background, analysis of her pragmatic development trajectory, and description of her cultural background, motivation and acculturation attitude, social activities and contextual factors that might aid or hinder her pragmatic development.

5. 3. 1 Amy's Profile

The second case participant is Amy, a 21-year-old Russian female student. "Amy" is the name I used for the sake of anonymity. She was in her third year in the Russian Altai State University, majoring in oriental studies involving Chinese history, economy and culture. She chose to apply for the exchange program from the Chinese Confucius Institute. She had received a stipend from this program of 2500 RMB per month and had free accommodations in the SISU hotel. When she heard that a Chinese doctoral student wanted to find a Russian student as her research participant, she volunteered to be the one. My contacts with her started in November 2015. She gave me the general impression that she was talkative and amiable.

Compared with Joy, Amy was from a very different family and educational background. Her parents were divorced, when she was very young. Her parents passed away two years ago, which made the situation worse. She was in a panic at that time, because she relied on them financially and emotionally. Since then she lived with her grandparents, who were in their 80s and had already retired. After her parents' death, she applied for the exchange program the first time. But she didn't come to China at that time, because she did not have enough money for a plane ticket. She began to make money by translating Chinese to Russian or from Russian to Chinese. Amy applied for this program once again, and this time she could afford the air ticket. She made the decision to change her life and solve problems all on her own. Strong-willed and independent as she was, she decided to make a bright future through her own efforts.

Amy didn't make up often and was very plain, and she didn't like to follow the trend. It was because that she had to save money for extra expenses. After winter vacation, she began to wear a headdress in March 2016, because she believed in Hinduism. She also felt safe under the headdress. She believed that friends were very important, and could help each other through tough times. She was open-minded and made friends with people from various countries. Outgoing and sociable as she was, she attended activities organized by the university and also searched for some interesting activities in Shanghai. She considered activities as important ways to make friends and know China. Consequently, she had lots of Chinese friends.

Amy began to learn Chinese when she was 15 years old. One of her friends was learning Chinese and told her that learning Chinese could help her to find a decent job and make big money. As the Chinese economy had been developing at a surprising speed in recent years, more and more Russians started to learn Chinese and do business with Chinese. Amy bought some books, and started to learn Chinese by herself for nearly one year. She stopped learning Chinese because of the heavy study burden in senior high school. However, she had become interested in the language and culture, and decided to choose Chinese as her future major. Her parents were both lawyers and helped her to search for information on university learning Chinese in Russia. Fortunately, she entered Altai State University to learn Chinese.

Amy was curious about China after learning Chinese, so she planned to study in China. Hopefully, she seized the opportunity to attend the exchange program. She regarded studying in China as the best way to improve her Chinese proficiency. As a result, she preferred to interact with me in Chinese every time we met. It seemed that she caught every possible opportunity to practice Chinese with people around her. She wasn't scared of making mistakes and was open to any criticism. She asked to correct whatever mistakes she made. Although she learned English in the elementary school, she didn't use it much in Russia or China. She preferred to use Chinese to communicate with her classmates from France, Japan, Greece etc, and only used Russian when she interacted with her Russian friends. As a result, she switched between Chinese and Russian whenever necessary.

Through interaction with her, I found she regarded me as her friend rather than a researcher. In order to help me, she bought a book named " Chinese View of Life Philosophy", which helped her understand Chinese people and culture. Sometimes, she would invite me to have a cup of coffee or meals with her, during which we happily chatted.

In the following subsections, focus is given to Amy's pragmatic features at the beginning, her pragmatic development trajectory, and the factors that might affect her pragmatic development.

5. 3. 2 Amy's pragmatic features of requests

The criteria for participant selection for case study were mainly based on the pragmatic features at the first test. According to Table 43, the most

frequently used formulae by Amy at the verybeginning were as follows:
"greeting", "title" and "name" for openers; "QP (1)", "performative" and
"QP (2)" for head acts; "G + H", "preparator" and "H + G" for external
modifications and "politeness marker", "appealer" and "hedge" for internal
modifications. It was obvious that the formulae used by Amy were similar to that
of the ones used by the majority of Russian subjects based on Table 43.

Table 43   Most frequently used formulae by Amy

	Ranking	Amy	RCL
Openers	1st	Greeting (n = 5)	Title
	2nd	Title (n = 5)	Greeting
	3rd	Name	Name/ Kinship terminology
Head acts	1st	QP (1) (n = 5)	QP (1)
	2nd	Performative (n = 3)	Performative
	3rd	QP (2)	Mood derivable
External Modifications	1st	G + H (n = 5)	G + H
	2nd	Preparator (n = 3)	Preparator
	3rd	H + G (n = 2)	H + G
Internal Modifications	1st	Politeness marker (n = 5)	Politeness marker
	2nd	Appealer (n = 3)	Appealer
	3rd	Hedge	Understater

Moreover, as mentioned above, Russian subjects tended to use "performative" for head acts, such as "qing ni ba lishike de neirong lu yixia yin!" (Please record the content of the class of history!) Amy had the similar feature based on the data collected.

To compensate for shortcomings of DCT, I recorded some naturally occurring data of requests made by Amy for triangulation. Amy visited me in Hangzhou in April. The following request was made by Amy to buy a rice cake on the street.

#Natural recording# (April 9th, 2016)

Nihao, qing gei wo yige, er…duoshao qian?

Hello, give one to me, please! How much is it?

It was obvious that Amy preferred to use "performative" for HA, and tended to apply "politeness marker" e. g. "qing" for IM. Thus, Amy could be viewed as a typical case for Russian subjects.

5.3.3 Amy's development trajectory

As stated in Joy's section, pragmatic competence is divided into two parts: pragmalinguistic competence and soicopragmatic competence. Thereby, pragmatic development involves pragmalinguistic and sociopragmatic development. The following subsections will describe Amy's development trajectory in detail.

5.3.3.1 Pragmalinguistic development

There are twelve scenarios in the DCT eliciting questionnaire, but the first three most frequently used formulae for openers by Amy had changed from T1 to T4. Amy tended to use "Greeting" to address unfamiliar equals and good friends in T1 and T2, but she changed to use "title" such as "tongxue" (同学, classmate) to address unfamiliar equals in T3 and T4. She chosed to use "name" to address good friends in T3 and T4. Moreover, Amy employed "popular alter" to address roommates rather than "name" in T3. As a result, the number of "name" decreased in T3 and T4. It seemed that she changed to be native like based on Table 44 and became stable from T3 on. Furthermore, according to the data displayed, Amy's pragmatic competence developed in a nonlinear way. Accordingly, Dynamic system theory (DST) could explain this phenomenon in this situation.

As shown in Table 45, "QP (1)" was most frequently used formulae for head acts from T1 to T4, which was similar to Chinese subjects. However, the number of "performative" reduced gradually from T1 to T4. As stated in Chapter 4, Russian subjects tended to be direct by using "performaitve" as head acts. Amy preferred to apply "performative" in group members', good friends and roommates' situations in T1. She began to choose "mood derivable" in good friends' or roommates' situations. Overviewing the data displayed in Table 45, Amy changed her formulae gradually through the course of my research and became similar to that of Chinese subjects.

Table 44   **Most frequently used formulae for openers by Amy**

	T1 (n = 12)	T2 (n = 12)	T3 (n = 12)	T4 (n = 12)	CNS
Opener	Greeting (n =5)	Greeting (n =5)	Title (n =5)	Title (n =5)	Title
	Title (n =4)	name (n =3)	Greeting (n =3)	Greeting (n =3)	Greeting
	Name (n =1)	Title (n =3)	Name (n =2)	Name (n =2)	Name

Amy preferred to use "G + H", "preparator" and "H + G" from T1 to T4 based on Table 46. However, the number of those formulae had changed each time. Amy's changes of formulae for external modifications were in a "U" shape manner. It was obvious that the formular produce by Amy approximated the NS data. As for formulae for internal modifications, Amy had not changed much. She was prone to use "politeness maker" and "appealer" from the beginning to the end. She considered it important to use "politeness marker" in requests, because she regarded "politeness marker" as the symbol of politeness in requests making actions.

Table 45   Most frequently used formulae for HA by Amy

	T1 (n = 12)	T2 (n = 12)	T3 (n = 12)	T4 (n = 12)	CNS
Head acts	QP (1) (n = 5)	QP (1) (n = 5)	QP (1) (n = 6)	QP (1) (n = 6)	QP (1)
	Performative (n = 3)	QP (2) (n = 3)	Mood derivable (n = 3)	Mood derivable (n = 3)	Mood derivable
	QP (2) (n = 2)	performative (n = 2)	performative (n = 2)	QP (2) (n = 2)	QP (2)

I would like to use "politeness maker" to mitigate my requests. This formula could make the sentences more polite. In Russian, "politeness maker" is always used in requests. As a result, I used to apply this formula in Chinese as well. (Amy T3)

Amy developed her pragmalinguistic competence to a great extent in term of the changes of the use of semantic formulae for openers, HA, EM and IM. Amy changed her formulae gradually from T1 to T4 and became more native like.

Table 46   **Most frequently used formulae for EM and IM by Amy**

	T1 (n = 12)	T2 (n = 12)	T3 (n = 12)	T4 (n = 12)	CNS
EM	G + H (n = 3)	G + H (n = 5)	G + H (n = 5)	G + H (n = 4)	G + H
	preparator (n = 2)	H + G (n = 4)	Preparator (n = 3)	Preparator/H + G (n = 2)	H + G
	H + G (n = 1)	Preparator (n = 3)	H + G (n = 2)		Preparator/ Gratitude
IM	Politeness marker (n = 5)	Politeness marker (n = 4)	Politeness marker (n = 4)	Politeness marker (n = 3)	Appealer
	Appealer (n = 4)	Appealer (n = 2)	Honorific (n = 3)	Appealer (n = 2)	Downtoner
	Hedge (n = 1)		Appealer (n = 2)	Honorific (n = 1)	Politeness marker

5.3.3.2 Sociopragmatic development

Sociopragmatic competence involves understanding of sociocultural aspects, cultural conventions and norms, which lays stress on thesociocultural respect of interaction. Therefore, learners' perception of politeness in diverse situations could reflect their sociopragmatic competence. This section attempts to describe and analyze the changes of Amy's perceptions of situational variables, such as power and social distance, from T1 to T4 mainly though qualitative analysis, which in turn reflects Amy's development of sociopragmatic competence.

＊Changes of perception of power

As stated above, Russian subjects showed deference and respectfulness to "teachers" and "administrators" in this survey. However they treated the hearers with equal or lower status in the same way, which was quite different from Chinese native speakers. The developmental trajectory of Amy's sociopragamtic competence will be illustrated as follows:

(1) Situation: ask to get a new student identity card [D + , P +]

T1: Nihao, laoshi! Qingwen wonali keyi banli xin xiaoyuanka? Kanqilai wo diu le wo de ka.

Good morning/afternoon, teacher Where could I get a new student identity card? It seems that I lost my card.

T2: Laoshi, nihao! Wo diule wo de xiaoyuanka, kebukeyi ban xinde?

Good morning/afternoon, teacher I lost my student identity card. Could I get a new one?

T3: Ninhao, laoshi! Wo diule wo de xiaoyuanka, zenme ban ge xinka?

Good morning/afternoon, teacher. I lost my student identity card. How to get a new one?

T4: Ninhao, laoshi! Wo diule xiaoyuanka, keyi ban xinde ma?

Good morning/afternoon, teacher. I lost my student identity card. Could I get a new one?

Concerning alerters, Amy used "nihao, laoshi" in T1, "laoshi, nihao!" in T2 and "ninhao, laoshi!" in T3 and T4. Although the sequence of formulae was reversed in comparison to those of Chinese native speakers, the addresser she employed became more native like. Furthermore, she used "nin" to show respect to administrators, and was indirect in requests making by applying "QP (1)" from T2 to T4. And she gave "grounder" before making requests in T3 and T4. Her pragmalinguistic and sociopragmatic competence developed at the same time.

I saw my Chinese friends show respect to administrators by employing "laoshi" or "nin". And I would like to do as the Romans do, when in Rome. Actually, administrators and teachers are quite different in Russian university. (Amy, T3)

According to Amy, she changed her perception of power in this situation by simulating the behaviors of Chinese native speakers.

(2) Situation: ask to copy PPT [D – , P +]

T1: Laoshi, ninhao! Duibuqi, wo xiang yao qing nin ba zhege kejian kaobei, keyima?

Good morning/afternoon, teacher. Sorry. Could I copy PPT?

T2: Jin jiaoshou, ninhao. Buhaoyisi, wo xiang qing nin ba jintian de kejian kaogeiwo, wo huijia zailaikankan. Jintian de ke man you yisi.

Good morning/afternoon, Prof. Jin. Sorry to trouble you. Could I copy PPT of today's class? I want to review when I go back home. The course was very interesting.

T3: Laoshi, ninhao, mafan nin ba jintian de kejian gei wo kaobei, henyou yisi, wo huijia zailaikankan, keyima?

Good morning/afternoon, teacher. Could you please permit me to copy PPT of todayVs course? It is very interesting. I want to review after going back home. Is it ok?

T4: Laoshi ninhao. Qing rang wo kaobei jintian de kejian, wo huijia zai kankan.

Good morning/afternoon, teacher. Please allow me to copy PPT of this course. I want to review after going back home.

With regard to openers, Amy employed the formulae frequently used by Chinese native speakers in this kind of situation. She also applied "grounder" after head act in T3 and T4, and used "sweetener" in T2. Moreover, she tended to use formulae for internal modifications, such as "mafan", "qing" and "buhaoyisi" to minimize the requestive imposition. However, she employed "performative" as head act from T2 to T4 As mentioned above, "performative" was popular among Russian subjects. Amy's example confirms quantitative data in section 4. It seems impolite to make requests by using "performative" in Chinese, and as if Amy didn't show respect to professor Jin in this situation.

Teachers or professors are knowledgeable and respected by others in the society. I think it is very important to show deference to them. As a result, I employed "nin", "buhaoyisi" and etc. , when I asked professors or teachers for help. (Amy, T2)

Therefore, in Amy's perception, she regarded professors as someone with high prestige, to whom she should show respect. She used to employ "perfomative" for the effect of L1 transfer.

(3) Situation: consult the place of school dormitory [D + , P =]

T1: Nihao! Buhaoyisi, wo zhaobudao sushequ. Ni zhibuzhidao zhege sushequ zai naer?

Good morning/afternoon, Sorry to disturb. I can't find the location of dormitories. Do you know where it is?

T2: Nihao, tongxue, ni qu naer? Wo zhaobudao xuyao de difang. Qing bang wo.

Good morning/afternoon, classmate. Where are you heading? I can't find the place that I want to go. Please help me.

T3: Nihao, tongxue, ni shi zhu zaisushi de ma? Wo milu le, dao sushe zenme zou?

Good morning/afternoon, classmate. Do you live in the dormitory? I am lost. How could I get to the location of dormitories?

T4: Tongxue, nihao! Ni qu naer? Nengbuneng dai wo qu xuexiao sushequ?

Good morning/afternoon, classmate. Where are you heading? Could you lead me to the location of dormitories?

As for openers, Amy started to use "tongxue" in T2, and most of the Chinese native speakers to address stranger students "tongxue". Amy employed "QP (1)" in T1, T3 and T4, because she was unfamiliar with the hearer. But she didn't use many internal or external modifications to minimize the impositive force of request.

(4) Situation: ask to take notes [D +, P -]

T1: Dajiahao, tongxuemen, women yao huibao. Wo juede meiyigeren keyi fuze yibufen neirong. Qing nimen xiexialai meigeren zuo shenme.

Hello everyone. Classmates, we need to make a presentation. I think that every one could take charge of the different parts of the task. Please write down every one's mission.

T2: Tongxuemen, women zai yiqi zuo huibao, women yiqi lai jueding shui zuo shenme.

Classmates. We are preparing for the presentation. Let's decide the mission of every one.

T3: Tongxue, qing ni ba jintian taolun de neirong xiexialai.

Classmate, please take notes of the content of our discussion.

T4: Tonxuemen, women dou zhunbei yixia, ni keyi jilu taolun de neirong?

Classmates, let's get ready for the presentation. Could you take notes of the content of our discussion?

With view to the head act in this scenario, Amy asked group member to write down the mission of each member in T1, and asked group member to decide everyone's task together in T2. However, she changed to use "performative" in T3 and "QP (1)" in T4. It seemed that she didn't understand the statement of this scenario at the beginning, and started to understand from T3 on.

I understand the description of the scenario at the very beginning, but I don't think it is proper to ask classmate to do something directly. However, when I confronted with this situation in reality, group leader arranged the mission for us directly. I was uncomfortable at first. But I think it is very efficient way to complete the task. Once in the class, my Chinese teacher told me that as a group leader, I am in charge of organizing the activities and arranging tasks, and other members have to follow me. (Amy, T3)

Amy's perception of power changed in terms of administrator's and group member's situation. She simulated Chinese native speakers' or friends' use of language, and then she realized the different perception of power between Russian and Chinese. She started to show deference to administrators by using "laoshi", "nin" and "qing", and became direct towards group member with lower status. Although Amy's pragmalinguistic competence approximated that of Chinese native speakers, she still employed "performative" for HA all the time in some situations. Generally speaking, Amy understood the sociocultural respects of social interaction gradually by immersion in studying abroad context.

Amy's dynamic or changing perception of social distance will be discussed in the following passages. There were some overlaps when discussing the perception of social distance and power. As a result, only two scenarios were illustrated and analyzed to explore Amy's changes of perception of social distance. The following examples were extracted from the data collected:

(1) Situation A: ask to take a photo [D + , P =]

T1: Nihao! Buhaoysi, ni nengbuneng bang wo paigezhao?

Hello! Sorry to trouble you. Could you help me to take a photo?

T2: Nihao! Nengbuneng bang women paigezhao?

Hello! Could you help me take a photo?

T3: Nihao! Duibuqi, mafanni bang women paigezhao, haoma?

Hello! Sorry. Will you please take a photo of us?

T4: Nihao, ni nengbuneng bang women paigezhao?

Hello. Could you help me take a photo of us?

(2) Situation B: borrow a pen [D – , P –]

T1: xx, wo zhaobudao bi, ni youmeiyou bi? Xiakehou huanni.

xx, I can't find my pen. Do you have pens? I will return it to you after class.

T2: xx, ni youmeiyou bi? Wo wangle.

xx, do you have a pen? I forgot to bring one.

T3: xx, wo meiyou bi, qing gei wo yige ba!

xx, I don't have a pen. Please give one to me!

T4: xx, wo meiyou bi. Jie yixia bi.

xx, I don't have a pen. Lend one to me.

As for Scenario A, Amy used "nihao" as opener, and "query preparatory" as head act from T1 to T4. Chinese native speakers tended to use "tongxue" as opener and "query preparatory" as head act in this situation based on the data from this survey. In scenario B, Amy used "name" to address her roommate, and she changed to be more direct in T3 by employing "mood devrivable" .

She stated that:

> I prefer to query the hearer, when I ask a stranger or friend for a small favor. My Chinese friends said I didn't need to be so polite. And they asked to be straight because we are friends. Otherwise, I tried to keep distance from them. (Amy, T3)

Amy's linguistic improvement was based on her perception of politeness in Chinese context. She knew how to apply diverse linguistic forms to interact with different types of persons. Both DCT data and interview data suggested that Amy selected the formulae consciously through observing native speakers' request behaviors or interacting with native speakers.

5.3.3.3 Subsection summary

As for the developmental trajectories of Amy's pragmatic competence, the findings show that Amy, a typical case of Russian subjects made big progress while studying in China. She improved her pragmalinguistic competence by applying native-like linguistic forms and formulae. Furthermore, Amy's perception of power and social distance changed towards that of Chinese subjects. Therefore, her pragmalinguistic competence and sociopragmatic competence developed almost at the same time. The next subsection aims at analyzing and discussing the factors that would facilitate or constrain Amy's pragmatic development.

5.3.4 Amy's cultural background

According to Wikipedia, Chinese is rated as one of the most difficult languages to learn for people whose native language is alphabet based or belongs to Indo-European language family, such as English, Russian, French, Spanish and etc. According to Amy, Chinese was difficult, but the most difficult part was how to use different linguistic forms in various situations.

All of my friends told me that Chinese is difficult to learn. I feel in the same way, but what makes the situation more complicated is that I don't know how to use proper expressions in different contexts. Chinese would call the female cleaners or administrators in the dormitories "ayi", which made me in confusion. When I confronted with this kind of situations, I was hesitated to address the persons for uncertainty of the exact words.

Pragmatic transfer could not be eradicated thoroughly, when learners are on the way to learning a second or foreign language. Chinese belongs to Sino-Tibetan language family, and has a far language distance from Russian. Therefore, Amy produced a negative pragmatic transfer sometimes. She had unforgettable experience caused by her L1 transfer in conversation with a Chinese teacher.

I sent a text message to my Chinese teacher and asked her to revise my article. She didn't reply. I felt strange, because she was tender and nice. I talked this to my Chinese friend, and asked her to read my message. I wrote: " laoshi, qing ni bangwo gai zhege wenzhang!" I translated Russian to Chinese directly in this situation. My friend told me to change into another expression, like this: "laoshi ninhao, buhaoyisi daraole! Wo you yipian wenzhang, neng qing nin bang wo Kankan ma?" I sent it to her again, and she replied me immediately.

Amy began to understand the different linguistic forms and functions in a specific situation. Because of language difficulty and distance, Amy took longer time to use Chinese appropriately in various situations. As for foreigners, native Chinese speakers tolerate their problems. However, this time it was her Chinese teacher who wanted to attract her attention to language usage under different circumstances. As illustrated in section 3, the questionnaire involving scenarios of requesting teachers for help, Amy changed her formulae for expression in the third and forth time. It was because of the incident occurred to her. Concerning European students, Chinese is far more difficult than any other language. The aftermath resulted in negative transfer and hindered her from making progress in pragmatic development.

5.3.5　Amy's motivation and acculturation attitude

As mentioned in the last subsection, Joy was motivated by job hunting and belonged to instrumental motivation. However, Amy also attempted to find a job after graduation at first for the prosperous economy in China. But she gradually found herself loving this language and its culture, and she was highly motivated by this emotion.

> At the beginning, I was told that learning Chinese could help me to find a decent job easily. Moreover, companies in Shanghai offer better payment than that in Russia. Russia and China are neighbors, and they interacted with each other economically, culturally and politically. My hometown is near Xinjiang. I become more and more interested in Chinese culture, and I found it was mysterious and attractive. Now, I want to learn Chinese not only to find a job, but also to make friends with native Chinese friends and integrated in its culture when I am in China.

According to Garner, Amy belonged to integrative motivation, which illustrates that learners learn a second language in order to interact with local people and immerse themselves in its culture. Furthermore, as for Amy's acculturation attitude, she was regarded as integration. She was maintaining her own cultural identity and extending relations with members of L2 community. Amy had a positive impression of China and Chinese people.

> China is a big and massive country with a great number of scenic spots in various cities. I like all types of Chinese food, which is diverse and delicious. Chinese people are friendly and warm-hearted in general. I went to Hangzhou in April, 2016, which is full of natural scenic spots. I also found G20 was coming soon in September in Hangzhou, which would make it more international. However, Chinese people like to eat western food, since a great number of western restaurants were open in Shanghai. Moreover, Chinese like spitting everywhere and they always rush to get a seat in subway or bus. Anyway, every coin has two sides. Generally speaking, I like China.

Amy preferred to share her feelings with both Russian and Chinese friends, and she was adapted to Chinese culture very well. She sometimes read books and wrote her journals in Chinese.

> I have several Chinese friends here, and we chat through Wechat everyday. We share interesting things. When I felt upset, I would turn to them whoever have time. I picked up Chinese native-like expressions through talking to them. They are the best teachers to me.

To sum up, Amy was at integrative functioning level in terms of intercultural interaction model. Thus, her pragmatic competence developed well in comparison to the Korean subject, Joy.

5.3.6 Amy's social activities

As mentioned above, learners' interaction with native speakers through social activities plays a crucial role in pragmatic development in terms of language socialization theory. "L2 learners are socialized through the use of language as well as how they are socialized to use language" (Ochs & Schieffelin, 1984, P49) . Activities are the focus of socialization. This subsection aims to analyze and display the major patterns of activities that Amy took part in that facilitated her development of pragmatic competence.

5. 3. 6. 1 Social interaction

As mentioned in Amy's biological profile, she was open-minded, independent, and extroverted by nature. She was always with friends in her spare time.

I think I am an easy-going girl, and I like to make different types of friends, regardless of the nationalities, personality, gender and etc. I knew a lot of international students here, and I always say "hello" to them whenever I met them. I think if we are polite to others, others will react in the same way. Life is boring without friends. As I am in China, I would like to make friends with native Chinese speakers.

According to my observation, I found Amy is a warm-hearted person. She likes to help others no matter who asked her. As stated above, she believed in Hinduism, and had been a vegetarian for nearly three years. Religion had shed light on her character building, since she described Hinduism as "inspiring" and "soul saving" .

I feel that my value is realized, when I help others. Love should be passed on to others one by one. Nobody would live on him/herself without others' help. I still remembered that I couldn't pay for my first year tuition fee for the university, because my parents passed away leaving nothing to me. My friends helped me to pay for it and introduced some part-time jobs to me. I think it very important to help others if you are able to.

As for my personal interaction with her, we still kept in touch with each other after she went back to Russia. She replied to me instantly and patiently whenever I had questions. She was the most helpful among the three case participants. Compared with Joy, Amy had totally different character. Amy was extroverted, independent, warm-hearted and strong-willed, which paved the way for her interaction with Chinese people.

As stated in Amy's profile, she was fond of making friends and preferred to speak Chinese regardless of the interlocutors' nationalities. There were mainly three types of social interactions: interaction with native Chinese speakers, interaction with classmates, and interaction with Russian friends.

According to Amy, her interaction with Chinese included topics such as: translation, academic problems, traveling, music and movies. Frequent interaction with Chinese friends informed her of Chinese culture and the use of formulae in various situations.

I went out with Chinese friends two or three times every week. My Chinese friends address me "qingaide", "meinv" or my name. Therefore, I addressed them in the same way, because I wanted to act like a native speaker. I was doing translation as my part-time job. Whenever I had problems, I would ask them for help. They also requested for help from me too. They requested me in a very direct way because of our intimate relationship. As a result, I knew how to request friends in Chinese.

It seemed that interaction with friends involving concrete matters would help learners develop pragmatic competence effectively. Even though her classmates were from all over the world, Amy preferred to use Chinese to communicate with them.

> Most of my classmates interact with each other both in Chinese and in English. As for me, I would like to speak in Chinese so as to improve my speaking and listening. I feel more relaxed, when I communicate with my classmates. It is because we are at the similar level and we are all making mistakes. But sometimes we all confuse about whether we use Chinese in a correct way or not.

Amy practiced with her classmates, but the outcome was not so clear as that with Chinese friends. Besides those two types of interaction, Amy interacted with her Russian friends almost everyday. Although they communicated with each other in Russian, they were learning Chinese together. They discussed about the language problems they encountered in daily life.

> We like to discuss language problems that we confronted with, and help each other to solve the problems. Sometimes, we even encounter with the similar problem. Chinese people preferred to end up with requests with "baituole" or "mafanle". There were no equivalences in Russian, so we were not quite sure of the meaning of these two formulae. After discussion with her, we found that they were employed to be polite.

Although Amy interacted with Russian friends in Russian, they talked about the topics involving the use of language and Chinese conventions or culture. Consequently, social interaction with others involving topics related to target language and its culture could to a great extent facilitate learners' pragmatic development.

5. 3. 6. 2　Classroom learning

As illustrated in Joy's section, international students had four periods per weekday. Because Amy had received a stipend from the Chinese government, she had to attend class on time and could not ask for leave without a reasonable excuse. With regard to Amy, these subjects were very useful and important for her. Classroom learning also informed her with Chinese culture implicitly and explicitly.

> My Chinese friends tell me that teachers are authoritative, and students act in a passive way in the class. My classmates are international students, who always challenge teachers from time to time. Teachers are inclined to make compromise in the classroom. But I still believe in what teachers teach because they are native speakers with profound knowledge.

Moreover, the curriculum was designed to cater to international students' needs. One of the subjects named "listening and speaking" involved events occurring during traveling, Chinese table manner or frequent mistakes that students would make. The same as Joy did, Amy considered classroom learning as the effective and efficient way to pick up Chinese.

> I learned a great number of new vocabulary, and useful expressions in the textbook. Moreover, teachers gave us feedback immediately and organized group work sometimes. We could practice our listening and speaking at the same time. It was very effective.

Amy's story reinforced the conclusion that classroom learning was very effective to achieve linguistic growth. The previous studies argue that learners with high language proficiency yield better pragmatic productions (Li, 2014).

Therefore, this type of activity played an indirect role in pragmatic development.

5.3.6.3 Activities on electronic platform

Apart from studying Chinese for nearly 2 – 3 hours per day, Amy had employed Chinese by using electronic platforms around 2 hours per day. The types of activities on electronic technology platform mainly included interacting with friends through Wechat and QQ, buying goods on "Taobao", watching Chinese movies and listening to music on "Youku".

> I am using Chinese on my laptop or cellphone everyday. I communicate with my friends through wechat or QQ. My Chinese friends helped me apply for a new QQ number. I prefer QQ for its convenience of sending my translation documents. I also buy lots of stuff on "taobao" (淘宝), and I would query about the condition of the products or bargin with sellers. The seller always called me "qing" (亲, dear). I found that some of my friends address people on Internet in this way too. As a result, I picked up unconsciously.

Moreover, Amy sent messages on Wechat Moments based on my observation. She had sent more than 100 messages during one year here and 95% of the messages were written in Chinese. The content of messages varies from introduction of places in China, emotional feelings for friends and descriptions of Chinese movies that she had watched. Amy was the only one among those three case participants who used wechat in a native-like way. There were two major reasons: (1) she had more Chinese friends, and she wanted to keep in touch with them; (2) she wanted to practise her Chinese whenever or wherever she could, and she was free to criticism. I often told her the mistakes that she made through Wechat, and she expressed gratitude to me.

Electronic technology platform functioned as an important instrument for international students to improve their language proficiency and develop their pragmatic competence.

5. 3. 7   Contextual factors

5. 3. 7. 1   School culture

* Administration mode

Compared with Joy, Amy had a stipend from the Chinese Government, which could be viewed as the primary reason that attracted her to study in China. Amy wished she could be arranged in the dormitories near to Chinese students' dormitories, which could help them make Chinese friends.

* Activities

Diverse students activities were organized officially to intensify communication and spread Chinese culture among international students who had received a stipend from Confucius Institution. Various types of activities had been organized to help international students understand its culture and language in-depth.

> Schoolar ranged us to visit different places, such as Nanjing, Suzhou and Dunhuang. When we were visiting the museums or famous places, guiders explained them in Chinese. I picked up lots of expressions in this respect. And School also asked a professional person to introduce teaism to us. It was very interesting.

After visiting those places, Amy kept diary in Chinese. All those activities stimulated her interests to learn Chinese, which helped her extend affection to China.

5. 3. 7. 2   Host members' attitudes

According to Amy, Chinese are passionate, friendly and helpful. Many

Chinese would say "hello" to her in the street, and even attempted to start a conversation with her. She felt respected and welcomed by local people.

I love Chinese for their friendness and kindness. They always smiled and even said "hello" to me, when I was walking on the road. Some of them like to talk to me in English because of my appearance. I mean that my physical appearance is different, so they thought I might speak English. English is my second language, so I could talk to them in English. Sometimes I would reply in Chinese, which surprised them.

She became more interested in Chinese partly for her pleasant experience in China. Chinese people were generous to her based on the interview data.

When I was having dinner with my friend in a small restaurant, a young woman came towards us. She was humorous and straitforward and told us that she wanted to make some foreign friends for practicing English. We chatted happily. She asked us to visit her someday and left her phone number to us. We called up and visited her a few days later. She invited us to a big dinner and gave us some gifts. She was so generous that we felt a bit uncomfortable.

Host members' attitudes played an important role in changing learners' acculturation attitude. Amy was motivated by job hunting at the beginning, and became curious and interested in Chinese for her experience in China.

I found that Chinese is very interesting, and Chinese culture is mysterious with five thousand years history. Chinese people make me feel at home or better than home. So I decided to work harder and pick up

Chinese culture, norms and conventions. I like speaking Chinese and feel the beauty of Chinese language.

Although this external factor didn't affect Amy's pragmatic development directly, it had impact on arousing her internal motivation, which triggered Amy to make linguistic growth. Unlike Joy's experience, Amy's personal experience with Chinese people had a positive impact on her willingness to interact with native Chinese speakers.

5.3.8   Section summary

According to the analyzed data, this section sorted out the general tendency of Amy's pragmatic development trajectory, and found out the factors that might aid or hinder Amy's pragmatic development. On the basis of my eight-month tracking of her linguistic behavior and social activities ethnographically in her daily life, along with the data collected from DCT and semi-structured interview, Amy's pragmalinguistic and sociopragmatic competence developed well and almost at the same time. The current data suggested that Amy's pragmatic competence developed in a smooth way compared with Joy, although it seemed that Joy's pragmatic competence was better than Amy at the beginning in light of the findings discussed in Chapter 4. It indicates that each learner's pragmatic development had its own trajectory regardless of their level at the beginning and cultural background.

This section also explored qualitatively the complicated and hidden reasons that resulted in Amy's particular pragmatic development trajectory. In light of the data discussed, the main factors were categorized into four groups: cultural background, Amy's motivation and acculturation attitude, Amy's social activities and contextual factors.

Through displaying the interview data, Amy's cultural background could be viewed as obstacles, which hindered Amy making smooth progress in respect of pragmatic competence. However, Amy was motivated to get a decent job at first, but changed to be motivated by the inner pursuit of integrating into Chinese culture through interaction with native speakers. Accordingly, her integrative motivation and acculturation attitude played a positive role in her pragmatic development. As discussed above, as an open-minded and independent girl, she was fond of making various types of friends. Socialization was regarded as a crucial process in the respect of language acquisition. Amy was sociable and interacted with native Chinese speakers, international classmates and Russian friends almost everyday, which helped her picked up native-like pragmatic strategies. Classroom learning and entertainment activities on electronic technology platform were described as regular activities involving Amy's use of Chinese language, facilitating her pragmatic development as well.

Furthermore, it suggests that contextual factors such as school culture and host members' attitude had played an importance role in Amy's pragmatic development. Officially organized student activities helped her improve Chinese and informed her of Chinese traditional culture. Chinese native speakers were willing to speak to Amy for practicing oral English. It was appearant that Amy had a pleasant experience with native speakers, which aroused her inner motivation to learn Chinese.

Many of the factors helped facilitate her to make improvements in respect to Chinese pragmatic competence. Furthermore, interation-oirented as she was, Amy created the chance to socialize with Chinese native speakers, which affected the development of pragmatic competence to a great extent. Thus, Amy's pragmalinguistic and sociopragmatic competence developed well at the same time.

5. 4   Eve-a French student: reserved, individualistic and experience-oriented

Eve was selected for its representative for Russian subjects in terms of pragmatic strategies in requests in Chinese. This section attempts to explore how Eve develop her pragmatic competence and understand the reasons leading to such outcomes. Reserved and individualistic as she was, her main purpose of studying in China was to get different experience. She rarely communicated with Chinese people, who kept on touch with Europeans, and she seldom took part in students' activities for her individualism. It was arranged in the following sequence: introduction of Eve's background, analysis of her pragmatic development trajectory, and description of her cultural background, motivation and acculturation attitude, social activities and contextual factors that might aid or hinder her pragmatic development.

5. 4. 1   Eve's Profile

The last case participant is Eve (pseudonym foranonymity), a 21-year-old female student. She was enrolled in the University of Lyon in France. She was in her third year in the University and she made a decision to study in China for one year. She applied to the exchange program supported by Confucius Institute, and she was accepted. As mentioned in Amy's section, Eve received 2500 RMB per month and got free accommodations in SISU hotel for one year. I knew her by accident, as I met her during my class observation. I invited her to have a coffee after accidentally meeting her during my class observation. After hearing about my research, she agreed to participate. Her Chinese was at intermediate level just like Joy and Amy. However, her speaking and listening was not as well as Joy and Amy, when I first met her. She had no confidence to communicate with people in Chinese.

Compared with Joy, Eve was born into an ordinary family in the suburb of East France, near the city called Mulhouse. And both of her parents were employees in a company. She had an older brother and an older sister. She described her family as an international one, since her brother worked in London and had a British girlfriend, and her sister was going to marry a New Zealander. Therefore, English was used as a communicative tool in her family. She was rather open to new things, and easily adapted to new circumstances. She was an easy-going, amiable and warm-hearted person, and she described herself as " international" and "crazy" . She told me that she tried duck tongue, pig liver and chicken claws, but none of her European friends dared to try. She was often seen hanging out with European students at various places, communicating, bonding, having coffee and having parties on campus and outside campus. But she was rarely seen hanging out with Chinese people. It seemed that she was open-minded and liked to taste new things. Actually, she was a little bit reserved and indirect in exchanging ideas and emotions. As a result, she was making lots of friends but not very close ones, and she preferred to be with European students in her spare time. Sarah, an Italian student was her best companion during her one year in China.

Eve learned English as a second language when she was little. As is known, France belongs to European Union, and many immigrants go to in France from various parts of Europe. As a result, since elementary school Eve always spoke English to her immigrant classmates. We met for the first time in November. When I tried to speak Chinese to her, she was unable to understand. As a result, I used English to introduce my research purpose. She spoke very fluent English with a large vocabulary. She started to learn Chinese in high school and decide to choose Chinese as her major in the university. It was because of her interest in Chinese and also an attempt to find a job related to Chinese after graduation. Although she studied Chinese for nearly three years in France, she could not speak Chinese in a fluent way. She explained that Frenchmen were not good at learning any kind of foreign language. She felt her teachers in France did not teach her in a way where she could learn Chinese effectively. She preferred to interact in English with international classmates and Chinese native speakers in Chinese.

I observed and interacted with Eve on various occasions in different places on or outside the campus. During the process of personal interaction, she regarded me as a researcher at first, but gradually she started to take me as a friend, as I often hung out with her for fun. Based on interview data and informal talks from time to time with her, over a period of 8 months, I had been able to record our communication in the form of field notes and interview transcription.

In the following subsections, I describe and analyze Eve's pragmatic development trajectory and the factors that might facilitate or constrain her development of pragmatic competence.

5. 4. 2   Eve's pragmatic features of requests

The criteria of participant selection for case study were mainly based on the pragmatic features at the first test. According to Table 47, the most frequent used formulae by Eve at the verybeginning were as follows: "attention getter", "title" and "greeting" for openers; "QP (1)", "QP (2)" and "Mood derivable" for head acts; "H + G", "G + H" and "preparator" for external modifications, and "politeness marker", "honorific" and "appealer" for internal modifications. It was evident that the formulae used by Eve were similar to that of the ones used by French subjects based on Table 47.

Although there were some subtle differences between the two columns shown in the following table, such as formulae for openers and head acts, Eve was still regarded as the typical case. For instance, Eve tended to use "attention getter" more often than "greeting", because she transferred her L1 into Chinese directly. It indicates that Eve's pragmatic features had strong connection to western culture.

Table 47　　　　　　　**Most frequently used formulae by Eve**

	Ranking	Eve	FCL
Openers	1st	Attention-getter	Greeting
	2nd	Title	Attention-getter
	3rd	Greeting	Title
Head acts	1st	QP (1)	QP (1)
	2nd	QP (2)	Mood derivable
	3rd	Mood derivable	Want statement
External Modifications	1st	H + G	H + G
	2nd	G + H	G + H
	3rd	Preparator	Preparator
Internal Modifications	1st	Politeness marker (n = 5)	Politeness marker
	2nd	Honorific	Honorific
	3rd	Appealer	Appealer

To compensate for shortcomings of DCT, I recorded some natural occurred data of requests made by Eve for triangulation. The following example was recorded during her visiting me in Hangzhou. Eve asked a stranger to take a photo of us.

#Natural recording# (April 9th, 2016)

Duibuqi, er…keyi bang women er.. pai zhao ma?

Excuse me, could you take a photo of us?

It was obvious that Eve preferred to use "attention getter" for alerters and "query preparatory" for HA. Thus, Amy could be viewed as a typical case for French subjects.

5. 4. 3   Eve's development trajectory

As stated above, pragmatic competence is comprised of pragmalinguistic competence and soicopragmatic competence. Thereby, pragmatic development involves pragmalinguistic and sociopragmatic development. The following subsections will describe Eve's development trajectory in detail.

5. 4. 3. 1   Pragmalinguistic development

As displayed in Table 48, the most frequently used formulae for opener by Eve were "attention getter", "title" and "greeting" in T1. But "attention getter" was less used gradually from T2 to T4. Instead, the number of "title", "greeting" and "name" increased steadily from T2 to T4. To take a close look at DCT data, Eve started to employ "title" to address stranger student, such as "tongxue" (同学, classmate) and use "name" to address good friends instead of "attention getter". According to Eve, because of diversity of semantic formulae for openers in Chinese, she had to intentionally pick this up through interaction with native speakers or observation of others' greetings in daily life.

I don't know how to address people in Chinese when I first arrived here. I learned from my friends and observed other's behavior. I found that I should call stranger student "tongxue" and call my friends "name". As a result, I picked up.

According to Table 49, Eve tended to use "QP (1)" and QP (2)" from T1 to T4, and had not changed much. She preferred to employ "QP (1)" and "QP (2)" in good friends' situation, while their Chinese counterparts tended to use "mood derivable". As analyzed and discussed in Chapter 4, Chinese used direct strategy among friends to enhance intimacy and relationship. However, according to Eve, only "query preparatory" was polite in requests regardless of the status of hearers. Eve started to use "mood derivable" more frequent in T3 and T4, and the number of "QP (2)" and "mood derivable" was even the same in T4. It seemed that Eve began to pick up the way that Chinese requested in different situations. But the interview data didn't support this prediction.

Table 48   Most frequently used formulae for openers by Eve

	T1 (n = 12)	T2 (n = 12)	T3 (n = 12)	T4 (n = 12)	CNS
Opener	Attention getter (n = 5)	Title (n = 5)	Title (n = 5)	Title (n = 7)	Title
	Title (n = 4)	Attention getter (n = 4)	Greeting (n = 3)	Greeting (n = 3)	Greeting
	Greeting (n = 1)	Greeting (n = 3)	Attention getter (n = 2)	Name (n = 2)	Name

I saw Chinese students make requests towards their friends directly sometimes, and they didn't use any query to mitigate the requests. So I began to use this kind of sentence structure sometimes for shorter and simpler expressions.

Eve made progress in applying the formulae for head acts in terms of the quantitative and qualitative data.

As stated in Table 50, Eve preferred to give grounders after making requests in T1 and T2, which was deductive way in discourse. However, she changed to use grounder before making requests more often in T3 and T4. Eve's use of formulae for external modifications became more native like through the course of my research. As for internal modifications, Eve preferred to employ "politeness marker" in T1, but gradually she preferred to use "appealer" as internal modifications. Moreover, she was prone to use "honorific" sometimes, because she considered "honorific" an important marker to show her respect to others. She even used "honorific" in unfamiliar equals' situations.

Table 49　　　　**Most frequently used formulae for HA by Eve**

	T1 (n = 12)	T2 (n = 12)	T3 (n = 12)	T4 (n = 12)	CNS
	QP (1) (n = 5)	QP (1) (n = 5)	QP (1) (n = 6)	QP (1) (n = 5)	QP (1)
Head acts	QP (2) (n = 3)	QP (2) (n = 3)	QP (2) (n = 4)	QP (2) (n = 3)	Mood derivable
	Mood derivable (n = 2)	Want statement (n = 2)	Mood derivable (n = 1)	Mood drivable (n = 3)	QP (2)

Table 50　　**Most frequently used formulae for EM and IM by Eve**

		T1 (n = 12)	T2 (n = 12)	T3 (n = 12)	T4 (n = 12)	CNS
EM		H + G (n = 5)	H + G (n = 5)	G + H (n = 5)	G + H (n = 4)	G + H
		G + H (n = 2)	G + H (n = 4)	H + G (n = 3)	H + G (n = 3)	H + G
		Preparator (n = 1)	Preparator (n = 2)	Gratitude/ Preparator (n = 2)	Gratitude (n = 2)	Preparator/ Gratitude
IM		Politeness marker (n = 3)	Appealer (n = 3)	Appealer (n = 3)	Appealer (n = 3)	Appealer
		Honorific (n = 2)	Honorific (n = 2)	Honorific (n = 2)	Honorific (n = 2)	Downtoner
		Appealer (n = 1)	Politeness marker (n = 1)	Politeness Marker (n = 1)	Politeness marker (n = 1)	Politeness marker

To sum up, Eve had improved her pragmalinguistic competence to a great extent based on both quantitative and qualitative data. As for the formulae for openers, HA, EM and IM, Eve had changed towards the way that Chinese make requests. However, Eve did best in the formulae for openers and EM. The following section analyzes her development of sociopragmatic competence.

5. 4. 3. 2　Sociopragmatic development

This section attempts to describe and analyze the changes of Amy's perceptions of situational variables, such as power and social distance, from T1 to T4 mainly through qualitative analysis.

＊Changes of perception of power

The following examples were extracted from the data collected:

(1) Situation: ask to get a new student identity card [D + , P +]

T1: Nihao! Wode xiaoyuan yikatong bujian le, wo buzhidao zainaer bu jian de. Suoyi wo xiang guashi, keyi chongxin mai yizhang xinde xiaoyuan yikatong ma?

Good morning/afternoon, I lost my student identity card. I want to report the loss of my identity card. Could I buy a new one?

T2: Ninhao! Wo xiang guashi, zenmeban? Wo (bukeyi) zhaodao wo de xiaoyuan yikatong.

Good morning/afternoon, I want to report the loss and get a new one. How could I manage it? I can't find my student identity card.

T3: Ninhao, wo jintian faxian wo de xiaoyuan yikatong bujian le, wo (bukeyi) zhaodao ta, suoyi wo xiang guashi bing chongxin banli yizhang xinde xiaoyuan yikatong, keyima?

Good morning/afternoon, Today, I find that I lost my student identity card. I can't find it. I want to report the loss and get a new one. Is it ok?

T4: Ninhao, wode xiaoyuan yikatong diule, (buneng) zhaodao. Wo ruhe chongxin banli yizhang xinde xiaoyuan yikatong? Xiexie nin!

Good morning/afternoon, I lost my student identity card and can't find it. How could I get new student identity card? Thank you!

Eve employed "nihao" as opener in T1, and changed to use "ninhao" in T3. "Ninhao" is used towards the hearer with high status in Chinese. Comparing with other subjects discussed above, Eve's requests were longer than any one of them. She preferred to give justification and reasons after making requests in T1 and T2. But she changed to give reasons before making requests in T3 and T4. As for the head act, she was indirect by employing "QP" from T1 to T4. Moreover, she applied "gratitude" in T4. The changes of linguistic forms didn't mean that she understood sociocultural respect of this context.

> I know the distinction between "ni" and "nin", because there are "tu" and "vous" in French. I don't know those administrators in the university, and they are not always friendly to us. If I want to get the service they provide, I need be polite. (Eve, T2)

(2) Situation: ask to copy PPT [D - , P +]

T1: Jiaoshouhao, nin de jiangshou henyou yisi, danshi wo de bilu butaihao, you hen xiao, suoyi wo qing wen nin, wo keyi kaobei zhemen ke de kejian ma?

Prof. Jin. Your course is very interesting. But my notes are not clear, and my writing is quite small. As a result, could I copy PPT of this course?

T2: Laoshihao, wo xiang kaobei zhemen ke de kejian, ranhou huijia fuxifuxi, keyima?

Good morning/afternoon, teacher. I want to copy PPT of this course, because I want to review after going back home. Is it ok?

T3: Duibuqi, Jinlaoshi, wo dui nin de ke hen gan xingqu, danshiwo you jige wenti, wo yu nin de ke bijiao shuxi, suoyi wo xiang kaobei zhemen ke de kejian, huiqu zai haohao xuexi, youmeiyou wenti?

Excuse me, Prof. Jin. I am very interested in this course, but I have one problem. I know you quite busy, so I want to copy PPT of this course and review after going back home. Is it ok?

T4: Jin jiaoshou, wo xiang kaobei zhemen ke de kejian, ranhou huiqu haohao xuexi, keyima?

Prof. Jin, I want to copy PPT of this course and review after going back home. Is it ok?

As far as formulae for openers were concerned, Eve addressed professor in the way that Chinese native speakers used to. However, she used "duibuqi" in T3, she said: "I would use 'excuse me' in this situation in French or in English, and the translation of this term is 'duibuqi' in Chinese." Effects of L1 transfer were inneglectable in analyzing learners' pragmatic competence. She was indirect by employing "QP" as head act, and preferred "grounder" before or after requests. It indicates that Eve showed respect to professors with high status.

(3) Situation: consult the place of schooldormitory [D +, P =]

T1: Nihao, duibuqi, mafannile. Wo yao kanwang wo de laotongxue, danshi wo buzhidao xuexiao sushe zai nali. Qing ni dailu, keyima?

Good morning/afternoon, Excuse me, Sorry to trouble you. I want to visit my classmate. But I don't know the location of dormitories. Could you lead me to that place?

T2: Duibuqi, tongxue, wo yinggai qu xuexiaosushe, danshi wo buzhidao zhege difang zai naer. Qing ni gaosu wo zenme zou.

Excuse me, Classmate. I should go to the school's dormitory. But I don't know the location of dormitories. Could you tell me how to get there?

T3: Qingwen, tongxue, wo xiang qu xuexiaosushe, qing ni shuoming zenme qu, duibuqi mafanle.

Excuse me. Classmate. I want to go to school's dormitories. Could you tell me how to get them? Sorry to trouble you!

T4: Duibuqi, tongxue, ni keyi gaosu wo ruhe qu xuexiaosushe ma? Xiexie.

Excuse me, classmate. Could you tell me how to get the location of dormitories? Thanks!

Regarding formulae for openers used by Eve, she always used " nihao", "duibuqi" and "qingwen" before "tongxue" . The reversed sequence of these two formulae was caused by L1 transfer. Eve preferred " performative" or "QP" in this situation. The sentence was especially long in T1, but became simpler and shorter in T4. She got rid of "grounder" in T4.

I find that stranger is not patient enough to know why I want to go to sushequ. Once I was lost in downtown, I asked a stranger about the direction. She wasn't interested in "my story" . I guess that she was busy. (Eve, T4)

(4) Situation: ask to take notes [D + , P -]

T1: Duibuqi, ni kebukeyi ba women taolun de neirong jilu xialai? Suoyi wo keyi kankan shibushi you zhongyao de xinxi. Xiexie ni.

Excuse me, Could you please take notes of the content of our discussion? And then we can take a look after discussion and highlight the important information. Thanks.

T2: Tongxuemen, women xiage xingqi yao huibao. Women taolun de neirong yinggai jilu, zheyang women jiu buhui wangji taolun de neirong. Shui xiang jilu?

Classmates. We have to give the presentation next week. We should take notes of the content of our discussion. We should take notes of our discussion. So we won't forget the content of our discussion. Who wants to take notes?

T3: Qingwen tongxue, ni keyi jilu taolun de neirong ma? Xiexie ni.

Excuse me, classmate. Could you take notes of the content of our discussion? Thanks!

T4: Tongxue, women yao zuo xiaozu huibao, ni kebukeyi ba women taolun de neirong jilu xialai? Xiexie ni.

Classmate. We need to make a presentation. Could you please take notes of the content of our discussion? Thanks!

Taking a close look at the requests made in this situation by Eve, she started to use "tongxue" in T2, but put "qingwen" before "tongxue" in T3 for L1 transfer. She mainly employed "QP" as head act. Although Joy was group leader in this situation, she was still indirect when making requests.

We are in the same group, and we have to cooperate with each other. I should be polite to them. Otherwise, they would not cooperate with me to complete the task. (Eve, T2)

Eve's perception of power remained stable in this situation. As stated above, Frenchmen tend to be egalitarian and individualistic. Thus, although Eve was group leader, she was indirect and treated them in a very polite way.

In short, Eve changed her perception of power in Chinese context to some extent. There were still some misuse of linguistic forms, for example, she used "kebukeyi" instead of "nengbuneng" in T2 and T3. Although it seemed that she understood the power in a specific situation, i. e. she was indirect and showed respect to administrators, her perception of power didn't change much. Her pragmalinguistic competence improved faster than her siciopramatic competence.

* Changes of perception ofsocial distance

The following examples are extracted to display:

(1) Situation A: ask to take a photo [D + , P =]

T1: Duibuqi, ni keyi gei women liangeren paizhang heying ma?

Excuse me, could you take a photo of us?

T2: Nihao! Duibuqi, qing ni gei women liangge paizhang heying, keyima? Xieixe ni!

Hello. Sorry to trouble. Will you please take a photo of us? Thanks!

T3: Tongxue, wo he pengyou xiang paige hezhao, ni keyi bang women pai yizhang ma? Xiexie ni!

Classmate, my friend and I want to take a photo together. Could you help us to take one? Thanks!

T4: Tongxue, ni keyi gei women liangren paizhang heying ma? Feichang ganxie!

Classmate, could you take a photo of us? Thank you very much!

(2) Situation B: borrow a pen [D - , P -]

T1: Duibuqi, wo faxian ziji wangji dai bi le. Kebukeyi jie ni de bi? Buhaoyisi, xiexie ni!

Excuse me. I find that I forget my pen. Could you lend one to me? Sorry to trouble you. Thanks!

T2: Duibuqi, wo wangle wode bi, keyi jie ni de bi ma? Xiexie!

Excuse me. I forgot my pen. Could you lend one to me? Thanks!

T3: Qingwen, wo xiangzuo biji, danshi wo wang daibile, wo keyi jie yizhibi ma? Xiexie ni!

Excuse me. I want to take notes. But I forgot to bring a pen. Could you lend one to me? Thanks!

T4: Pengyou, wo ziji wangdai bile. Wo keyi jie nide bi ma? Xiexie ni!

Friend, I forget to bring a pen. Could I borrow one from you? Thanks!

Concerning scenario A, Eve used "nihao" and "duibuqi" as opener in T1 and T2, and changed to use "tongxue" in T3 and T4 like her Chinese counterparts. She preferred "query preparatory" in this situation and applied "gratitude" in T2, T3 and T4 as external modifications. Her pragmalinguistic competence improved based on the Scenario A. As for scenario B, she employed "duibuqi" as openers in T1 and T2 for L1 transfer (discussed in last section). Moreover, although the hearer was her roommate, she was indirect by using "query preparatory" as head act, and applied "gratitude" from T1 to T4 in this situation.

I try to be polite, so I use query to ask for help. Although we are close, I think I should be polite so as to maintain the interpersonal relationship. (Eve, T2)

French subject, Eve's perception of social distance had not changed much. She still tried to be polite by applying "query preparatory" and "gratitude" among friends.

5.4.3.3 Subsection summary

As for the developmental trajectories of Eve's pragmatic competence, the findings show that Eve, as a representative of French subjects, employed formulae that differed from that of Chinese subjects at the beginning, but developed towards native-like at the end of the semester. Although it seemed that she understood the power and social distance in a specific situation for her native-like use of formulae, her perception of the situational variables didn't change much based on the interview data and my observation. Therefore, it was concluded that the development of Eve's pragmalinguistic competence preceded that of her siciopragmatic competence. The following subsections will focus on analyzing factors that might affect Eve's pragmatic development trajectory.

5.4.4   Eve's cultural background

As mentioned in Amy's section, people whose native language is alphabet based or belongs to Indo-European language family, regard Chinese as one of the most difficult languages to learn. Regarding Eve, Chinese was difficult for its totally different linguistic forms and functions from that of French. And what made the situation more complicated was that the use of different linguistic forms in various situations varied considerably.

> Frenchmen are not good at learning any kind of foreign language. Chinese is the most difficult language in the world. It is rather challenging to learn a language that differed from our native one thoroughly. Furthermore, I don't know how to use proper expressions in different context.

As is known that Chinese belongs to Sino-Tibetan language family, and shows far language distance from French. The language distance together with cultural distance affected Eve's pragmatic competence. As Rafieyan et al. (2014) point out that cultural distance plays a significant role in learners' pragmatic comprehension. Eve experienced negative pragmatic transfer sometimes.

> Once I requested for a coffee in cafe by using the sentence "duibuqi, qing gei wo yibie kafei" (Sorry, please give me a coffee) I went to the cafe frequently, so I acquainted with the waiter very well. He joked, " dangran, buguo ni buyong daoqian, ni meicuo. " (Sure, but you needn't apologize, you have no fault) I blushed at once and felt embarrassed. "duibuqi" is translated from "Excuse me" in English or "excuser moi" in French. I didn't realize it until the waiter told me.

It seemed that Eve took longer time to use Chinese appropriately in various situations caused from far distance between Chinese and French. Eve experienced more negative pragmatic transfer compared with Joy. Thus, language difficulty and distance played a negative role in Eve's pragmatic development.

5.4.5   Eve's motivation and acculturation attitude

As mentioned in the last two subsections, Joy was motivated by job-hunting, which belonged to instrumental motivation, while Amy was motivated by her inner interests in Chinese after her studying in China. As far as Eve was concerned, her instrumental motivation was to get a job.

Although a small number of Frenchmen learn Chinese, I am quite interested in this language. Furthermore, China is a massive country with sufficient sources, and China's economy is developing at a surprising speed. China is far away from our country, so the culture, customs and scenic views are totally different. I would like to learn something new and special. Moreover, there are many Frenchmen doing business with Chinese but a few Frenchmen are good at this language. As a result, I could get a job easily in market no matter the economy is good or not.

According to the interview data, Eve didn't like to interact with Chinese people much, taking her poor Chinese and limited vocabulary as an excuse. According to Garner (1979), Eve belonged to instrumental motivation. Furthermore, as for Eve's acculturation attitude, she was regarded as separation in light of the data collected. She was showing greater interests in maintaining their home culture over the host one implicitly.

I go to parties organized by my European friends every weekend. It made me feel better, because of the spaghetti, alcohol… I missed French food very much. I do like Chinese food, and I want to taste all the eight types of Chinese cuisine. You know I have a French stomach, and need some bread and pasta (laughters).

Eve had a neutral impression of China and Chinese people. Although she was learning Chinese, she thought it a bit strange to speak Chinese with European friends.

China is huge compared to France with various types of fruits and dishes. Chinese food is very diverse and delicious. Chinese people are friendly and curious about foreigners. However, Chinese people like spitting on the road. What's more, it was too crowded in big cities.

Eve preferred to share her feeling with Sarah (her Italian friend mentioned in her profile), when she felt upset or homesick. She sometimes read books and wrote her journals in French in order to record the interesting events that she experienced in China. To sum up, Eve belonged to instrumental functioning in terms of Intercultural Interaction model. As a result, her pragmatic competence was developed slower than Amy.

5.4.6   Eve's social activities

The types of learners' social activities played an important role in Learners' pragmatic development. Activities are the focus of socialization. This subsection aims to illustrate the major patterns of activities which Eve took part in that affected her pragmatic development.

5.4.6.1   Social interaction

As described in Eve's profile, she was open-minded and curious about new things. Her family background influenced her significantly. Therefore, she attempted to understand Chinese conventions, customs, and culture by experiencing the things Chinese people do.

> I like to try different things and understand various cultures in the world. As you know, my family had impact on me, since my brother has a British girlfriend and my sister has a New Zealander bride. They chatted with me about the fascinating stories happened to them when they travelled in different countries. Therefore, I was dreaming of travelling or studying in China someday. Now my dream come true, so I would like to make best use of it.

It seemed that Eve was open to others, as she was smiling towards others and making friends all around. However, as a matter of fact, she was introverted and reserved in nature according to my observation and communication with her.

[Field notes 16th, March 2016]

When I asked her about her family background, she changed her face and reacted with a big laugh. She told me the location of her hometown and changed the topic. Moreover, when I asked her about her impression of China and Chinese people. She replied with neutral words, such as great, large, comfortable etc. We were having lunch together in a cafe. When I chatted with her, she stopped eating and replied with me carefully⋯

As a matter of fact, Eve tended to be reserved and keep her emotions inside. However, as a European girl, she didn't need to make efforts to make friends with Chinese people. It was because many Chinese students would like to practice English with her or may be curious about foreigners. As a result, she reported that she had many "nodding" acquaintances on campus but no Chinese friends.

I like to smile to others. As a result, I knew lots of Chinese people on campus, such as a waiter or waitress in Bella, Easy cafe, administrators in the hotel and some Chinese students that I often meet in the library. They would chat with me for a while each time we meet. I learned some expression in oral Chinese from them, for example, " meinv", "laoshi nihao" and "mafanle".

Although Eve didn't make any real Chinese friends, her pragmatic competence improved a lot for the sake of these nodding acquaintances on campus. Her perception of politeness remained the same from the beginning to the end, because she didn't understand the Chinese culture thoroughly. She didn't make in-depth conversation with any Chinese, which could be regarded as the main reason that hindered the development of her sociopragamtic competence.

5. 4. 6. 2 Classroom learning

As illustrated in Joy and Amy's section, international students had four periods per weekday. Eve had received a grant from the Chinese government, so she had to attend class on time and could not ask for leave without a reasonable excuse. As far as Eve is concerned, the teaching method of Chinese teachers helped her pick up language quickly.

> In France, my Chinese teachers were from Taiwan and France. They taught us new vocabulary every time, and never reviewed the old ones in class. As a result, I couldn't find the right words to express myself in daily life. Here, teachers teach in a very different way, which not only help us pick up new words, but also help us to review old ones. Moreover, the textbooks are designed with the words that we just learned.

The spiral way of teaching method could reinforce the knowledge that had just learned, and transit to new knowledge on the basis of the old ones. Furthermore, the classroom learning also informed her of Chinese culture implicitly and explicitly.

> My Chinese teacher would integrate Chinese culture in the class, and informed us of Chinese conventions sometimes. For example, when my teacher gave the class about "table manner", our teacher would like to tell us what Chinese usually do, when they were invited to a meal. I appreciate the teaching method of our Chinese teachers.

Moreover, teachers gave feedback to Eve instantly in the classroom, which was important to learners. Eve considered classroom learning as an effective and efficient way to learn Chinese.

Teachers are authoritative with profound knowledge. As a result, I always trust what Chinese teachers have taught us. Moreover, they helped us to correct our pronunciation, expressions and tone whenever we made mistakes in class. It was very efficient and helpful. Sometimes, I am not sure whether my utterances are correct or not, and become hesitate to use Chinese in daily life. However, I feel relaxed and free to speak Chinese in class.

Eve preferred to useEnglish when I interviewed her each time. She told me that she was too nervous to speak Chinese with me. She was afraid of making mistakes and felt safer speaking in English. Eve regarded classroom learning as an important way to learn Chinese. In addition, classroom instruction helped improve her language proficiency, which in turn might facilitate her pragmatic competence indirectly.

5. 4. 6. 3　Activities on electronic platform

In addition to studying Chinese fornearly 2 – 3 hours per day, Eve used Chinese through electronic platform nearly 1 – 2 hours per day. The types of activities on electronic technology platform mainly involved interacting with friends through Wechat, watching Chinese movies on "Youku" and listening to Chinese songs on the phone or MP4.

I chat with my friends through Wechat here, and using Facebook with my friends back in France. I like listening and singing songs. I regard singing songs as an effective way to learn a foreign language. I picked up English in this way. As a result, I download some Chinese songs on my phone, and try to learn to sing.

She asked me to make a list of some beautiful Chinese songs and send them to her through Wechat. We went to Karaoke once near the campus. To my surprise, she could sing several Chinese songs very well. Electronic technology platform served as an important instrument for international students to improve their language proficiency and develop their pragmatic competence.

5.4.7 Contextual factors

5.4.7.1 School culture

Administration & activities

Eve was pleased with the facilities of the accommodation in SISU, since it was a hotel and free for her to stay. However, she viewed it as a barrier to interact with Chinese students.

> I really appreciate with facilities of school accommodation, but I couldn't meet any Chinese student nearby. I read some articles about study abroad for linguistic growth, which emphasize interaction with native speakers for language improvement.

Eve seldom attended students' activities, since she consider them uninteresting. She preferred to hang out with her European friends.

> I don't like to attend those activities organized by school, because I like to arrange things for myself. I have to meet friends in my spare time, so I don't have time to take part in those activities.

Eve considered it important to live with some native speakers for linguistic growth, which could provide a pleasant environment for interaction. But she preferred to arrange her own personal activities, which could be seen as her emphasis on individualism.

5. 4. 7. 2   Host members' attitudes

As a European girl, Eve had been warmly welcomed in China. She described Chinese people as "warm-hearted", "friendly" and "kind" . She could get help anywhere in China, but she also felt uncomfortable by their overreaction.

> Chinese people are very generous and helpful. They would say "hello" to us and talked to us in English. Some of them would ask us to take photos together, and some even take photo of me without permission. I was annoyed at the beginning and felt disrespected. But now I adapt to be a "celebrity" here.

Shanghai is a metropolitan city, in which a great number of foreigners study, do business, travel, etc. Therefore, people in Shanghai are familiar with Europeans. However, people from smaller and secondary cities don't have much chance to meet foreigners. Below Eve describes a very strange way they would react.

> I went to xx with my friends in March. When we were walking in the street in downtown, everybody looked at us as if we were animals in the zoo. Some kids even attempted to touch us. Although we knew that they were just curious with us, we still felt extremely uncomfortable. But now I begin to enjoy Chinese friendness and kindness, which helped me overcome some barriers here.

Although Eve felt uncomfortable for some Chinese people's overreaction and curiosity, she still enjoyed being respected and welcomed. Many Chinese would take initiative to chat with her in English. Thus, she gradually used to speak

English to Chinese people. It would be for this reason that Eve felt strange speaking Chinese with her European friends. As a result, she didn't make efforts to seek Chinese friends for linguistic growth. Moreover, most of Chinese people were nodding acquaintances to her without in-depth interaction. Host members' attitudes helped her to get chances to interact in Chinese but also hindered her from using Chinese frequently. Therefore, Eve's pragmalingutistic competence developed better than her sociopragmatic competence.

5.4.8 Section summary

Based on the analyzed data, this section sketched Eve's pragmatic development trajectory and sorted out the factors that influenced on their pragmatic development. Eve made progress in terms of pragmalinguistic and sociopragmatic competence. But her pragamlinguistic and sociopragmatic competence were developed in an uneven way. The findings indicate that Eve's development of pragmalinguistic competence preceded her development of sociopragmatic competence. As for the formulae for openers, HA, EM and IM, Eve approximated Chinese norms in request making. For examples, she changed to use "title" such as "tongxue" (同学, classmate) for openers, and started to give reasons before making requests. But her perception of power and social distance had not changed much in light of interview data. The factors that resulted in Eve's particular development trajectory could be grouped into four categories: Eve's cultural background, Eve's motivation and attitude, Eve's social activities and contextual factors.

As discussed above, it is clear that Amy's cultural background hindered her from making smooth progress in respect to pragmatic competence on the basis of the qualitative data. Moreover, Eve was motivated to get a job related to Chinese, which belonged to instrumental motivation. And she was described as separation in terms of acculturation attitude. Accordingly, Eve's motivation and acculturation attitude had seemingly played a negative role in her pragmatic development.

It seemed that Eve was open and warm-hearted by the first impression. As a matter of fact, she was reserved and refrained from talking about her emotions and ideas. She had many Chinese nodding acquaintances on campus, but she didn't make efforts to establish intimate relationship with them. Those small talks and greetings indeed helped her pick up native-like pragmatic strategies. However, her interaction with native speakers remained very superficial, which could not help her understand Chinese culture and norms comprehensively. Moreover, classroom learning was regarded as an effective way to pick up Chinese language by Eve. In her spare time, she preferred to use Wechat to communicate with friends and listen to Chinese songs on the cellphone. Apart from that, it seems that Chinese people's overreaction made Eve too proud to use Chinese in daily life. Eve attempted to maintain her identity by hanging out with European friends and speaking English.

It is evident that most of these factors facilitated her improvement in Chinese pragmatic competence. However, Eve lacked the opportunities to socialize with native Chinese speakers in-depth. As a result, her perception of politeness in Chinese had not changed much. Therefore, Eve's pragmalinguistic competence was better developed than her sociopragmatic competence.

5. 5　The overview of cross-case study: convergences and divergences

This section compares and contrasts development trajectories and factors that might facilitate and constrain pragmatic development among those three case participants: Joy, Amy and Eve. The following passages aim to clarify and discuss convergences and divergences of the three participants.

The three case participants had developed their pragmatic competence in general, which could be viewed as their convergence. However, Joy, Amy and Eve developed their pragmalinguistic competence and sociopragmatic competence in different ways. Joy's development of sociopragmatic competence preceded her development of pragmalinguistic competence, while Eve's development of pragmalinguistic competence preceded her sociopragmatic competence, and Amy developed her pragmalinguistic and sociopragmatic competence at the same time.

Table 51　　　　　　　　　　　**Types of factors**

Categories	Subcategories		Joy	Amy	Eve
Cultural background (Compared with Chinese culture)	Long distance			√	√
	Short distance		√		
Motivation and acculturation attitude	Instrumental		√		√
	Integrative			√	
Social activities	Social interaction			√	√
	Travelling around China		√		
	Classroom learning		√	√	√
	Activities on electronic platform		√	√	√
Contextual factors	School culture	Administration	√	√	√
		Activities		√	
		Textbook contents	√		
	Host members' attitude		√	√	√

As shown in Table 51, main factors were found out in terms of ethnographic interview data, field notes and memos. Four main categories were identified as follows: cultural background, motivation and acculturation attitude, social activities and contextual factors. The four categories affected the three focal case participants' pragmatic development, which could be regarded as convergence. However, divergence was also identified as follows: 1) Subcategories varied from each other among those three cases (see Table 51); 2) The same factor had exerted different influence on each individual.

According to Table 51, those three case participants varied from each other in the subcategories of four main categories. As a Korean girl, the distance between her culture and Chinese culture was quite near, while the distance between Russian participant's culture/French participant's culture and Chinese culture was further. Both Joy and Eve belonged to instrumental motivation and acculturation attitude, but Amy held integrative motivation and acculturation attitude. Joy travelled around China frequently, and regarded classroom learning as the most important way to learn Chinese. Amy and Eve interacted with Chinese people from time to time in daily life, and actively participated in classroom learning. Three of them interacted with friends, buying goods, or watching movies on electronic platform almost everyday. Contextual factors, school culture, host members' attitude and textbook contents had impact on shaping Joy's attitude towards Chinese language and culture. Host members' attitudes toward Joy made her refrain from frequent contacting with Chinese people. But Amy viewed school culture and host members' attitudes as important factors that changed her attitudes towards Chinese people and formed integrative motivation gradually by sojourn in China. Only Eve regarded host members' attitude as the significant factor that affected her interaction with Chinese.

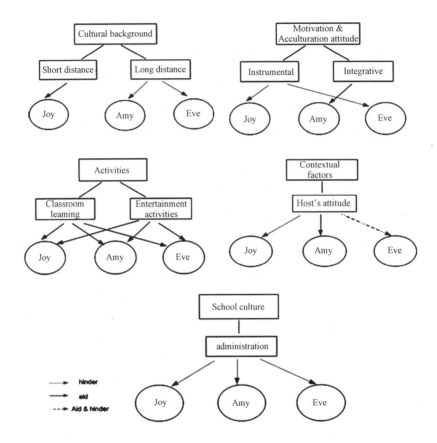

Figure 8   Functions of identical subcategories of factors

As displayed in Figure 8, the same factor shared by those three participants would exert a different influence on them. As far as cultural background concerned, Joy was from Korea, whose culture was similar to that of Chinese culture. Therefore, she developed her sociopragmatic competence far better than her pragmalinguistic competence. However, despite Amy and Eve both being from European culture, their cultures differed from each other in some aspects. Amy, as a Russian girl, had very different perception of politeness, which sometimes constrained her from making progress in pragmatics. So was Eve. As for motivation and acculturation attitude, Joy and Eve belonged to instrumental one, so they had a lower concern of contacting with Chinese for linguistic growth. Amy tended to be integrative; she delved herself into Chinese culture through an intensive interaction with Chinese friends. Moreover, the social activities such as classroom learning and entertainment activities those three participants attended seemed to facilitate their pragmatic development. School administration didn't have positive impact on students' pragmatic development. Host me members' attitudes would change international students' attitudes towards Chinese culture. Joy had unpleasant experience with Chinese native speakers, so she didn't interact with Chinese much, which in turn constrained her pragmatic development. Amy changed from separation acculturation attitude to integrative acculturation attitude for her pleasant experience with host members in China. As for Eve, she had many nodding acquaintances for her cultural background and host members' attitudes, which seemingly facilitate her pragmatic development in some respects. Therefore, Even the same factor would have different impact on learners' pragmatic development.

5. 6   Summary

This chapter illustrates the major findings from the two research questions, based on which trajectories of pragmatic development and factors are drawn in relation to cultural and individual differences. Pragmatic competence was divided into two parts: pragmalinguistic competence and sociopragmatic competence. According to case studies, the Korean participant's soicopragmatic competence was better developed than her pragmalinguistic competence. The Russian participant developed pragmalinguistic and soicopragmatic competence at the same time. The French girl showed great pragmalinguistic development, but her sociopragmatic competence lagged behind. This chapter also demonstrated major factors that might affect their pragmatic development.

Finally, convergence and divergence across the three case participants had also been illustrated. In the next chapter, features of pragmatic strategies from three different cultures in requests, participants' trajectories of pragmatic development and complicated major factors are discussed. To follow, the researcher puts forward a new model that could be used to study the dynamic and complicated process of L2 learners' pragmatic development.

Chapter 6

General Discussion

6.1 Introduction

This chapter attempts to interpret and discuss the findings presented in the previous two chapters. The findings are recapitulated for the three research questions, and then results are comprehensively discussed. Finally, the findings of this study are reconceptualized to construct a theoretical model for implications.

In response to the first research question, the pragmatic strategies of three different cultural groups in L2 requests are summarized, and then the different formulae for openers, HA, EM and IM for Russian, Korean and French participants are discussed. It suggests that learners from various cultures tended to use different types of formulae in Chinese requests. In response to the second research question, it shows that learners from different cultural backgrounds developed their pragmatic competence at different speed, and their development trajectories varied individually. In answer to the third research question, three case participants were investigated longitudinally to explore the factors that might facilitate or constrain learners' pragmatic development. A model is drawn to elaborate the dynamic interrelation between main factors and learner's pragmatic development.

6.2 Features of pragmatic strategies

This section summarizes the major findings for the first research question: What are the features of pragmatic strategies in requests among Korean, French and Russian Students? First, it presented the general semantic formulae for openers, HA, EM and IM used by Chinese users, and then compared and contrasted the differences between Chinese groups and other three cultural groups in terms of semantic formulae. Finally, learners' perceptions of situational variables were also compared to understand their different perceptions of politeness. In other words, both pragmalinguistic and sociopramatic aspects of pragmatic competence were discussed to address the distinctions and similarities among those four cultural groups.

6.2.1 Pragmatic strategies of Chinese native speakers

Chinese native speakers tended to use "title", "greeting" and "name" as formulae for openers. The findings of this study show that Chinese speakers were prone to use "title" or "title + PM" towards the hearer with higher status, and preferred to use "name" to address friends or roommates. In this study, when superiors were professors and administrators, most of the users were prone to employ "laoshi" or "laoshi ninhao" to address the superiors. It suggests that Chinese people tended to use the openers with up grading function to address the hearer with higher power. However, Chinese speaker tended to use "xx" (name) or "tongxue" to address friends, roommates or strangers with equal power. The results echoed the findings of a previous study conducted by Rue and Zhang (2008), who state that openers with upgrading functions were applied towards people with higher status in Chinese requests, when openers applied toward juniors, neutral formulae were extensively used by Chinese speakers.

More than half of Chinese subjects used "query preparatory" as head act in this study (64. 6%). It could be explained from the Chinese philosophical perspective. Chinese speakers attempt to protect both their own face and hearers' face by requesting in an indirect way. He (1993) argues that Chinese users believe that nobody should be obliged to do what you request, so they tend to behave polite towards whomever they ask for an act and refrain from acting arrogantly or in an authoritarian way. Rue and Zhang (2008) argue that Chinese users are prone to use more query preparatory for head act in requests than their Korean counterparts.

Based on quantitative data in this study, contemporary Chinese young speakers were prone to use "want statement" towards "administrators" . Since administrators in the university were regarded as having a high status, the students behaved in a polite way when making requests. However, it contradicted the convention in this survey. Students were more likely to consider the administrators who work in the office as being obligated to provide service for them. It suggests that Chinese young users showed more respect to professors than administrators. Chinese people have admired knowledgeable persons since ancient China. This is deeply rooted in Chinese culture. Furthermore, Chinese were prone to be more direct by using "mood derivable" towards friends or roommates. Chinese culture focuses on collectivism, and regards smooth interpersonal relationship as the most important issue. Chinese speakers tended to apply direct strategies to show intimate relationship (Wang & Li, 2007).

According to the data, Chinese users favored using reasons or justifications before making requests rather than after making requests. Chinese people are inclined to be inductive in conversational discourse. As a result, they preferred to give reasons before making requests. Zhang and Wang (1997) confirm the findings of this study, and argue that Chinese users were inclined to be inductive by applying external modifications before requests, while westerners were proned to be deductive by employing external modifications after requests. Moreover, "Gratitude" (20. 8%) was used frequently towards the hearers with equal status as the speakers, which implicates that Chinese users were prone to express their appreciation to the hearer with the equal power when making requests. However, "sweetener" (21. 8%) was used frequently towards the hearers with lower status. Although the speakers had higher power, they tended to use "sweetener" to hide their status and protect hearer's negative face.

Furthermore, Chinese users applied some polite words such as "baituole" (拜托了, please), "xinkule" (辛苦了, thanks) and "buhaoyisi" (不好意思, sorry to have troubled you) in the [power +], [power =] and [power -] situations. This type of strategies had not been shown in previous studies, which focused on Chinese requests. This current study viewed this kind of strategies with Chinese characteristics, when compared with other cultural groups. Moreover, "modal particles" such as "aini" (爱你, love you), "memeda" (么么哒, the sound of "kiss") appeared in this study had not been found in similar studies either. It could be explained by the influence of English learning among youngsters. And those formulae were only used towards friends or roommates, who were close to the speaker.

Chinese speakers were prone to employ "downtoner" as formulae for IM between friends or intimate relations. And "qing" was frequently used in almost all kinds of situations. In 1993, He states that Chinese users tend to apply "qing" in requests under any kind of circumstances. Moreover, "honorific" was used towards the hearer with higher status. The data indicates that Chinese showed politeness and deference to the person who had higher power, and also evidenced once again that Chinese tend to be hierarchical.

In short, the findings implicate that power and social distance affect the choice of semantic formulae significantly in requests, which also confirms that

Chinese people tend to be indirect, hierarchical and reserved.

6.2.2   Comparison among cultural groups

As mentioned in Chapter 4, types of formulae and strategies Korean subjects employed were the most similar to that of Chinese native speakers among those three foreign cultural groups based on both frequency calculation and examination of significant difference. However, as learners, Korean subjects misused some formulae. The findings of this research indicate that Korean speakers chose to use "attention-getter" to alter hearers' attention sometimes, overused "politeness marker" and apply "duplication", which was not found in Chinese native speakers' requests. Generally speaking, the effects of power were more systematic and significant than that of social distance for Korean learners. Formulae applied by both Chinese and Korean groups were similar, which were affected by power significantly (Rue & Zhang, 2008).

Concerning Russian subjects, they preferred to use "kinship terminology", which differed from other three cultural groups. "Kinship terminology" is the type of formulae that is used to address relatives, but speakers use this type of formulae to shorten the distance from the hearer. Russian speakers tended to employ "kinship terminology", such as "xiongdi" (兄弟, brother), "meimei" (妹妹, sister) and "pengyou" (朋友, friend), which were barely used by Chinese native speakers. In 2015, Kotorova states that the Russian culture lays more stress on solidarity than distancing. Therefore, they preferred to use this type of formulae to shorten the distance between interlocutors. Moreover, Russians turned out to be the most direct among those four cultural groups, when they made requests in Chinese. Kotorova argues that Russians do not perceive the act of request as a serious face threat act because of the short distance between Russian speakers. According to Kotorova's study, Russians tend to be more direct than German based on the wording of request. In this survey, it was found that Russians tended to use "performative" as head act in this study, which is similar to previous studies. Power and social distance works almost equally on the use of formulae in requests made by Russian subjects, which was quite different from that of Chinese or Korean counterparts.

As for French subjects, Chinese and French belong to two different language families, and their cultures differed from each other significantly. The number of types of formulae used by French speakers differing from that of Chinese speakers was biggest among the three cultural groups based on examination of log-likelihood ratio. As for the formulae for opener, they tended to choose "greeting" and "attention-getter", which could be regarded as the effects of L1 transfer. As a common phenomenon in L2 speech act, pragmatic transfer had been explored in a variety of speech acts involving various types of languages and cultures (Wannaruk, 2008). Moreover, the percentage of "query preparatory (1)" (67. 2%) was particularly high. It indicates that French subjects were indirect, which was also found in previous studies. In 1996, Mulken states that French users are prone to apply "query preparatory" as the main strategy in request making. Moreover, Like Korean, French subjects favored overuse "honorific" due to different function of "tu" and "vous" in French (Ismail et al. , 2014). However, "tu" and "vous" are different from "ni" and "nin", since "vous" is also used in the situations that speakers and hearers are equal but strangers. Consequently, the use of formulae by French speakers differed from that of Chinese most significantly in the survey. As for the situational variables, power affected the use of formulae by French speakers to some extent but not so systematic. French people are more egalitarian and individualistic, which conforms the previous studies (Cohen & Shively, 2007b; Warga & Schölmberger, 2007).

In 2004, Byon points out that Korean used to be more hierarchical and collectivistic than Americans. Since French and Americans belong to Western cultures, while Chinese and Korean all originated from Confucius culture, and both belong to Eastern cultures. Thus, along with the findings in this study, Chinese and Korean tend to be hierarchical, collectivistic, and reserved in comparison to their French and Russian counterparts. Accordingly, the patterns or pragmatic features of those four cultural groups found in this study are reasonable.

6. 3   Cultural differences of pragmatic development

Case study was applied to explore the learners' pragmatic development. Generally speaking, all the participants' developed their pragmatic competence to a certain extent. However, according to the analysis of data, the speed and trajectories of pragmatic development of those three learners differed from each other considerably. It seemed that the Korean participant's pragmalinguistic competence was not as well developed as their sociopragmtic competence; while the French participant's pragmalingutistic competence was better than their sociopragamtic competence at the end of the research; the Russian participant developed their pragmalinguistic and sociopragamtic competence at the same time. According to Chang (2011, P786), "the relation between sociopragmatic competence and pragmalinguistic competence is a complex and interwoven one rather than a simple, liner 'which precedes-which' kind of relation. "

6. 3. 1   Pragmalinguistic development

In this study, Chinese proficiency of those three participants was all at the intermediate level. The three cases were selected based on DCT completed at the beginning. They were representatives of those three cultures to some extent. In order to examine the development of their pragmalinguistic competence, they were tested at one-month interval during one semester. The scenarios of DCT questionnaire remained the same from T1 to T4, but the sequence of them were randomly arranged to decrease the negative influence. The most frequent used formulae produced by participants from those three cultural groups were compared with that of Chinese native speakers to investigate their development trajectories.

Generally speaking, their pragmatic development trajectories are not linear, but dynamic and complicated. The up and downs of the statistics based on frequency of those selected formulae reflected the dynamic process of pragmatic development. According to DST (Dynamic System Theory), language acquisition is unpredictable and far more complicated than a linear state could illustrate. Furthermore, the following types of variables working together bring about the influence on language learning of individuals, such as variables within the linguistic system, social context and personal psychological conditions (De Bot et al. , 2007). As the initial condition, learning motivation and capacity, social network and learning context were all considered as possible variables to different individuals. And the small difference at the beginning would cause a big consequences at the end. As a result, the findings of this current research are reasonable in light of DST.

Cultural variation was considered as a significant variable at the beginning based on the data in response to the first research question. Korean, Russian and French subjects employed different types of semantic formulae for openers, HA, EM and IM. Although participants were all at the same proficiency level, French subjects had the more types of formulae that differed from Chinese native speakers than that of Korean and Russian subjects. As discussed in the last section, cultural difference was considered as the main factor that resulted in the diverse characteristics of those three groups. According to the DST, the initial condition affects the development significantly, and minor differences in the beginning may lead to dramatic effects in the long run (De Bot et al. , 2007).

However, based on the analysis of the developmental data, Korean subjects whose requests were the most similar to that of Chinese speakers, developed slowest among those three cultural groups. Russian subjects developed fastest based on the longitudinal data, followed by the French subjects. The unpredictable results indicate that cultural difference might play a role in pragmatic development, but not a decisive one, which would interrelate with other variables to facilitate or constrain their pragmalinguistic or sociopragmatic development.

As for the Korean student, Joy did develop her pragmalinguistic competence to some extent in term of the changes of the use of semantic formulae for openers, HA, EM and IM. However, the outcomes of her pragmatic development were not dramatic. Concerning the Russian student, Amy developed her pragmalinguistic competence to a great extent in terms of the changes of the use of semantic formulae. Amy changed her formulae gradually from T1 to T4 and approximated native norms. With regard to the French student, Eve improved her pragmalinguistic competence to some extent based on both quantitative and qualitative data. However, Eve did best in the formulae for openers and EM.

Several reasons would result in the different developmental speed of learners' pragmalinguistic competence. On the one hand, it indicates that natural conversation with native speakers would be the vital element in pragmatic development. Some types of semantic formulae emerged and became popular recently would rarely appear in any kind of learning materials, such as "tongxue" for addressing unknown students. To establish close interpersonal relationships with native speakers are important for acquiring native-like pragmatic strategies. On the other hand, learners should pay attention to their overuse of certain formulae in various speech acts. It also suggests that teachers should integrate pragmatic strategies in teaching to enhance learners' overall pragmatic competence.

6.3.2   Sociopragmatic development

The development of sociopragmatic competence is far more complicated than that of pragmalinguistic competence. In this survey, quantitative data was mainly used to examine learners' pragmalinguistic development, which was compensated by interview data. However, qualitative analysis of DCT questionnaire along with interview data was used to explore learners' changes of perception of politeness in Chinese context. In order to understand in-depth the cultural variations of the changes of perception of politeness, three case participants were selected from each culture.

6.3.2.1   The changes of perception of +P

All learners showed great respect to the hearer with higher status, such as teachers from the beginning to the end. Although the Korean subject, Joy didn't address professors in a proper way, she tended to be indirect by applying "query preparatory". Russian subject, Amy addressed professors in a native-like way by employing "query preparatory" from the beginning to the end. So did the French subject, Eve.

Professors and administrators were designed to be superior in thisresearch, and administrators were unfamiliar superiors. It seemed that speakers should show more respect to unfamiliar superiors. However, when learners made request to administrators, they didn't show as much respect as they did to teachers in terms of semantic formulae. Joy considered an administrator as someone who provided a service. It indicates that obligation exerted great influence on the use of formulae. In 2010, Economidou-Kogetsidis suggests that power is tightly associated with rights and obligations within the role. Take the customer-waiter relationship as an example, since the waiter has to offer service to the customer, the waiter has less power than the customer. As a result, Joy seemingly used more direct strategies to make requests towards administrators. Russian subject changed her perception towards administrators by learning from Chinese native speakers. And French subject tried to be polite in order to get service from administrators.

6. 3. 2. 2   The changes of perception of = P

Learners treated strangers with equal power almost in the similar way as that of Chinese native speakers. Korean learners misused the alerters, but employed "query preparatory" just as Chinese speakers. It seemed that Amy used more external modifications than her Korean counterpart, but the use of formulae in this scenario is similar to that of Chinese speakers. Eve tended to be more talkative towards the strangers, but she became aware of the distance and changed her perception towards strangers.

6. 3. 2. 3   The changes of perception of – P

Learners from Eastern and Western cultures had a different perception of politeness in [p –] situation. Joy was direct towards the group members, because she was the group leader. Both qualitative data extracted from DCT and interview data showed that Joy regarded power as a significant variable that affected her use of formulae. Korean speakers as well as Chinese users applied more direct strategies towards the persons with lower status in natural communication (Rue & Zhang, 2008). The findings of this study confirmed previous studies. However, some misuse of formulae still existed for her unfamiliarity with the frequent formulae in Chinese. Amy changed to be direct by applying " performative " after immersion in China for two months. She changed perception of power, and became more hierarchical based on her interview data. Eve didn't change much in this situation. She regarded egalitarianism as an important principle to communicate with others.

In short, learners from different cultural backgrounds made requests in the similar way towards the hearer with high power. Moreover, learners from similar cultural backgrounds had a similar perception of power, but learners from different cultural backgrounds perceived the situational variables in various ways. Some of the latter changed their perception of politeness like Amy. But Eve did not change her perception of politeness very much. It was very difficult for learners to change the rooted conventions and perception of politeness, when the cultural norms of the target community differed from their own considerably.

6.3.2.4 The changes of perception of +D

As mentioned above, Chinese speakers tended to employ indirect head act such as "query preparatory" to unfamiliar equals. It was consistent with Sifianou study of 1992. Moreover, Korean subject showed a strong tendency to use direct strategies such as "performative" at the beginning, and didn't show changes through the course of research. However, according to her interview data, she noticed the social distance and attempted to be polite by using "qing" instead of applying indirect strategies. Her linguistic forms could not reflect her perception of politeness. Amy employed the similar formulae as Chinese speakers in this situation. French subject changed her formulae for openers gradually through the course of immersion. However, the effects of L1 transfer were quite strong on Eve's language use based on DCT questionnaire. In this situation, learners tended to use non-conventionally indirect strategies toward unfamiliar equals at the end of the research, expect the Korean subject. Their perceptions of unfamiliar equals were similar to that of Chinese speakers based on the data collected.

6.3.2.5 The changes of perception of −D

Chinese speakers showed strong tendency to employ direct head act such as "mood derivable" towards familiar equals. The study was inconsistent with previous studies. In 2008, Rue and Zhang argued that Chinese were more likely to apply indirect strategies as head acts towards familiar equals than that of Korean users, regardless of power. However, Chinese preferred to use direct strategies towards close friends in this survey.

The Korean subject, Joy became direct from T3 to T4, and employed "meimei" to address roommates. Although Chinese did not use it, Joy tended to maintain the intimate interpersonal relationship with her roommate by using kinship terms. In 1992, Sifianou suggested that Japanese attached more importance to establish and maintain bonds of solidarity by applying direct strategies in requests towards familiar equals, as in this manner could they be considered to be taken as in-group members. Chinese, Korean and Japanese had some conventions and sociocultural perceptions in common. Thus, Joy changed her linguistic forms to reflect her perception of situational variable, social distance.

Amy changed her formulae for openers and head acts gradually towards native like expressions. Based on her interview data, Amy changed her perception of social distance through interacting with her Chinese friends. As for the French subject, Eve preferred to use "query preparatory" towards acquaintance. She considered it important to maintain smooth interpersonal relationships with friends. Therefore, her perception of politeness in familiar equals' situation had not changed throughout.

To sum up, social distance was an effective situational variable, which affected the use of formulae by learners. Korean sociopragmatic competence was stable and remained similar to Chinese. However, the use of formulae for different situations was still blurred in her mind. It was overwhelming to find that the Russian subject changed her perception of social distance greatly, she even performed in a native-like way in request making. The perception of French subject towards familiar and unfamiliar equals remained the same and hadn't changed much. The reasons were explored and discussed in the following sections.

6.3.3 Cultural distance and pragmatic developmental trajectories

It seemed that the degree to which the distance between learners' own culture and the L2 culture had impact on the level of pragmatic comprehension (Rafieyan et al. , 2014). Cultural distance refers to the degree in which the shared conventions and norms in one community is different from those in another, and it is composed of five dimensions: " collectivism versus individualism, femininity versus masculinity, uncertainty avoidance, power distance, and Confucian dynamism or long term versus short-term orientation in life" (Hofstede, 2003, P163). As is known, Korean culture and Chinese culture are grouped into Asian culture and share some similarities in many respects, which tend to be collectivistic and hierarchal. However, Russian culture and French culture are grouped in European culture, which have a long cultural distance from Chinese culture, and tend to be individualistic and egalitarian.

The quantitative analysis of this present study indicates that international students from three cultural groups tended to apply certain types of pragmatic strategies in requests. On the other hand, the quantitative results show that Korean learners demonstrated the most similar pragmatic features, followed by Russian learners and French learners in sequence, in comparison to that of Chinese speakers. Accordingly, it seems that the distance between learners' culture and target community culture has impact on their pragmatic competence.

Based on case study, the current study found that Korean participant, Joy developed her sociopragmatic competence faster than her pragmalinguistic competence, and Russian participant, Amy developed her sociopragmatic and pragmalinguistic competence almost at the same time, while French participant,

Eve developed her pragmalinguistic competence faster than her sociopragmatic competence. The short cultural distance between Korean and Chinese culture determined that Joy understood cultural norms and conventions better, which in turn facilitated her sociopragmatic development. However, the long cultural distance between Chinese and French culture made Eve act differently in requests. Moreover, she refrained from shifting her perception of politeness by maintaining her own cultural identity. As a result, her sociopragmatic development lagged behind. Although the distance between Russian and Chinese culture is vast, Amy was aware of the different cultural difference took initiative in delving herself into Chinese culture (the reasons behind will be explained and discussed in-depth in following sections). As a result, she developed her sociopragamtic and pragmalinguistic competence evenly. When learners become familiar with and aware of the culture characteristics of the target language community, the cultural gap between their native cultural norms and the ones of the target language could be bridged significantly, which eventually bring about the development of pragmatic comprehension (Rafieyan et al. , 2014).

In conclusion, cultural background is likely to play a crucial role in pragmatic competence and pragmatic development. This study argues that cultural background worked as a determining factor at the initial stage of international students' pragmatic competence in study abroad context, and played an important role in pragmatic development in general. However, learners' awareness of the cultural features between their own culture and target language culture, along with other factors would affect the development trajectory in the long term.

6. 4   The integrated model of motivation and acculturation attitudes

Research topics associated with adaptation to a target culture in study abroad and second language acquisition are often studied from psychological and linguistic perspective (Culhane, 2004). Sojourners' motivation towards targeted language is likely to impact on their patterns of interactions and the relationship with native speakers they establish and maintain in host culture, which could in turn effect on acculturation attitudes. This section attempts to discuss the interrelationship between motivation and acculturation attitudes and its effect on pragmatic development.

6. 4. 1　The inner relation of the model

The findings postulate that the types of motivation determine the types of acculturation attitude. According to Gardner, there are two types of motivation relating to SLA in host culture: instrumental and integrative motivation. As stated in Chapter 5, instrumental motivation refers to the importance an individual attaches to personal linguistic improvement rather than interacting with native speakers; while integrative motivation concerns an individual engaging himself or herself in communication with members of the target language community for linguistic improvement (Gardner & Lambert, 1959). Acculturation attitudes refer to L2 learners' attitudes toward acculturation in study abroad context, which affect outcomes of language learning considerably. According to Berry in 1986, four types of acculturation attitudes were generated: integration, assimilation, separation, and marginalization. The definition of those four types of patterns was illustrated in Chapter 4.

According to the data collected, Joy was motivated to get a job related to Chinese by learning Chinese. She regarded the Chinese economy as prosperous and developing at a surprising speed. Trade between Koreans and Chinese has expanded quickly during this decade. Since Joy's father exported products to China, she was motivated by her father to learn Chinese in case she could help her father after graduation. However, she didn't regard it important to interact with Chinese for linguistic growth based on interview data. As a result, Joy belonged to instrumental motivation and held the attitude that classroom learning and the immersion experience were enough for linguistic growth. She didn't engage in delving herself into sociocultural aspects of Chinese community with lower concern for contacting Chinese, which could be regarded as separation acculturation attitude. Although Joy attempted to make friends with Chinese, she wanted to get a language partner for linguistic growth rather than acknowledgment of Chinese culture through interaction with Chinese based on interview data and field notes. Unfortunately, she had not made friends with Chinese during the year in China. This was due in part to her personality, school administration mode, Chinese attitudes towards Korean students, etc. However, her psychological adaption attitude was viewed as the primary barrier for her having less contact with Chinese.

Concerning Eve, she received a grant from the Chinese government monthly, which could be viewed as an important reason that she chose to study in China for one year. According to her, the fast developing economy in China made her feel that learning Chinese was a correct choice. Shanghai is an amazing metropolitan city with its internationalized plaza, restaurants and business center. Moreover, she was astonished by the beautiful city, Hangzhou, where the big event G20 had been held. However, since English is lingua franca in the world, English becomes an obligatory subject beginning in primary school in China. Language and culture are intertwined, which could hardly be separated (Stewart & Strathern, 2017). Therefore, the young generation in China has been affected by western culture exclusively. The findings showed that western culture boosted globally in a decade in China, which might make foreigners uncertain of the core content of Chinese traditional culture. It was likely that Eve considered it not necessary to make changes. Cohen and Shively (2007b) argue that learner's cultural identity had significant impact on language acquisition. The attributes of motivation, such as to what extent learners' native culture is preferred over the second one and what kind of learning attitudes they hold towards target language and culture, play an important role in L2 acquisition (Gardner & Lambert, 1959). As a result, Eve was not strongly motivated to delve into Chinese culture based on my observation and interview data. Although Eve had many Chinese nodding acquaintances on campus, she hadn't made any close Chinese friends during her year in China. Therefore, the findings show that instrumental motivations seemingly result in separation acculturation attitude, which seemingly hindered her pragmatic development.

As far as Amy is concerned, her parents passed away, so she had to struggle for her own future. According to the interview data, she found companies in Shanghai could offer better salary for her than in Russia. As a result, she attempted to get a job in China after graduation. Time has elapsed, she became more and more interested in Chinese culture, and she considered it important to make friends with Chinese for cultural acquisition. Moreover, if she wanted to settle down in China, she had to pick up both Chinese and its culture. As a result, she became dedicated to bond with Chinese both for linguistic growth and cultural acknowledgment. However, Amy also thought of maintaining her cultural identity based on interview data. Therefore, it was evident that Amy belongs to integrative motivation and integrative acculturation attitude.

Basedon above discussion of the findings, there are two points that we could make: (1) All of the participants were motivated to study in China mainly for its peaceful environment, fast-developing economy and well-funded education for international students. However, when they studied in China, their motivation turned out to change into various ways for personal and contextual factors, such as popularity of western culture in China, job-hunting in China after graduation; (2) it seems that the types of motivation had significant impact on the types of acculturation attitudes. Learners with instrumental motivation were not interested in contacting with native speakers in the host community (separation); learners with integrative motivation acquired language and culture by seeking opportunities of interaction with members of the host culture so as to delve into the new socio-cultural milieu (integration). The result confirms the model produced by Culhane (2004). In this current study, instrumental and integrative functioning levels were found, which proved Culhane's model empirically.

6. 4. 2   The interrelation between the model and social interaction

To comprehend target language implicatures learners need to be informed with the target cultural normsembedded in that language, which indicates that the pragmatic competence related to the knowledge of cultural conventions of target language (Rafieyan et al. , 2015). As stated in the last section, learners with an instrumental functioning level (instrumental motivation and separation attitude) don't consider it important to interact with native speakers, which is vital to acquire cultural aspects of the target language. In 2015, Rafieyan et al point out to what degree learner's acculturation attitudes towards target language and culture determined the level of pragmatic competence. Therefore, it might be safe to conclude that motivation and acculturation attitude have significant impact on pragmatic development in study abroad context.

In this present study, Amy with integrative functioning level developed her pragmatic competence most soundly among the three case participants. She developed her pragmalinguistic competence and sociopragmatic competence almost at the same time based on the analysis of quantitative and qualitative data. However, Joy and Eve with instrumental functioning level developed their pragmatic competence to some extent but unevenly. As is known, soiciopragmatic competence involving cultural norms and conventions requires learners to understand situational variables, such as power and social distance. Only through interaction with native speakers in the targeted community, learners can become familiar with the cultural aspects of the target language. Amy had strong desire to interact with Chinese and attempted to make friends with Chinese as much as possible, because she was strongly motivated to acquire cultural knowledge and was aware of the importance of cultural difference in language learning. However, Joy and Eve didn't take initiative to make friends with Chinese, or didn't consider it important to interact with Chinese. Both of them regarded classroom learning as an important way to acquire Chinese language, but they neglected the cultural knowledge of the target language, which played a significant role in pragmatic production and comprehension.

It was suggested that language learners should explore the culture of the target language through interaction with native speakers so as to develop their pragmatic competence (Rafieyan et al. , 2015). However, it seems that only learners in study abroad context were highly motivated to learn a foreign/second language and developed a positive acculturation attitude, they could accept the advice to interact with native speakers and delve in the target culture for pragmatic development.

6. 5   Routinized social activities

Socializing activities are regarded as the core of language socialization research. In 2002, Garrett and Baquedano-López claim that activities that take place in daily life are viewed as the core of language socialization research, which is rarely described explicitly but regarded as the highly productive aspects. As a result, focus was given to the socializing routines the three case participants were involved in their daily life in this study based on language socialization theory, which allowed me to penetrate the major patterns of activities that involving learners' Chinese learning and use of the language. Social activities in daily life functioned as important input for learners in target community. In this present study, concerning pragmatics, interaction stood out as the main activity that affected learners' pragmatic comprehension and acquisition, while other activities worked as supportive factors for pragmatic development.

6. 5. 1   The main role of social interaction

In 2001, Bardovi-Harlig and Bastos state that intensity and quality of interaction play a crucial role in conversation expressions produced by learners, which in turn enhances their L2 pragmatic competence. The results of this study show that intensity of interaction with native speakers in study aboard context had significant impact on learners' both pragmalinguistic and sociopragmatic development.

According to the data, Korean learner, Joy didn't interact with Chinese except for a short conversation with drivers or members of tourist groups during her trip around China. Furthermore, the topics of conversation involved were almost the same, such as cosmetic surgery and cosmetics. As far as was Amy concerned, she had established intimate relationships with many Chinese speakers, and contacted them on Wechat or face to face almost everyday. Since she worked as a part-time translator in her spare time, she discussed with her Chinese or Russian friends the usage of Chinese frequently. The topics in conversation involved academics, translation, asking for help, greetings, bonding, all promoted Amy's employment of pragmatic strategies approximating Chinese pragmatic norms. With regard to Eve, she had some nodding acquaintances on the campus. She greeted them in daily life from time to time, but seldom talked in-depth. Therefore, Eve made a big progress in her pragmalinguistic competence, but not in her sociopragmatic competence, which involves cultural conventions and norms in Chinese. Accordingly, it could be safe to conclude that both intensity and quality of interaction function as a decisive mediate tool for pragmatic improvement.

In conclusion, the intensity and quality of interaction played a primary role in developing learners' pragmalinguistic and sociopragmatic competence. L2 socialization believes that those who are more competent in target language and informed with cultural norms would help those who are less competent in language and unfamiliar with cultural conventions in target culture (Duff, 2011; Vygotsky, 1978). Furthermore, most socialization occurs implicitly, but not through participants' repeated practices of pragmatic strategies explicitly in targeted language community. Thus, socializing with various types of native speakers constantly could help learners acquire pragmatic knowledge.

6.5.2 The supportive role of other activities

These three cases took part in classroom learning and entertainment activities on electronic technology platform involving acquisition of Chinese. Those activities were categorized as a group for their indirect effect on pragmatic development.

Classroom learning provided with sufficient and correct language input for those learners. In 2002, Kasper and Rose suggest that there are two types of pragmatic learning in classroom: explicit pragmatic learning based on pedagogical teaching plan, and implicit pragmatic learning through use of the target language in the classroom. In this study, the first type of pragmatic learning had not taken place. The second type of learning would occur, but classroom alone cannot involve all the topics that occurred naturally in daily life (Taguchi, 2015). Furthermore, input of pragmatic routines, cultural facets and conventions were very limited in classroom. According to the interview data, Chinese teachers would give pragmatic feedback in classroom, which was inconsistent with previous studies (Barron, 2003) . However, three case participants all regarded classroom learning as an important aspect for their own pragmatic improvement. In addition, according to Vygotsky (1978), an individual's ability could be enhanced with the help of a more capable adult or more capable peers through taking part in collaboration activities. Therefore, the participants enhanced their pragmatic competence in instructional setting. In contrast, it was because the classroom learning had positive impact on their language proficiency, which indirectly promoted their pragmatic comprehension. Numerous studies had found that high proficiency language level produced better pragmatic competence (Bardovi-Harlig, 2009; Taguchi, 2011; Xu et al. , 2009) . Therefore, classroom learning did facilitate learners' pragmatic development to some extent.

Based on interview data, electronic technology tools served as a primary platform for learning pragmatics through entertainment activities. Learners made use of technology platform bonding, information searching, watching films, buying goods and etc. Taguchi (2015) argues that online activities have offered many opportunities for pragmatic learning because learners can establish relationship with the members of the target community. All the three participants reported that they communicated with Chinese native speakers through Wechat on mobile phones. Amy and Eve watched Chinese films frequently on laptop. Films consist of natural occurred conversation in the movies, could help learners acquire pragmatic strategies in complex situations. Since films provide with sufficient discourse-length and contextualized conversations, it can be regarded as an effective material to analyze speakers' pragmatic features of the language they use (Abrams, 2014). Moreover, Amy sent short messages on friend micro circle frequently, which enabled her to construct their thoughts in advance before making them public, thereby helping her acquire pragmatic strategies. More engagement in activities on technology platform had been made by Amy, thereby her pragmatic competence developed fastest among those three cases.

Other activities had offered some chances for learners to acquire target language and its culture, but played a secondary role in pragmatic development, because other activities affected learners' pragmatic improvement indirectly, while naturally occurred interaction promoted their pragmatic awareness and acquisition directly. In a word, activities mentioned above served as mediation means that mediated native speakers and learners. According to Frawley (1997), communication with teachers or peers could be regarded as other-regulated activities, which serves to connect individuals to the outside world and enable them to develop their potentials. In this study, learners were sojourners in China, who took advantage of this environment to take part in such activities, could achieve pragmatic development eventually.

6. 6　Contextual factors

Besides the factors mentioned above, contextual factors such as host members' attitudes and school culture played an important role in learners' pragmatic development. Furthermore, host members' attitudes would affect learners' acculturation attitudes through frequent interaction. And school culture might provide opportunities for learners to learn Chinese culture and conventions, and would also constrain learners' pragmatic development by its specific administration mode.

6. 6. 1　Host members' attitudes as a reflective mirror

English as a lingua franca in the process of globalization is an obligatory subject since primary school in China. Language is composed of a system of signs, which are intertwined with cultural value (Stewart & Strathern, 2017). According to Leppanen and Pahta (2012), English could be disruptive to the purity of the Finnish language and culture, since the popularity of English will destroy the cultural identity and integrity embedded in Finnish national language. Western culture associating with English has a significant impact on Chinese culture. It seemed that Chinese youngsters have become more westernized since they prefer KFC, steak or pizza to Chinese dumplings or baozi, based on the interview data. Apart from that, Chinese have a positive attitude towards foreigners, which has existed for quite a long time. Although it has received criticism from scholars and promoters of Chinese traditional culture, this kind of attitude was deeply rooted in Chinese people's mind. Some previous studies suggest that learners' interaction with members of the target language community is seemly to affect their attitudes towards the host members and the target language itself (Culhane, 2004). Therefore, Chinese people's attitudes towards international students would impact their perception of Chinese culture and their acculturation attitude, which worked as a reflective mirror.

In this current study, learners from various cultural backgrounds had different experience with Chinese native speakers. Eve and Amy felt that they were warmly welcomed, while Joy's experience in China was not so pleasing. Eve was French, but she could speak English fluently. Many Chinese had a strong desire to make friends with her, because they wanted to practice oral English. However, Eve didn't make close friends with Chinese. The results show that Eve seemingly attempted to maintain her cultural identity by sticking to her previous life style, because she felt that western culture was popular in China. Moreover, Chinese responded to Eve warmly, which made her feel comfortable being French. As she said that she felt like a celebrity in China, lots of Chinese took photos of them in the streets. The findings contrasted the argumentation put forward by Du (2015), who argued that learners seemed to be more open minded and less likely to maintain their own cultural identity, if host environment is pleasant and supportive to sojourners. The reason could be that the cultural community learners were born and raised in had strong impact on their motivational orientation and culture attitudes toward the target language, its culture, the members of the target community (Gardner, 1979; Gardner & Lambert, 1959). Eve was born and raised in western culture, which was prevalent in China. Thereby she remained the similar lifestyle and living habits in China. Thus, host members' attitudes towards learners' culture and language affected learners' motivation and acculturation attitudes to a great extent.

Amy was a Russian, and she had a high proficiency in English as well. She held instrumental motivation and acculturation attitudes at the beginning. Amy had received a warm welcome from Chinese during her year in China. She changed her attitudes towards Chinese and Chinese culture through interaction with Chinese people. She preferred to make friends with Chinese and acted like Chinese in many aspects. Amy was strongly motivated to integrate herself in Chinese community as she wanted to work and stay in China after graduation. However, according to the data, Amy developed much tighter bonds with Russian friends, as she still preferred to share her feelings and travel around with her Russian friends other than Chinese friends. Compared with Eve, Amy was more flexible in respect of acculturation attitudes, but her motivation and acculturation attitudes belong to integrative but not psychosocial functioning level (highest level) in terms of Intercultural Interaction model based on the analyzed data.

As for Joy, she was also welcomed, but she was annoyed by questions about cosmetic surgery in Korea. She sometimes refrained from communicating with Chinese. As a result, she didn't often interact with Chinese during her year in China. Therefore, host members' attitudes toward their own culture and towards learners played an important role in forming or changing learners' motivation and acculturation attitudes in study abroad context.

In short, the three case participants didn't have strong willingness to delve into Chinese culture, probably because Chinese culture was not the dominant culture in comparison to western culture. Moreover, the majority of Chinese attitudes toward international students affected international students' acculturation attitudes, which in turn had impact on their pragmatic development.

6.6.2   The school culture as a double-edged sword

The present study indicates that school culture in SISU was diverse for catering different requirements. Administration mode, textbook contents and students activities were found to be the most important factors that affected learners' pragmatic development.

According to interview data, international students were arranged in a separation area on the campus, which reduced the chance for the communication with Chinese students. Case participants suggested that school provide a free location to encourage interaction with native speakers. Numerous studies have been conducted to suggest that home stay could improve learner's pragmatic development during learners' sojourn in study abroad (Cohen & Shively, 2007; Hassall, 2013; Shively, 2015). Based on interview data with a teacher (working at SISU School of Chinese Studies and Exchange), the reasons led to such administration pattern in university could be as follows: (1) Chinese universities take more responsibility for students security. There are certain regulations for administration in the dormitories for Chinese students, which could not be accepted by foreigners. (2) International students would have very different life styles and hold total different values, which would cause conflicts, if they were arranged in one dormitory. Sociocultural patterns and values determined the manner of school administration. According to Erickson (1987, P32), "cultural difference is regarded as tracing lines of status, power, and political interest within and across institutional boundaries found in the total social unit." Such school educational administration would seemingly hinder learners' pragmatic development. Based on interview data, Joy was willing to live with some Chinese students, which could help her make some Chinese friends. Eve and Amy also found it a good way to communicate with Chinese daily through living together with Chinese students.

Activities organized for international students were quite diverse in SISU, such as speech competition, festival celebrations, visiting museums, trips to different cities and lectures on Chinese culture. Amy benefited from these activities a lot in her pragmatic improvement. Hymes (1972) regarded language as culturally grounded and contextualized human activities. Those activities increased her knowledge of Chinese culture through interaction with Chinese or observing daily life habits. However, without much contact with Chinese, Joy considered the textbook contents as the major input for acquisition of Chinese. However, the out-of-date pragmatic formulae in the book prevented her from making requests in a native-like way. Joy was dependent on language program, and expected to get a language partner through officially organized programs, however there was no such language program to meet her needs. Eve was individualistic, thereby she didn't care about students' activities organized. Therefore, school culture in this current study worked as double-edged sword in learners' pragmatic development.

6.7　A model for pragmatic development

Based on the discussion in this chapter, the tentative conceptual framework in chapter two was revised as shown in Figure 9. Development of pragmatic competence comprises two aspects: development of pragmalinguistic competence and sociopragmatic competence. In order to examine the development trajectories, the use of semantic formulae for openers, HA, IM and EM in requests had been illustrated and analyzed. Cultural variation was a significant variable at the beginning of immersion program regarding pragmatic competence, but which was not the only crucial variable in the process of pragmatic development.

As displayed in Figure 9, international students' pragmatic development in SISU is related to cultural background, motivation and acculturation attitudes, social activities and the contextual factors. Learners' language and cultural background determined their initial stage of sociopragmatic competence and affected the changes of perception of politeness, cultural conventions and norms. Motivation & acculturation attitudes worked as a psychological engine that determined learners' socializing patterns and behaviors. Although personality could not be changed, motivation and acculturation attitudes should be directed towards an ideal condition through promotion of Chinese traditional culture worldwide and construction of more pleasant learning context.

Contextual factors such as host members' attitudes and school culture such as administration mode, textbook content and activities would affect pragmatic development implicitly and explicitly. Chinese attitudes towards international students affected learners' acculturation attitudes. Therefore, the cultivation of admiration of our own traditional Chinese culture among the young generation would help them form proper attitudes towards Chinese and western culture, which could in turn affect the perception of Chinese culture by foreigners. School administration determined by sociocultural patterns, political facets, could find a middle place to create more pleasant environment for catering international students. Moreover, learners should be aware of the out-of-date pragmatic strategies in conversations or dialogues illustrated in textbooks. Activities such as classroom learning, entertainment activities on electronic technology platforms, travelling and social interactions determined the quality and quantity of the pragmatic knowledge learners could acquire. Social interaction was crucial to develop both pragmalinguistic and sociopragmatic competence thoroughly. Activities on technology platforms were integrated into learners' life, because nobody could live without them in modern society. Other activities also involving interactions with native speakers or more competent learners functioned as scaffolding, which helped learners develop their pragmatic competence. The framework could also be applied to other studies concerning L2 pragmatic development.

It is strongly suggested that international students' motivation and acculturation attitudes shaped by their cultural background and contextual factors, which associated with sociocultural patterns, ideology, values people hold and the process of globalization, seemingly determine the quality and intensity of the interactions they engage in, which would in turn affect their pragmalinguistic and sociopragmatic development.

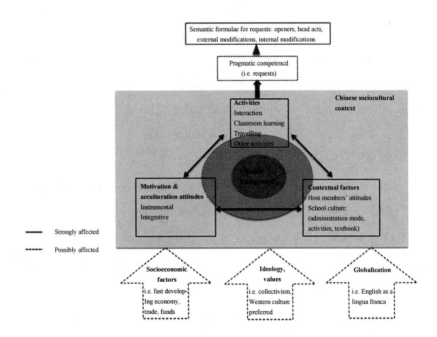

Figure 9　A model for international students' pragmatic development in SISU

6. 8 Summary

This chapter generalizes and discusses the major findings for the three research questions, based on which, cultural variations of the features ofpragmatic strategies and pragmatic development trajectories, and factors had been discussed. On the basis of the discussion, a theoretical model was constructed, which could be applied to study the dynamic process of L2 learners' pragmatic development. In the next chapter, the significance of the study, contributions, potential limitations and implications are discussed. At last, I would point out the directions of future research.

Chapter 7

Conclusions and Implications

7.1 Introduction

This chapter briefly recapitulates the findings for the three research questions, and discusses the contributions of this research to the existing literature concerning the field of interlanguage pragmatics. Limitations of the study are reviewed, including participants' selection, methodological weakness and other limitations. Pedagogical and other implications are discussed according to the findings. Finally, the directions of future research are proposed.

7.2 Major findings of the research

This section reviewed and recapitulated the answers to the three research questions in light of DCT data, interview data and field notes. This study employed requests speech act to address the problems concerning pragmatic competence based on previous studies (Blum-Kulka & House, 1989; Bruner et al., 1982). The study aims to find out the difference of pragmatic development trajectories among learners from various cultures so as to get pedagogical implications. Although international students were all at the same proficiency level, their pragmatic knowledge in a natural setting differed considerably. The semantic formulae they preferred in requests made in Chinese differed from Chinese speakers, and carried their own cultural characteristics. Learners from various cultural backgrounds developed pragmatic competence in different ways. Factors had been explored to extend the understanding the learners' acquisition of pragmatic knowledge and pragmatic development.

7. 2. 1   Research question 1: What are the features of pragmatic strategies in requests among Korean, French and Russian students in SISU?

DCT questionnaires were completed and analyzed to investigate the pragmatic features of Chinese speakers first. Generally speaking, Chinese were indirect in request making action, and regarded interpersonal relationships as an important capital in social interactions. Power affected the use of formulae systematically and significantly, and social distance primarily had impact on the use of formulae among interlocutors with equal status. Based on the DCT data, Chinese native speakers tended to use "title", "greeting" and "name" as formulae for openers, preferred indirect strategies by employing "query preparatory", favored using reasons or justifications before making requests, and were prone to employ "downtoner" as formulae for IM between friends or intimate relations. Moreover, although some formulae, such as "kinship terminology", "popular alerters", "politeness word" and "modal particle", were not extensively used, they were characterized as special terms with Chinese characteristics in comparison to similar research in requests conducted internationally (Blum-Kulka & Olshtain, 1984; Hong, 2009; Hong, 1996; Koc, 2011; Lee, 2005; Li, 2000; Lin, 2009; Rue & Zhang, 2008).

According to the analysis of DCT data, types of formulae and strategies Korean subjects employed were the most similar to that of Chinese native speakers in terms of frequency calculation and log-likelihood examination. Situational variables such as power and social distance were embedded in the scenarios designed in DCT to examine learners' understanding of the sociocultural aspects of interactions in Chinese. Korean subjects had the similar understanding of the situational variables based on the quantitative analysis of the data. However, some types of formulae preferred by Korean subjects, such as "attention-getter" to alter hearers' attention, "politeness marker" and "duplication", differed from that of Chinese.

Russian subjects tended to be more direct than Chinese subjects fortheir strong tendency for applying "performative" as head act. Moreover, power and social distance worked equally on the use of formulae in requests made by Russian subjects, which was quite different from that of Chinese or Korean counterparts. As for the frequent formulae used by Russian subjects, they preferred to use "kinship terminology", which was identified as terms with Chinese characteristics. However, the formulae for "kinship terminology", such as "xiongdi" (兄弟, brother), "meimei" (妹妹, sister) and "pengyou" (朋友, friend) they used in this survey, were seldom used by Chinese native speakers. They tended to use "politeness marker" such as "qing" (请, please) to show respect to the hearers, which was found in all learners' data in this survey regardless of their cultural backgrounds.

As for French subjects, they were the most indirect in making requests among those three cultural groups. It confirms the previous studies conducted by Mulken (1996) who argued that French people favored to apply "query preparatory" strategy as head act in requests. Power had not been effective in making requests by French subjects. As for the types of formulae, they tended to choose "greeting" and "attention-getter" for openers, "query preparatory (1)" for head acts, "politeness marker" for internal modifications. Moreover, French subjects preferred to use "honorific", which could be explained by the difference between "tu" and "vous" in French (Ismail et al., 2014).

In short, the descriptions of the features of pragmatic strategies in this survey supported the argumentation that Chinese and Koreans tend to be more hierarchical and collectivistic, while French and Russians were more egalitarian and individualistic.

7.2.2   Research Question 2: In what way do their pragmatic strategies of requests change?

Many studies have been conducted to investigate L2 learners' pragmatic development in studying abroad context (Cohen & Shively, 2007; Hassall, 2013; Ishida, 2005; Taguchi, 2008; Xu et al. , 2009). However, pragmatic development of L2 learners from various cultural backgrounds in studying abroad context had not been explored yet. This study selected learners in terms of the number of students from a specific country in SISU and cultural distance between the learner's own culture and Chinese culture. Korean subjects produced the most similar formulae for requests to that of Chinese speakers, but their development speed was unpredictable based on this study.

For the limitation of time and resources, after reading and examining of the data collected, Joy (Korean), Amy (Russian) and Eve (French) were chosen based on their features of pragmatic strategies, which were representation of Korean, Russian and French cultures respectively, and allowed for the characteristics of cultural difference of pragmatic development longitudinally to be explored. The three learners' pragmatic development was analyzed and discussed in terms of pragmalinguistic and sociopragmatic competence.

As far as the development of pragmalinguistic competence is concerned, DCT questionnaires had been completed at one-month intervals. According to both quantitative and qualitative analysis of the data collected, the Russian participant developed fastest in comparison to other two, followed by the French learner. Surprisingly, Korean subject who tended to be the most similar to Chinese native speaker in the first DCT test, developed slowest by comparing the data horizontally and vertically.

With regard to the development of sociopragmatic competence, data from the DCT were analyzed qualitatively. The Korean subject's perception of power and social distance remained stable and was similar to that of Chinese subjects. However, the development of Korean subject's pragmalinguistic competence lagged behind that of her sociopragmatic competence.

The Russian subject changed her perception of power in various situations. She simulated Chinese native speakers' or friends' use of language, and then she was aware of the different perceptions of power and social distance in Russia and China. Moreover, both of her pragmalinguistic and sociopragmatic competence developed very well and almost at the same time.

The French subject had not changed much her perception of power and social distance in Chinese. Although it seemed that she understood the power and social distance in a specific situation from her native-like use of formulae, her perception of the situational variables didn't change much based on her interview data. Her pragmalinguistic competence was improved faster than her sociopragmatic competence.

In short, the pragmatic development trajectories of those learners from different cultures differed from each other considerably. The findings of the study showed that the development of pragmalinguistic and sociopragmatic competence was not always at the same time.

7.2.3 Research Question 3: What factors affect the changes of their pragmatic strategies?

In response to this research question, the same three focal case participants were selected base on their performance in DCT and pilot interview data. The main factors had been determined based on ethnographic interview data, field notes and memos. Four main categories had been identified as follows: cultural background, motivation & acculturation attitude, social activities and contextual factors. Motivation and acculturation attitude had significant impact on the three participants' pragmatic development. With view to activities, social interaction, classroom learning and entertainment activities on electronic technology platforms served as the major activities that shed light on their pragmatic changes. Concerning contextual factors, host members' attitudes played a crucial role. Although those subcategories had been illustrated as common among the three cases, they had different impact on their pragmatic development.

As for Joy, a Korean girl, her perception of politeness was similar to that of Chinese. As a result, her sociopragmatic competence was native-like from the beginning to the end. Quiet and submissive as she was, Joy was a typical and traditional Korean girl who depended on others for the linguistic growth. She thought that textbook content and language programs had significant impact on her pragmatic development. Moreover, although she didn't make many Chinese friends, she was fond of travelling around China, which helped her to some extent make improvements.

Amy is a Russian girl, who was independent, extroverted, helpful and strong-willed. She was capable of solving problems, which helped her make great progress in learning Chinese. Russian culture is quite different from Chinese culture, and those two languages belong to two different big families, which hindered her from making smooth progress in pragmatic development. However, her pragmatic competence developed the quickest among the three participants. This might be a result of her frequent interactions with Chinese friends and her strong motivation to integrate herself in Chinese community.

Eve, as a European girl, had experienced language difficulty in China. She avoided speaking Chinese in daily life and maintained her French identity. She also had lots of Chinese nodding acquaintances for her cultural background and English proficiency. But she didn't like to make close friends with Chinese, which hindered her from understanding Chinese conventions and sociocultural elements. As a result, her sociopragmatic competence improved slower than her pragmalinguistic competence.

7.3 Contributions of the research

The findings of this current study have made a significant contributions to the existing literature mainly from four aspects. First, based on the literature review documenting pragmatic strategies of L2 learners' requests in diverse languages, this study, in an effort to investigate pragmatic strategies of requests made in Chinese by L2 learners' with various cultural backgrounds, adopted DCT with 12 scenarios. The findings of the study indicated that learners from a specific culture made requests in a specific way and had the same problems or misuses of semantic formulae in requests performance made in Chinese. Furthermore, the paradigm of this study shift from the static to the dynamic speech act theory as so to theorize the pragmatic development of learners' speech acts of request. The present study adopting DCT questionnaire intermittently to examine learners' changes of pragmatic strategies in requests along with interview data, focused on the development trajectories of learners. Moreover, most of the speech act studies adopted quantitative measures with a focus on the changes of learners' requesting strategies rather than explored in depth the reasons behind it. This study not only investigated the development trajectories of learners with various cultural backgrounds on the basis of both quantitative and qualitative method, but also explored the reasons causing the different trajectories of learner's pragmatic development in light of qualitative data from ethnographic case studies. In this sense, this study contributed to the existing literature on interlanguage pragmatic development by employing a longitudinal case study.

Second, this study supported the argument that study abroad context had played a positive role in L2 pragmatic development. In light of literature review, scholars had not achieved agreement on this issue (Freed, 1990; Matsumura, 2001; Khorshidi, 2013). Based on the data collected in this study, DCT was conducted every month to test learners' changes of request strategies. Generally speaking, all the participants selected in this study changed their pragmatic strategies towards more native like. Therefore, this present study added to the literature to reinforce the advantages of study abroad programs.

Third, the results of this research show that the development of L2 learners' pragmalinguistic competence and sociopragmatic competence was not at the same speed, and cultural variation was not the vital element in pragmatic development. In light of literature review, pragmatic competence is divided into two aspects: pragmalinguistic and sociopragmatic competence (leech, 1983; Thomas, 1983). The development of L2 learners pragmalinguistic competence could both precede or after their sociopragmatic competence (Chang, 2011). Those participants developed their pragmalinguistic and sociopragmatic competence at different speeds. Moreover, short cultural distance had a positive impact on the use of pragmatic strategies in requests at the beginning but did not affect the development inn the long term. It was because the Korean participant made requests like that of Chinese but developed slowly in respect of pragmalinguistic competence; while the Russian participant distinguished her performance in requests with the progression of the research and developed her pragmalinguistic and sociopragmatic competence almost at the same speed.

Fourth, drawing on the empirical findings of the three case participants, the study dug out the complex factors that might hinder or aid learners' pragmatic development in Chinese context. There was not one certain reason that caused the outcomes of pragmatic development, but complicated factors and socializing activities that learners took part in led to unpredicted results. Hence, this investigation added knowledge to the literature of pragmatic development in the interlanguage pragmatics, which would be the only study so far that explored both pragmatic development and the reasons behind it in Chinese context. At last, this investigation has proposed a synthetic theoretical model of L2 pragmatic development in Chinese context, which may benefit learners' linguistic improvement and acquisitions of pragmatic knowledge among international students in China.

7. 4 Limitations of the research

Despite the current methodological design was based on the review of prevalent research methods in the field of interlanguage pragmatics such as Discourse Completion Test (DCT), role-plays, and naturally recording data in certain speech acts (Cohen & Shively, 2007; Hong, 2005; Khorshidi, 2013), the present study is not without limitations.

First, Discourse Completion Task (DCT), a written form, was attacked for its limitations mentioned in Chapter three. As Wolfson (1989) pointed out DCT was targeted to get the data about what learners wanted to say instead of capture their actual language used in real context. Moreover, the same scenarios were used to test learners' changes of pragmatic strategies four times. Negative influence of repetition of test questions would have impact on the accuracy of the results.

Second, in response to the second research question, only three participants were investigated longitudinally. Although the three participants were selected in terms of their performance at the first DCT test and their representing three different cultures, the small number of participants could not generalize the results. Moreover, in order to examine their sociopragmatic competence, three of them were chosen to explore qualitatively. However, the limited number of participants could not reveal the complicated, dynamic and changing factors that affected learners' pragmatic development.

Third, the present study was longitudinal in order to explore the development process of learners' pragmatic development. As a matter of fact, the data collection lasted eight months. This length of time was not long enough to explore such a complicated phenomenon.

Fourth, the interpretation of the data might suffer from subjectivity. The analysis of the qualitative data was mainly based on the researcher's subjective interpretation of the interview data, field notes and memos. Although participants confirmed the transcriptions of the interview data, and the interpretation of the data was double checked by an expert of qualitative research and my supervisor, some misinterpretation of the data could still exist.

Finally, the analysis of the changes of requeststrategies was most frequently used formulae rather than all the formulae involved in this research. Although those types of formulae were typical, the limited number of formulae was far from enough. Therefore, the investigation of the pragmatic development was explorative, and results of the examination were representative in some sense.

7.5 Implications

The findings of this current study have quite a lot of pedagogical implications for international students and Chinese teachers in terms of both classroom pedagogy and curriculum design, and implications for administrations of international students. This section discusses these implications in light of the findings on learners' pragmatic strategies in requests, development of pragmatic competence, and factors that affected pragmatic development in general.

First, teachers need to be aware of the different pragmatic features of international students from various cultural backgrounds. As mentioned in this study, learners from France, Russia and Korea had a strong tendency for certain types of semantic formulae for openers, HA, IM, and EM. Therefore, teachers need to guide and correct learners' misuse of such formulae in requests, and keep an eye on the input of pragmatic knowledge and cultural conventions so as to enhance learners' overall pragmatic competence. Moreover, the findings of this study show that learners' development of pragmalinguistic competence precedes that of sociopragmatic competence or verse visa. Teachers should not neglect Asian students' development of pragmalinguistic competence for shorter cultural distance between Asian learners' culture and Chinese culture, and pay more attention to European students' sociopragmatic competence by inducing pedagogical content of the effects of situational variables on the choices of the formulae for requests, aside from grammatical knowledge. Some types of semantic formulae with Chinese characteristics, such as "politeness words" and "modal particle" for EM, "kinship terminology" for openers, should be introduced to learners explicitly in classroom. In 2007, Uso-Juan argues that language used in a natural setting is far more sophisticated than simply conveying the meaning by applying expressions from textbook. Therefore, teaching practice should focus on sociocultural conventions, norms and pragmatic rules of the targeted language and expose learners to authentic input in the classroom. Instant feedback for learners' pragmatic mistakes is needed in the classroom as well.

Second, L2 learners should be aware of the pragmatic rules in the target language, under which the cultural conventions regulate. Learners with a mature system of pragmatic knowledge in their native language could easily fall back on their pragmatic knowledge of L1 in learning and use of L2 (Li, 2009). However, individual learners may get rid of the L1 transfer by being aware of the transfer through constant exposure to authentic conversations in everyday life. The results of this study could also make learners with various cultural backgrounds be aware of the misuse of formulae or transfer in requests. One more important note, L2 learners should not think that sojourn in study abroad context could lead to pragmatic development naturally. In this study, three case participants developed their pragmatic competence at different speeds. Socializing with Chinese native speakers would be considered as the most important factor that facilitated learners' pragmatic development, as Kasper (2001, P231) states that "learners' exposure to rich and contextually appropriate input is a prerequisite for the development of their pragmatic competence in the target language". Furthermore, learners should not only rote memorize the pragmatic routines and frequent formulae that they acquired in communications, but also understand the situational variables underlying the context. It is proposed that learners should form positive acculturation attitudes towards the target language and its community, and make most use of the "study abroad context" so as to enhance their pragmalinguistic and sociopragmatic competence at the same time.

Third, Universities should make efforts to provide more support. The findings of the study indicated that socializing with native speakers played a crucial role in informing learners' of pragmatic knowledge and use of formulae in certain kind of situations. However, Joy reported that she could not find Chinese friends and suggested officially organized language programs or activities, which advocated both Chinese native speakers and international students to take part in. In many universities, language centers was established to provide services for international students. International students could apply for a native language partner for psychological and academic needs. Moreover, the participants reported that cultural elements were not often integrated in the classroom. As a result, it is suggested that universities should organize activities to spread Chinese culture.

Last but not least, pragmatic competence is related to cultural norms and conventions. Improvement of international students' pragmatic competence should depend on their knowledge of Chinese culture. The findings of this study show that international students were not highly motivated to delve into Chinese culture for personal and contextual reasons. Although a great number of funds have been devoted to education for international students, they were not highly motivated to learn Chinese. Therefore, policies should be made to change this phenomenon. Chinese traditional culture should be advocated among young generations in China. When Chinese are fully informed with our own traditional culture, we could spread our culture to international students. On the one hand, the promotion of Chinese culture could reinforce Chinese national identity, and protect our own culture in the process of globalization. On the other hand, international students would change their perception towards Chinese culture by our own attitudes toward it.

The implications discussed above are intended to make contributions to pragmatic teaching, studying in abroad context and school administrations for international students. Developing pragmatic competence is of great importance to all language learners in smooth L2 conversations involving complicated various speech acts such as requests.

7. 6 Suggestions for future research

The scope of the present study was to investigate the pragmatic features of learners from Korea, Russia and France, learners' pragmatic development and the possible factors affecting learners' pragmatic development. The research scope is still limited and could not address other issues that might be relevant to the topic. Thereby, this study may illustrate a number of possible directions for future research.

First, compared to remedy the methodological limitations in this present study, future research should target to collect natural occurring data of speech acts. Future research might apply authentic data, corpus data or role play data to validate the DCT elicited data so as to reinforce the reliability of the study. Moreover, one university was chosen as a case study, the future research would select participants from various universities from south to north in China. The number of participants was limited in respect of the investigation of learners' pragmatic development. Hence, another direction of future research would increase the number of the participants to generalize the results and establish the theoretical model systematically. As a longitudinal empirical study to examine learners' pragmatic development, eight month is far from enough. Therefore, future research would lengthen the time of data collection to enhance the validity of the study.

Second, learners were chosen primarily from Korea, Russia and France in this present study. Relations between Cultural variations and the development of pragmatic competence could not be drawn comprehensively. Thereby, future research would encompass learners from more types of cultural backgrounds, which could provide sufficient knowledge for the teaching of pragmatics in the classroom, and implications for L2 learners.

At last, this study can be duplicated to examine whether the same results can be captured in other languages, in other speech acts such as apologies, gratitude, compliments and so on. To what extent that the proposed theoretical model would work in such duplicated study, it would help retest the correctness of the results of this current study.

7.7   Concluding remarks

This present study supports the argument that the SA context has positive correlation with L2 learners' pragmatic development. Requests in Chinese produced by learners from various cultural backgrounds had their own characteristics and varied from culture to culture. It seemed that the pragmatic strategies made by Korean subjects was similar to that of Chinese due to shorter cultural distance, Russian and French subjects had more types of formulae differing from that of Chinese than their Korean counterparts. However, the Russian subject improved her use of linguistic form quickest and changed her perception of situational variables towards that of Chinese through the course of this research, thereby the Russian participant distinguished herself in terms of development of pragmatic competence. The results of the current study also show that the development of pragmalinguistic competence and the development of sociopragmatic competence are not always at the same time. It is strongly suggested that international students' motivation and acculturation attitudes shaped by their cultural background and contextual factors, seemingly determined the quality and intensity of interaction they engaged in, which would in turn affect their pragmalinguistic and sociopragmatic development.

Reference

Abolfathiasl, H. , & Abdullah, A. N. (2015). Pragmatic consciousness-raising activities and EFL learners' speech act performance of ' making suggestions' . *Journal of Language Teaching and Research*, 6 (2), 333.

Abrams, Z. I. (2014). Using film to provide a context for teaching L2 pragmatics. *System*, 46, 55 – 64.

Al-Gahtani, S. , & Roever, C. (2015). The development of requests by L2 learners of standard Arabic: a longitudinal and cross-sectional study. *Foreign Language Annals*, 48 (4), 570 – 583.

Alcón Soler, E. (2005). Does instruction work for learning pragmatics in the EFL context? *System*, 33 (3), 417 – 435.

Alcón-Soler, E. (2015). Pragmatic learning and study abroad: Effects of instruction and length of stay. *System*, 48, 62 – 74.

Alemi, M. , Eslami, Z. R. , & Rezanejad, A. (2014). Rating EFL learners' interlanguage pragmatic competence by non-native English speaking teachers. *Procedia-Social and Behavioral Sciences*, 98, 171 – 174.

Allami, H. , & Naeimi, A. (2011). A cross-linguistic study of refusals: An analysis of pragmatic competence development in Iranian EFL learners. *Journal of Pragmatics*, 43 (1), 385 – 406.

Austin, J. L. (1962). *How to do things with words?* Oxford: The Claredon Press.

Bardovi-Harlig, K. (1999). Exploring the interlanguage of interlanguage pragmatics: A research agenda for acquisitional pragmatics. *Language Learning*, 49 (4), 677 –713.

Bardovi-Harlig, K. (2009). Conventional expressions as a pragmalinguistic resource: Recognition and production of conventional expressions in L2 pragmatics. *Language Learning*, 59 (4), 755 –795.

Bardovi-Harlig, K. (2013). Developing L2 Pragmatics. *Language Learning*, 63, 68 –86.

Bardovi-Harlig, K., & Bastos, M. T. (2011). Proficiency, length of stay, and intensity of interaction and the acquisition of conventional expressions in L2 pragmatics. *Intercultural Pragmatics*, 8 (3), 347 –384.

Bardovi-Harlig, K., & Griffin, R. (2005). L2 pragmatic awareness: Evidence from the ESL classroom. *System*, 33 (3), 401 –415.

Bardovi-Harlig, K., & Vellenga, H. E. (2012). The effect of instruction on conventional expressions in L2 pragmatics. *System*, 40 (1), 77 –89.

Baron, J., & Celaya, M. L. (2010). Developing pragmatic fluency in an EFL context. *EUROSLA Yearbook* (10).

Barron, A. (2003). *Acquisition in interlangauge pragamtics: Learning how to do things with words in a study abroad context.* Amsterdam/Philadelphia: John Benjamins.

Barry, D. (2001). Development of a new scale for measuring acculturation: The East Asian Acculturaion Measure (EAAM). *Journal of Immigrant Health*, 3 (4), 193 –197.

Bataller, R. (2010). Making a request for a service in Spanish: Pragmatic development in the study abroad setting. *SPRING*, 43 (1).

Bayley, R., & Schecter, S. (Eds.). (2003). *Language Socialization in Bilingual and Multilingual Societies.* Clevedon, UK: Multilingual Matters.

Beebe, L., & Takahashi, T. (1989). *Do you have a bag?: Social status and partterned variation in second language acquisation.* Clevedon: Multilingual Matters.

Beebe, L. M. , Takahashi, T. , & Uliss-weltz, J. (Eds.). (1990). *Pragmtic transfer in ESL resufals.* New York: Newbury House.

Beebe, L. T. , Takahashi, S. , & Weltz, U. (Eds.). (1990). *Pragmatic transfer in ESL refusals* Newbury House: Bandrege MA.

Bella, S. (2011). Mitigation and politeness in Greek invitation refusals: Effects of length of residence in the target community and intensity of interaction on non-native speakers' performance. *Journal of Pragmatics*, 43 (6), 1718 – 1740.

Berry, J. W. (1986). The acculturation process and refugee behavior. *Contest: Southeast Asians in California*, 10 (75), 25 – 37.

Berry, J. W. , Kim, U. , & Boski, P. (Eds.). (1987). *Psychological acculturation of immigrant.* Newbury Park: Sage.

Blum-Kulka, S. (1997). *Dinner Talk.* Mahwah, NJ: Erlbaum.

Blum-Kulka, S. , & House, J. (1989). *Cross-cultural pragmatics: Requests and Apologies.* Norwood, N. J. : Alex.

Blum-Kulka, S. , & Olshtain, E. (1984). Requests and apologies: A cross-cultural study of speech act realization patterns (CCSARP) . *Applied Linguistics.*

Blum-Kulka, S. , Shoshana, Olshtain, & Elite. (1989). *Investigating Cross-cultural Pragmatics: an Introductory Overview.* Norwood: Ablex.

Bodycott, P. , & Walker, A. (2000). Teaching abroad: Lessons learned about inter-cultural understanding for teachers in higher education. *Teaching in Higher Education*, 5 (1), 79 – 94.

Brown, H. D. (1994). *Principles of Language Learning and Teaching.* NJ: Prentice Hall Regents.

Brown, P. , & Levinson, S. (1978). *Universals in Language Usage: Politeness*

Phenomena. Cambridge: Cambridge University Press.

Brown, P. , & Levinson, S. C. (1987). *Politeness: Some Universals in Language Usage.* Cambridge: Cambridge University Press.

Brown, R. , & Gilman, A. (1972). Pronouns of power and solidarity. In P. Gigliogli (Eds.), *Language and social context.* Harmondsworth: Penguin.

Bruner, J. , Roy, C. , & Ratner, N. (1982). *The Beginnings of Request.* New York: Garden Press.

Bu, J. (2010). Study of pragmatic transfer in persuasion strategies by Chinese learners of English. *The Southeast Asian Journal of English Language Studies,* 16 (93 – 114).

Bu, J. (2011). A study of pragmatic transfer in suggestion strategies by Chinese learners of English. *Studies in Literature and Language,* 3 (2), 28 – 36.

Byon, A. S. (2004). Sociopragmatic analysis of Korean requests: Pedagogical settings. *Journal of Pragmatics,* 36 (9), 1673 – 1704.

Chang, Y. -F. (2011). Interlanguage pragmatic development: The relation between pragmalinguistic competence and sociopragmatic competence. *Language Sciences,* 33 (5), 786 – 798.

Chomsky, N (1980). *Rules and Representations.* New York: Columbia University Press.

Cohen, A. D. (2008). Teaching and assessing L2 pragmatics: What can we expect from learners? *Language Teaching,* 41 (02).

Cohen, L. Manion, L. & Morrison, K. (2011). *Research Methods in Education* (7ᵗʰ ed.). New York: Routledge, 289.

Cohen, A. D. , & Shively, R. L. (2007). Acquisition of requests and apologies in Spanish and French: Impact of study abroad and strategy-building intervention. *The Modern Language Journal* (91).

Coulmas, F. (Ed.). (1981). Poison to your soul. In F. Columas (Eds.),

Thanks and apologies contrastively viewed. The Hague: Mouton.

Creswell, & Plano Clark, V. (2007) . *Designing and Conducting Mixed Methods Research.* Thousand Oaks: Sage.

Creswell, J. (1998). *Qualitative Inquiry and Research Design: Choosing among Five Traditions.* Thousand Oak: CA: Sage.

Crystal, D. (1985) . *A Dictionary of Linguistics and Phonetics.* Oxford: Blackwell.

Crystal, D. (1997). *Cambridge Encyclopedia of the English Language.* New York: Cambridge University Press.

Culhane, S. F. (2001) . Assessing Intercultural Competence in SLA. *Polyglossia* (4), 40 – 52.

Culhane, S. F. (2004) . An intercultural interaction model: Acculturation attitudes in second language acquisition. *Electronic Journal of Foreign Language Teaching*, 1 (1), 50 – 61.

Curl, T. , & Drew, P. (2008). Contingency and action: A comparison of two forms of requesting. *Research on Language and Social Interaction*, 41 (2), 129 – 153.

De Bot, K. , Lowie, W. , & Verspoor, M. (2007). A dynamic systems theory approach to second language acquisition. *Bilingualism: Language and Cognition*, 10 (01), 7.

DeCapua, A. D. (1998) . *Complaints: A comparison between German and English.* Concordia College Dissertation.

Dogancay-Aktuna, S. , & Kamisli, S. (1992) . Pragmatic transfer in interlanguage development: A case study of advanced EFL learners. Paper presented at the National Linguistics, Turkey.

Du, H. (2015) . American college students studying abroad in China: Language, identity, and self-presentation. *Foreign Language Annals*, 48 (2), 250 – 266.

Duff. (2007). Second language socialization as sociocultural theory: Insights and issues. *Language Teaching*, 40, 309 – 319.

Duff, P. A. (2003). New directions in second language socialization research. *Korean Journal of English Language and Linguistics* (3), 309 – 339.

Duff, P. A. (2008). *Case Study Research in Applied Linguistics*. New York: Lawrence Erlbaum Associates.

Duff, P. A. (2011). Second language socialization. In A. Duranti, E. Ochs & B. B. Schieffelin (eds.), *The Handbook of Language socialization*. United Kingdom: Blackwell.

Duff, P. A., & Talmay, S. (2011). *Language Socialization Aprroaches to Second Language Acquistion: Social, Cultural, and Linguistic Development in Additional Languages*. London: Routledge.

Duranti, A., Ochs, E., & Schieffelin, B. B. (2012). *The Handbook of Language Socialization*. United Kingdom: Wiley-Blackwell.

Economidou-Kogetsidis, M. (2008). Internal and external mitigation in interlanguage request production: The case of Greek learners of English. *Journal of Politeness Research. Language, Behaviour, Culture*, 4 (1).

Economidou-Kogetsidis, M. (2010). Cross-cultural and situational variation in requesting behaviour: Perceptions of social situations and strategic usage of request patterns. *Journal of Pragmatics*, 42 (8), 2262 – 2281.

Erickson, F. (1987). Conceptions of school culture: an overview. *Educational Administration Quarterly*, 23 (4).

Evans, M., Alano, C., & Wong, J. (2001). Does a short language course in an immersion setting help teachers to gain in communicative competence? In P. Bodycott & V. Crew (Eds.), *Language and cultural immersion: Perspectives on short term study and residence abroad*. HongKong: The Hong Kong Institute of Education.

Eve, A. S. , & Josep, G. P. (2010). The effect of instruction on learners' pragmatic awareness. *International Journal of English Studies*.

Fang, B. & Wu, Y. (2016). On changing trends of China's foreign students of higher education—an analysis of statistic data of the past 15 years. *Journal of Higher Eduction*, 2, 20.

Farashaiyan, A. , Tan, K. H. , & Subakir, M. (2014). An investigation of Iranian instructors' methods and techniques in teaching interlanguage pragmatics. *Procedia-Social and Behavioral Sciences*, 118, 61 – 67.

Felix-Brasdefer, J. (2004). Interlanguage refusals: Linguistic politeness and length of residence in the target community. *Language Learning*, 54 (4), 687 – 653.

Félix-Brasdefer, J. C. , & Hasler-Barker, M. (2015). Complimenting in Spanish in a short-term study abroad context. *System*, 48, 75 – 85.

Franch, P. B. (1998). On pragmatic transfer. *Studies in English Language and Linguistics*, 1 – 16.

Fraser, B. (1983). The domain of pragmatics. In J. C. Richards & R. W. Schmidt (Eds.), *Language and communication*. New York: Longman.

Frawley, W. (1997). *Vygotsky and Cognitive Science: Language and the Unification of the Social and Computational Mind*. Cambridge, MA: Harvard University Press.

Freed, B. F. (Ed.). (1990). Language learning in a study abroad context: the effects of interactive and non-interactive out-of-class contact on grammatical achievement and oral proficency. In J. Alatis (Eds.), *Language teaching and language acquisition: the interdependence of theory, practice and research*. Washington, DC: Georgetown University Press.

Fukushima, S. (2000). *Requests and Culture: Politeness in British English and Japanese*. Berlin: Peter Lang.

Gao, H. (1999). Features of request strategies in Chinese. *Working Papers*

(47), 73 – 86.

Gardner, R. C. (1979). Social psychological aspects of second language acquisition. In H. Giles & St. Clair (Eds.), *Language and social psychology*. Oxford: Blackwell Press.

Gardner, R. C., & Lambert, W. (1959). Motivational variables in second language acquisition. *Canadian Journal of Psycology*, 13, 266 – 272.

Garrett, P. B., & Baquedano-López, P. (2002). Language socialization: Reproduction and continuity, transformation and change. *Annual Review of Anthropology*, 31 (1), 339 – 361.

Ghanbari, H., Gowhary, H., & Azizifar, A. (2015). Investigating apology strategy among Kurdish bilinguals: a case study in Ilam. *Procedia-Social and Behavioral Sciences*, 199, 204 – 210.

Glaser, K. (2013). A Case for explicit-inductive instruction in teaching pragmatics in ESL. *TESL Canada Journal*, 30.

Goffman, E. (1967). *Interaction Ritual: Essays in Face-to-face Behavior*. New York: Anchor.

Gu, y. (1990). Politness phenomena in modern Chinese. *Journal of Pragamtics*, 14, 237 – 257.

Gu, y. (1992). Politeness, pragmatics and culture. *Foreign Language Teaching and Research*, 92 (4), 10 – 17.

Halenko, N., & Jones, C. (2011). Teaching pragmatic awareness of spoken requests to Chinese EAP learners in the UK: is explicit instruction effective? *System*, 39 (2), 240 – 250.

Hashemian, M. (2012). Cross-cultural differences and pragmatic transfer in English and Persian refusals. *The Journal of Teaching Language Skills*, 4 (3), 23 – 46.

Hassall, T. (2003). Requests by Australian learners of Indonesian. *Journal of Pragmatics*, 35 (12), 1903 – 1928.

Hassall, T. (2013). Pragmatic development during short-term study abroad: The case of address terms in Indonesian. *Journal of Pragmatics*, 55, 1 – 17.

He, M. (1993). *Zhongguo yinyong liyi da quan* [*The Encyclopedia of Practical Chinese Courtesy*] . Shanghai: Shanghai Culture Press.

He, Z. (1996). What is interlanguage pragmatics. *Foreign Linguistics* (1), 1 – 6.

He, Z. (2010). *A Brief Introduction to Pragmatics*. Beijing: Beijing University Publisher.

Hofstede, G. (2003). *Culture's Consequences: Comparing Values, Behaviors, Institutions and Organizations across Nations*. Thousand oaks: SAGE.

Holmes, J. (1995). *Women, men and politeness*. London: Longman.

Holtgraves, T. (2005) . Social psychology, cognitive psychology, and lingusitic politeness. *Journal of Politeness Research* (1).

Hong, G. (2005) . *Research Methodology in Cross-Cultural Pramgatics: An Iquiry into Data Collection Procedures*. Beijing: Foreign Language Teaching and Research Press.

Hong, G. (2009). Features of request strategies in Chinese. *Working Papers in Linguistics*, 47, 73 – 86.

Hong, W. (1996). An empirical study of Chinese request stragegies. *Int'L. J. Soc. Lang.* , 122, 127 – 138.

House, J. , & Kasper, G. (Eds.). (1987) . *Interlanguage pragmatics: requesting in a foreign language*. Tubingen: Narr.

Huang, M. -C. (1996) . *Achieving Cross-cultural equivalence in a study of American and Taiwanese Requests*. University of Illinois Press.

Huang, Q. (2010). Interlanguage pragmatics theory and its implications for foreign language. *Journal of Language Teaching and Research*, 1 (5).

Hymes, D. (1972). *On communicative competence*. New York: NY: Penguin.

Ifantidou, E. (2013). Pragmatic competence and explicit instruction. *Journal of Pragmatics*, 59, 93 – 116.

Isabelli, C. A. , & Nishida, C. (2005). *Development of the Spanish subjuncitve in a nine-month study-abroad setting.* Selected proceedings of the 6th conference on the acquisition of Spanish and Portuguese as First and Second Languages. Somerville, MA: Cascadilla Proceedings Project.

Ishida, M. (2005). Acquisition in interlanguage pragmatics: learning how to do things with words in a study abroad context. *Journal of Pragmatics*, 37 (5), 737 – 741.

Ismail, I. R. S. , Aladdin, A. , & Ramli, S. (2014). Vous ou tu?: towards understanding the politeness concept in French. *Procedia-Social and Behavioral Sciences*, 118, 184 – 189.

Iwasaki, N. (2008). Style shifts among Japanese learners before and after study abroad in Japan: becoming active social agents in Japanese. *Applied Linguistics*, 31 (1), 45 – 71.

Jebahi, K. (2011). Tunisian university students' choice of apology strategies in a discourse completion task. *Journal of Pragmatics*, 43 (2), 648 – 662.

Johnson, R. B. , & Onwuegbuzie, A. J. (2004). Mixed method research: a research paradigm whose time has come. *Educational Researcher*, 33 (7), 14 – 26.

Kahraman, B. , & Akkus, B. (2007). The use of request expressions by Turkish learners of Japanese. *Journal of Theory and Practice in Education*, 3 (1), 122 – 138.

Kasper, G. (1991). Research methods in interlanguage pragmatics. *SSLA* (13), 215.

Kasper, G. (1992a). Introduction: interlanguage pragmatics in SLA. *Studies in Second Acquistion*, 18 (2), 145 – 148.

Kasper, G. (1992b). Pragmatic transfer. *Second Language Research*, 8 (3), 203 – 231.

Kasper, G. (2001). Four perspectives on L2 pragmatic development. *Applied Linguistics*, 22 (4), 502 – 530.

Kasper, G. (Ed.). (1989). *Variation in interlanguage: speech act realization.* Clevedon: Multilingual Matters.

Kasper, G., & Rose, K. R. (2002). *Pragamtic development in a sceond language.* Oxford: Blackwell.

Kasper, G., & Schmidt, R. (1996). Developmental issues in interlanguage pragmatics. *SSLA* (18).

Kecskes, I. (2014). *Itercultural Pragmatics.* New York: Oxford University Press.

Kim, H. (2008). The semantic and pragmatic analysis of South Korean and Australian English apologetic speech acts. *Journal of Pragmatics*, 40 (2), 257 – 278.

Kim, J., Dewey, D. P., Baker-Smemoe, W., Ring, S., Westover, A., & Eggett, D. L. (2015). L2 development during study abroad in China. *System*, 55, 123 – 133.

Kinginger, C. (2008). Language learning in study abroad: Case histories of Americans in France. *The Modern Language Journal.*

Kinginger, C. (2011). G. Schauer: interlanguage pragmatic development: The study abroad context. *Applied Linguistics*, 32 (5), 572 – 574.

Kinginger, C., & Farrell, K. (2003). Assessing development of meta-pragmatic awareness. *Frontiers.*

Koc, E. M. (2011). Politeness in requests: A cross-cultural study of Turkish and British natives. *Eurasian Journal of Educational Research* (42), 153 – 166.

Koike, D. A., & Pearson, L. (2005). The effect of instruction and feedback in the development of pragmatic competence. *System*, 33 (3), 481 – 501.

Koc, E. M. (2011). Politeness in requests: a cross-cultural study of Turkish and British natives. *Eurasian Journal of Educational Research* (42), 153 – 166.

Kotorova, E. (2015). Expressing REQUEST in German and Russian: A communicative-pragmatic field analysis. *Procedia-Social and Behavioral Sciences*, 206, 36 – 45.

Kvale, S. (1996). *Interviews*. Thousand oaks: Sage.

Lafford, B. A. (1995). *Getting into, through and out of a survival situation: a comparison of communicative strategies used by students studying Spanish abroad and at home.* Amsterdam: John Benjamins.

Lantolf, J. P. (2000). Introducing sociocultural theory. In J. P. Lantolf (Eds.), *Sociocultural thoery and second language learning.* New York: Oxford University Press.

Lee, C. (2005). A cross-linguistic study on the linguistic expressions of Cantonese and English requests. *Pragmatics*, 15 (4), 395 – 422.

Lee-wong, S. M. (1994). Imperatives in requests: direct or impolite— observations from Chinese. *Pragmatics*, 4 (4), 491 – 515.

Leech, G. (1983). *Principles of Pragmatics.* London: Longman.

Leech, G. (2007). Politeness: Is there an East-West divide? *Journal of Politeness Research*, 3.

Leppanen, S. , & Pahta, P. (Eds.). (2012). Dangerous Multilingualism. In J. Blommaert (Eds.), *Finnish Culutre and Language Endangered – language ideological debates on English in the Finnish Press from 1995 – 2007.* Palgrave Macmillan UK.

Levinson, S. C. (1983). *Pragmatics.* Cambridge University Press.

Levisons, S. C. (2006). Cognition at the heart of human interaction. *Discourse Studies*, 8 (1), 85 – 93.

Li, C. (2009). *Chinese EFL learners' pragmtic and discourse transfer in the discourse of L2 request.* The University of Hong Kong Dissertation.

Li, D. (2000). The pragmatics of making requests in the L2 workplace: a case study of language socialization. *The Canadian Modern Language Review*, 57 (1).

Li, S. (2012). The effects of input-based practice on pragmatic development of requests in L2 Chinese. *Language Learning*, 62 (2), 403 – 438.

Li, S. (2014). The effects of different levels of linguistic proficiency on the development of L2 Chinese request production during study abroad. *System*, 45, 103 – 116.

Li, J. & Xue, Q. (2007) Interlanguage and its application. *Applied Linguistics* (1).

Li, Y. (2013). Thoughts and advice on futuredevelopment of international students education. *China Higher Educaiton Research* . 9, 27.

Lin, C. Y. , Woodfield, H. , & Ren, W. (2012). Compliments in Taiwan and Mainland Chinese: the influence of region and compliment topic. *Journal of Pragmatics*, 44 (11), 1486 – 1502.

Lin, M. -F. (2014). An interlanguage pragmatic study on Chinese EFL learners' refusal: perception and performance. *Journal of Language Teaching and Research*, 5 (3).

Lin, Y. -H. (2009). Query preparatory modals: Cross-linguistic and cross-situational variations in request modification. *Journal of Pragmatics*, 41 (8), 1636 – 1656.

Lincoln, Y. S. , & Guba, E. (1985). *Naturalistic Iquiry*. Beverly Hills: CA: Sage.

Liu, J. & Huang, S. (2013). A study of correlation between field dependence/independence cognitive style and interlanguage pragmatic competence. *Foreign Languages in China*, 10 (1).

Liu, S. & Liao, F. (2006). A survey of studies in Chinese pragmatics outside China. *Journal of Foreign Languages* (2).

Llanes, À. , & Muñoz, C. (2009). A short stay abroad: Does it make a difference? *System*, 37 (3), 353 – 365.

Lundell, F. F. , & Erman, B. (2012). High-level requests: A study of long residency L2 users of English and French and native speakers. *Journal of Pragmatics*, 44 (6 – 7), 756 – 775.

Mao, L. (1994) . Beyond politeness theory: ' Face ' revisited and renewed. *Journal of Pragmatics*, 21, 451 – 486.

Matsumura, S. (2001). Learning the rules for offering advice: A quantitative approach to second language socialization. *Langauge Learning*, 51 (4).

Maxwell, J. A. (1996). *Qualitative research design: An interactive approach.* Thousand Oaks: Sage.

Mehmet, D. (1991). Pragmatics and language teaching. *Hacettepe universitesl egitim fakutesl dergisl*, 6.

Merriam, S. B. (1998). *Qualitative Research and Case Study Applications in Education: Revised and Expanded from Case Study Reserach in Education.* Thousand Oakds: Sage.

Mills, S. (2003) . *Gender and politeness* (Vol. 17): Cambridge University Press.

Ministry of Education of the People's Republic of China (2017). The statistics of the international students in China of 2016. Online: http: // www. moe. gov. cn/jyb_ xwfb/xw_ fbh/moe_ 2069/xwfbh_ 2017n/xwfb_ 170301/170301_ sjtj/201703/t20170301_ 297677. html

Ministry of Education of the People's Republic of China (2017). The increasing number of international students from the countries along "the Belt and Road" . Online: http: //www. moe. edu. cn/jyb_ xwfb/xw_ fbh/moe_ 2069/xwfbh_ 2017n/xwfb_ 170301/170301_ mtbd/201703/t20170302_ 297943. html.

Moon, Y. -i. (1996) . *Interlanguage features of Korean EFL leanrers in the communicative act of complaining.* Indiana University.

Morris, C. W. (1938). *Foundations of the Theory of Signs.* Chicago: Univeristy of Mouton Press.

Mulken, M. V. (1996). Politeness marker in Dutch and French requests. *Language Sciences*, 18 (3 –4), 689 – 702.

Nguyen, T. T. M. , Pham, T. H. , & Pham, M. T. (2012). The relative effects of explicit and implicit form-focused instruction on the development of L2 pragmatic competence. *Journal of Pragmatics*, 44 (4), 416 – 434.

Nishida, H. (1985). Japnanese Intercultural communication competence and corss-cultural adjustment. *International Journal of Intercultural Relations*, 9, 247 – 269.

Nureddeen, F. A. (2008). Cross cultural pragmatics: Apology strategies in Sudanese Arabic. *Journal of Pragmatics*, 40 (2), 279 – 306.

Ochs, E. (1988). *Culture and language development.* Cambridge, UK: Cambridge University Press.

Ochs, E. (2000). Socialization. *Journal of Linguistic Anthropology*, 9 (1 – 2), 230 – 233.

Ochs, E. , & Schieffelin, B. B.. (1979). *Developmental Pragmatics.* New York: Academic Press.

Ochs, E. , & Schieffelin, B. B. (1984). Language acquisition and socialization: Three developmental stories and their implications. In R. A. Sheweder & R. A. LeVine (Eds.), *In culture thoery: essays in mind, self and emotion.* New York: Cambridge Univ. Press.

Onwuegbuzie, A. , & Johnson, R. B. (2006). The validity issue in mixed research. *Rsearch in the Schools*, 1.

Özdemir, Ç. , & Rezvani, S. A. (2010). Interlanguage pragmatics in action: Use of expressions of gratitude. *Procedia-Social and Behavioral Sciences*, 3, 194 – 202.

Pan, X. (2015). *A Study on Cultural Differences of Acculturation Adapation among American and Japanese Students in China.* China Social Sicence Press.

Pfingsthorn, J. (2012). Teaching and Learning Pragmatics: Where Language and Culture Meet. *Journal of Pragmatics*, 44 (4), 538 – 540.

Poole, D. (1992). Language socialization in the second language classroom. *Langauge Learning*, 539 – 616.

Qu, R. & Jiang, Q. (2011). Location selections by international students in China and analysis of reasons. *Journal of Higher Education*. 3.

Rafieyan, V., Behnammohammadian, N., & Orang, M. (2015). Relationship between acculturation attitude and pragmatic comprehension. *Journal of Language Teaching and Research*, 6 (3), 504.

Rafieyan, V., Sharafi-Nejad, M., Khavari, Z., Damavand, A., & Lin, S. E. (2014). Relationship between cultural distance and pragamtic comprehension. *English Language Teaching*, 7 (2), 103 – 109.

Rasouli Khorshidi, H. (2013). Study abroad and interlanguage pragmatic development in request and apology speech acts among Iranian learners. *English Language Teaching*, 6 (5).

Regan, V. (1995). The acquisition of sociolinguistic native speech norms: Effects of a year abroad on L2 learners of French. In B. Freed (Eds.), *The linguistic impact of study abroad.* Amsterdam/Philadephia: John Benjamins Publisher

Rintell, E. M. (1997). Getting your speech act together: The pragmatic ability of second language learners. *Working Papers on Bilingualism* (17), 98 – 106.

Roever, C., Wang, S., & Brophy, S. (2014). Learner background factors and learning of second language pragmatics. *International Review of Applied Linguistics in Language Teaching*, 52 (4).

Rose, K. (1999). *Teachers and students learning about request in Hong Kong.*

In E. Hinkel (Eds.), *Culture in second language teaching and learning.* Cambridge: Cambridge University Press.

Rose, K. R. (2000). An exploratory cross-sectional study of interlanguage pragmatic development. *SSLA* (22), 27 – 67.

Rue, Y., & Zhang, G. Q. (2008). *Request Strategies: A Comparative Study in Mandarin Chinese and Korean.* America: John Benjamins B. V.

Sa'd, S. H. T., & Mohammad, M. (2014). Iranian EFL learners' sociolinguistic competence: refusal strategies in focus. *Journal of Language and Linguistic Studies*, 10 (2), 48 – 66.

Saasaki, M. (1998). Investigating EFL students' production of speech acts: a comparison of production questionnnaires and role plays. *Journal of Pragmatics* (30).

Schauer, G. A. (2009). *Interlanguage Pragmatic Development.* Great Britain: Continuum.

Schauer, G. A., & Adolphs, S. (2006). Expressions of gratitude in corpus and DCT data: Vocabulary, formulaic sequences, and pedagogy. *System*, 34 (1), 119 – 134.

Schieffelin, B. B., & Ochs, E. (1986). *Language Socialization across Cultures.* Cambridge: Cambridge Universtiy Press.

Searle, J. (1979). *Expression and meaning.* Cambridge: Cambridge University Press.

Searle, J. (Ed.). (1976). *A classification of illocutionary acts.* Language Society (1), 1 – 23.

Seidman, I. (2006). *Interviewing as Qualitative Research.* New York: Teachers College Press.

Seyyed, H. T. S., & Mohammad, M. (2014). Iranian EFL learner's sociolinguistic competence: Refusal strategies in focus. *Jounal of Language and Linguistic studies*, 10 (2), 48 – 66.

Shang, X. (1997). Interlanguage and second language acquisation. *Foreign Language Research* (1).

Shively, R. L. (2011). L2 pragmatic development in study abroad: A longitudinal study of Spanish service encounters. *Journal of Pragmatics*, 43 (6), 1818 – 1835.

Shively, R. L. (2015). Developing interactional competence during study abroad: Listener responses in L2 Spanish. *System*, 48, 86 – 98.

Sifianou, M. (1992). The use of diminutives in expressing politeness: Modern Greek versus English. *Journal of Pragamtics*, 17 (22), 155 – 173.

Soler, E. A. , & Martinez-Flor, A. (Eds.). (2008). *Investigating Pragmatics in Foreign Language Learning, Teaching and Testing*. Great Britain: Cromwell Press.

Spencer-Oatey, H. (1993). Conceptions of social relations and pragmatics research. *Journal of Pragmatics*, 20 (1), 29 – 47.

Spencer-Oatey, H. (1996). Reconsidering power and distance. *Journal of Pragmatics*, 26 (1), 27 – 47.

Spradley, J. P. (1980). *Participant Observation*. United states of America: Holt, Rincart and Winston.

Spradley, J. P. (1979). *The Ethnographic Interview*. United states of America: Holt, Rincart and Winston.

Stewart, P. J. , & Strathern, A. J. (2017). Language and cultureIn J. Pamela & J. S. Andrew (Eds.), *Breaking the frames* (pp. 69 – 78). Springer International Publishing.

Su, D. (2014). Request Strategies: A Comparative Study in Mandarin Chinese and Korean. By Yong-Ju Rue and Grace Qiao Zhang. (Pragmatics & Beyond 177.) PA: John Benjamins, 2008. Pp. xv, 320. *Language and Linguistics*, 15 (4), 597 – 600.

Taguchi, N. (2008). Cognition, language contact, and the development of pragmatic comprehension. *Language Learning*, 58, 33 – 40.

Taguchi, N. (2011). The effect of L2 proficiency and study-abroad experience on pragmatic comprehension. *Language Learning*, 61 (3), 904 – 939.

Taguchi, N. (2015). "Contextually" speaking: A survey of pragmatic learning abroad, in class, and online. *System*, 48, 3 – 20.

Takimoto, M. (2009). Exploring the effects of input-based treatment and test on the development of learners' pragmatic proficiency. *Journal of Pragmatics*, 41 (5), 1029 – 1046.

Tan, K. H., & Farashaiya, A. (2012). Utilizing formulaic request strategies in an ESL classroom. *Procedia-Social and Behavioral Sciences*, 59, 42 – 46.

Tashakkori, A., & Teddlie, C. (Eds.). (2003). *Adavanced mixed methods research designs*. Thousand Oaks: Sage.

Thelen, E. (2005). Dynamic systems theory and the complexity of change. *Psychoanalytic Dialogues*, 15 (2), 255 – 283.

Thomas, J. (1982). Cross-cultrual pragmatic failure. *Applied Linguistics*, 4 (2), 91 – 112.

Thomas, J. (1995). *Meaning in Interaction—an Introduction to Pragmatics*. London: Longman.

Turnbull, W., & Saxton, K. (1997). Modal expressions as facework in refusals to comply with requests: I think I should say ' no ' right now. *Journal of Pragmatics* (27), 145 – 181.

Uso-Juan, E. (Ed.). (2007). The presentation and practice of the communicative act. In E. Soler & M. P. S. Jorda (Eds.), *Intercultural language use and language learning*. Springer.

Uso-Juan, E., & Martinez-Flor, A. (2006). *Current Trends in the Development and Teaching of the Four Language Skills*. Berlin: Walter de Gruyter.

Vygotsky, L. S. (1978). *Mind in Society: the Develompent of Higher Psychological Processes*. Harvard University Press.

Wang, C. (2010). Toward a second language socialization perspective: issues in study abroad research. *SPRING*, 43 (1).

Wang, J. (2002). *Cross-cultural interlanguage study between Chinese and English.* Fudan University Dissertation.

Wang, S. & Li, W. (2007). An empirical study on pragmatic transfer in the performance of refusals. *Foreign Language Research* (4).

Wannaruk, A. (2008). Pragmatic Transfer in Thai EFL Refusals. *RELC Journal*, 39 (3), 318 – 337.

Warga, M. , & Schölmberger, U. (2007). The acquisition of French apologetic behavior in a study abroad context. *Intercultural Pragmatics*, 4 (2).

Watt, M. , & Ebbutt, D. (1987). More than the sum of the parts research method in group interviewing. *British Educational Research Journal.*

Watts, R. J. (2003). *Politeness*: Cambridge University Press.

wolfson, N. (1989). The social dynamics of native and nonnative variation in complimenting behavior. In M. P. Eisenstein (Eds.), *The dynamic interlanguage: epirical studies in second language variation.* New York: Plenum Press.

Wood, D. J. , Burner, J. , & Ross, G. (1976). The role of tutoring in problem-solving. *Journal of Child Psychology* (17), 89 – 100.

Xie, C. , He, Z. , & Lin, D. (2005). Politeness: myth and truth. *Studies in Language.*

Xu, M. (2015). An experimental study on interlanguage instruction based on pragmatic memes. *Foreign Language Education*, 36 (3).

Xu, P. & Ma, T. (2002). A historical review on Chinese pragamtics and discussion on application of pragmatic theories in China. *Foreign Language Research* (3).

Xu, W. , Case, R. E. , & Wang, Y. (2009). Pragmatic and grammatical competence, length of residence, and overall L2 proficiency. *System*, 37 (2), 205 – 216.

Yang, J. (2005). *A study on international students' cultural adaption in China.* East China Normal University Dissertation.

Yang, J. (2006). The characteristics and influencing factors of construction of international students in China. *Journal of South-Central University for Nationalities (Humanitites and Social Sicence)*. S1, 13 – 14.

Yang, L. (2009). Acquisition of expressions of gratitude by American learners of Chinese in the target language environment. *Chinese Teaching in the World*, 29 (4).

Yuan, Y. (2001). An inquiry into empirical pragmatics data-gathering methods: writtern DCTs, oral DCTs, field notes, and natural conversations. *Journal of Pragmatics* (33), 271 – 292.

Yule, G. (1996). *Pragmatics.* Oxford: Oxford University Press.

Yusefi, K., Gowhary, H., Azizifar, A., & Esmaeili, Z. (2015). A pragmatic analysis of thanking strategies among Kurdish speakers of Ilam based ongender and age. *Procedia-Social and Behavioral Sciences*, 199, 211 – 217.

Zhang, S., & Wang, X. (1997). A comparison study on request speech act. *Modern Foreign Languages* (3).

Zhang, Y. (Ed.). (1995). *Indirectness in Chinese requesting.* Honolulu: University of Hawai'i Press.

Zheng, X., & Ying, J. (2015). A study on inference quality of mixed methods research in foreign language education research. *Technology Enhanced Foreign Language Education* (3).

Acknowledgement

Upon the completion of my dissertation in Shanghai International Studies University (SISU), I owe a debt of gratitude to numerous people who support me all the way around.

First, express my gratitude to my supervisor Professor Zheng Xinmin. He is an insightful and knowledgeable person, who led me to the academia. Under his instructon, I learned how to conduct a study and complete a research article in a more scientific manner. He offered me guidance whenever I felt confused and puzzled about my research. Thanks to his open-mindness, I was allowed to choose any research topic for my dissertation, which is crucial to me to persist for such a long time. All those qualifications that he has exerted tremendous influence on me.

Second, I would like to extend my heartfelt thanks to Miss Li Qinping and Mr Lu Qinning who helped me to find the participants in SISU. Thanks also to the 60 international students and 20 Chinese students who regarded as participants in my study, especially the three case participants for their willingness to share their life stories and learning experiences. This study could not be completed without their time, help and contributions.

Third, I am extremely obliged to Dr. Li Citing, Dr. Zhao Guanfang and Dr. Xie Xiaoyan, who offered valuable suggestions to my proposal confirmation. Since then, Dr. Li Citing helped me sort out many problems concerning my disseration and provided me with piles of research articles and works related to my research. She even went through my dissertation during her years in the United States. I also express graditude to Prof. Hong Gang, who spent his time offering suggestions and discussing with me. Due to their noble, and academic support, I could write my dissertation in a relatively smooth way.

Fourth, my gratitude goes to my research collegues in Simon's Learning and Research Community (SLRC): Sun Qinmei, Wang Yushan, Zuo Xiuyuan, Yang Chunhong, Zheng Qiong, Ning Qiang, Wang Jingli, Jing Feilong, Xu Bin, Zhang Junmin, Ihsan Ali, Dang Quynh Dzung, Jing Jin, Ruan Xiaolei, etc. Our academic discussions and casual chats are helpful, enlightening and fun. Peer support and corroboration works as scaffolding that helps me develop my full potential. Our friendship established during the past three year go beyond academic area. My special thanks go to Ning Qiang who helped me to find a native speaker to proof read through my disseration.

Last, my great appreciation goes to my beloved parents, husband and son. My heart-felt gratitude goes to my parents for showing me love and care all the time. I thank my dear husband, Lin Jianlin who has been a continual source of support all those years, to my little son, Lin Yinan who behaves quite well from kindergarten to primary school, which is very important and allowed me to concentrate on my disseartation writing.